A HISTORY OF
WINCHESTER

The City Cross.

A HISTORY OF
WINCHESTER

Barbara Carpenter Turner

Phillimore

1992

Published by
PHILLIMORE & CO. LTD.
Shopwyke Hall, Chichester, Sussex

ISBN 0 85033 737 2

Printed and bound in Great Britain by
BIDDLES LTD.
Guildford, Surrey

Contents

List of Illustrations

Frontispiece: The City Cross

Preface and Acknowledgements

The writing of Winchester's history will never be complete, but I hope that this book will be a useful introduction to the city's history. It has been made possible by the enthusiastic interest of all kinds of people; that interest is sometimes academic, sometimes a keen and affectionate perception, an awareness of Winchester's past found, to use the old term, in alien and native alike. I record my debt to one 'alien' who combined great academic qualities with much perception: the late Bishop of Winchester, Dr. A. P. Williams, 'History Bill', for it was he who suggested that I ought to write this book, and that a short narrative history would be useful. I thank too my publisher, Phillimore, for accepting a text which deals with many topics and raises many questions. Some of these questions will never be answered, others await detailed investigation; some answers will undoubtedly be provided with the completion of the *Winchester Studies* series.

It is a long time now since I first saw the City Archives, and I want to record my gratitude to those people who helped me in many ways, beginning with my predecessor as Honorary Archivist J. S. Furley, and our mutual friend the late R. H. McCall, then Town Clerk of Winchester. Without Robin McCall the City Record Office as it is today, albeit housed by the County Council, would never have existed. I want particularly to thank the late Frank and Eleanor Cottrill, the one our first museum curator, and the other Hampshire's first County Archivist: both renowned for the generous way in which they always helped other people, a tradition continued by their successors, and indeed all the staff of the City Museum and the Hampshire Record Office.

John H. Harvey gave me much help, particularly concerning Wintonians recorded in the archives of Winchester College, whose successive wardens and fellows I thank for many kindnesses over the years. I thank the Dean and Chapter of Winchester Cathedral for permission to consult their archives and for the kindness of their librarians, the late Canon A. W. Goodman, the late Dr. W. F. Oakeshott, the late Canon J. Boden and the late Canon F. Bussby. Thanks must also be given to John Crook for his help with picture research.

Though I cannot imagine a life uninvolved with Winchester's history, I should probably have never put pen to paper had it not been for the editor of the *Hampshire Chronicle* who encouraged me to write *Medieval Churches* and who later published many of my articles on local subjects. I thank her and her staff not least for the contribution which the *Chronicle* is making today by publishing material on current events for future historians. Finally, and above all, I thank my late husband, for it was he who taught me to look at Winchester.

Barbara Carpenter Turner

Illustration Acknowledgements

The following are thanked for permission to use illustrations: Dick Amey, 74, 75; Mrs. J. Chorley, 50; John Crook, 1-10, 12-21, 23, 24, 28-37, 39-45, 47, 48, 51-6, 68, 81, 82, 86, 87; the Dean and Chapter of Winchester Cathedral, 65; Hampshire Record Office, 26, 60, 62, 64; Bertram Hutchings, 85; St John's Hospital, 22; 'Printed Page', George Watson, 77; Winchester, 46; E. A. Sollars, 27, 49; Winchester City Museums, frontispiece (PWCM 5823), 63, 67 (PWCM 4825), 71 (PWCM 10147), 72 (PWCM 7499), 80 (PWCM 5666), 83 (PWCM 6402), 84 (PWCM 5200); Winchester City Record Office, 11, 25.

Introduction

Nature has endowed the site handsomely. Human skills and achievements have added to the endowment, though the contributions of some 60 generations of mankind have not always improved or enhanced the Winchester scene. The city lies on a restricted site in a fold of the downs, at a point between two ridgeways where the River Itchen can be crossed with ease. To the east, over the river, is the great height of St Giles' Hill; on the opposite side of the town, the slopes of St Paul's Hill and of the western downs are less severe and easier to develop. To the north and south there are wide, flat, marshy areas of much beauty, watered by the river and by Winchester's lesser streams, acres which could be irrigated as water meadows, or built on if man were sufficiently skilled and secure from attack. On the southern horizon the river valley is broken into abruptly by the great mound of St Catherine's Hill and the heights of Hockley, by the downland beyond the village of Compton and the districts now called Stanmore and Oliver's Battery. Early man lived on the downland around the city for many generations before Winchester had any written history. He inhabited St Catherine's Hill, and his life there was the subject of one of the most famous excavations of all time.[1] St Catherine's was found to have been an Iron Age hill fort, with traces of an undeveloped settlement of the same period. The site was probably abandoned *c*.150 B.C., after parts of the fort walls had been stormed and burnt. Less famous farm settlements of the Iron Age have been traced at Worthy Down and at Stanmore; recent excavations in Winchester itself have found traces of occupation, but as yet there is little evidence to suggest the complete nature or extent of the settlement of Winchester before the coming of the Romans.[2] Nature's restrictions on the growth of Winchester, though handsome, are severe, to be overcome only by much ingenuity and technical skill.

It was this ingenuity which enabled generations of Winchester men to build their city with the materials that nature had provided. The great historic buildings rely partly on 'foreign' materials – Caen and Quarr stone, Purbeck marble, roofing slates and tiles from the West Country – but smaller domestic buildings and even parts of the great monuments were constructed from flints gathered by hand on neighbouring fields and downs, from quarried chalk, the natural 'stone' of the Winchester area, and from wattle used with daub, a mixture usually including chalk, dung and straw. Many of these buildings were timber-framed, an economical method of construction which lingered on into the 17th century, as in the so-called Bargee cottages on Wharf Hill. Internal timber-framing for partitioning, where the filling was cheap brick nogging, not daub, continued to be used into the present century, and the unwarned eye may sometimes deem a fairly recent building to be older than it really is.

Conversely, the fronts of some Winchester houses are younger than they appear to be if judged only on architectural appearance. Winchester house-holders tended to be conservative in taste, to alter their property in a manner which was clearly 20 or 30 years behind the London style (for example, the demolished 79 High Street). Many buildings, though, are much older than their façades suggest: from St Giles' Hill those Chesil Street houses which are grouped to the north of St Peter Chesil church can be seen to be gabled houses with much later fronts. Another perfect example is 6 Great Minster Street; Winchester citizens have not always been able to afford expensive and complete rebuilding. Until the 19th century, renovation and repairs were more common than completely new construction, which tended to be limited to sites where there had been no previous development.

Even on the restricted central sites, however, expansion or contraction of individual buildings was often possible. The closing of small lanes, particularly in the 16th century, allowed some householders to enlarge their properties. Lawful and unlawful encroachments onto the highway were quite common until the 18th and 19th centuries, when the paving commissioners regulated these matters. Properties were divided and redivided, smaller groups made into larger single units, and groups of cottages 'under one roof' became single units. The Queen Anne Guildhall, in its medieval origin, was a clutter of smaller buildings. Winchester, therefore, is what it is today because of the natural environment and because of the varied skills, differing prosperities and diverse architectural needs of many generations of the city's inhabitants. Winchester itself tells its own story.

The wider narrative of historic events and circumstances also affected the growth of the city. Winchester was a Roman town, and its great wall offered safety but also restriction which continued until the 19th century. When the Romans had gone, Winchester became a royal town and a cathedral city, endowed from the early 10th century with three great church communities whose precincts occupied a vast proportion of the south side of the High Street – Old Minster, New Minster and Nunnaminster. The western down was partially covered by a great royal fortress; the centre of the city was dominated by build-ings in the hands of the Church. Moreover, the earliest benefactors were so liberal in their support of Mother Church in general and of the Old Minster (cathedral priory) in particular, that much property in the city and almost all the land around it belonged to ecclesiastical landowners. The great priory manor of Chilcombe, a vast area of farmland, produced the wool on which so much of Winchester's medieval prosperity was based; much of what is now thought of as Winchester formed the bishop's soke, and was free from municipal interference. The dissolution of the monasteries put a partial end to all this when Hyde Abbey (New Minster) and St Mary's (Nunnaminster) were demolished, but the bishop's soke lingered on into the mid-19th century, and the cathedral and diocese survived as owners of real estate for many years to come. The decision of the ecclesiastical commissioners to sell their land around Winchester at Winnall, Weeke, and in the district of Stanmore has had far-reaching results in terms of Winchester's growth and expansion.

The historic fact that Winchester, as distinct from the soke, emerged at the beginning of the Norman period as a city of burgesses, able to dispose of their own real estate without the interference of a manorial overlord, has also been important. The presence of a royal court, of discriminating and often wealthy clerics, of other communities, including the Jews until 1290, the various schools and hospitals, the prison, and the fact that Winchester has continued to be a centre of county administration and an assize town are all historic factors which have helped to make the city what it is today. Combined with Winchester's obvious importance as a county market, these are factors which have often brought much prosperity and a successful local economy, reflected in the individual efforts of local shopkeepers and small manufacturers.

The city's early prosperity was largely derived from its natural environment. Roman Winchester was a market town, and food surpluses were sent to the city long after grain crops had given way to wool. The two earliest Winchester craft guilds were those of the weavers and fullers, men whose prosperity was largely the result of an environment which offered them an excellent and suitable water supply, plenty of wool, and a great cosmopolitan market via the Bishop's Fair on St Giles' Hill. Nor should the proximity of the port of Southampton be forgotten: communication with the coasts of England and of Europe was much easier even for medieval men than has sometimes been suggested.

The gifts and the restrictions of its natural environment, the energies and skills of hundreds of individual citizens, and the passage of history have made Winchester what it is today.

Chapter One

Roman Winchester

No one knows when or how the Romans first came to Winchester. Coins of Claudius and Nero found locally suggest an early occupation, and the name, *Venta Belgarum*, 'the market town of the Belgii', indicates that the settlement they found was substantial. Roman Winchester continued to rely for much of its prosperity on the surrounding agricultural district, and *Venta* was one of the two capital centres of the canton of the Belgii, the second being *Aquae Sulis* (Bath).[1]

It had long been suspected that the walls of the medieval city were Roman in origin, and recent excavations have confirmed this. The wall was probably con-structed in about A.D. 200, replacing an earlier earthen enclosure. In the western part of the town, on the site of the extension to the Hampshire County Council offices, excavation in 1951 showed a great Roman embankment (on coin evidence not earlier than A.D. 180), some 45 ft. wide, on top of which the later wall was constructed. In Colebrook Street, to the east, the wall also proved to be of Roman origin, and can be seen on the Weirs below the Scott Garden. In 1959 some 300 ft. were excavated in North Walls and the core, flint rubble bound together with typical pinkish mortar, was revealed clearly. To the south, investigations made

1. Second-century Roman mosaic pavement from the Brooks excavation, discovered in 1988 and now in Winchester City Museum.

1

near Wolvesey in 1960 confirmed that section to be Roman, subjected to two medieval refacings.[2] This wall was pierced by gates, one of which, Southgate, was excavated in 1971.[3] Northgate led to Silchester, the *Sarum* (Salisbury) road came to Westgate, and Southgate marked the end of the way from *Clausentum* (Bitterne); *Venta* was thus an important road centre. Within the walled area, fragments of the street pattern and traces of Roman buildings have emerged.

Venta was a centre for trade and markets, an important administrative centre, and a meeting place for Romans and Britons from a wide area. There were substantial farmsteads in the neighbourhood, villas at Itchen Abbas and Sparsholt, with fine mosaic floors.[4] The port *Clausentum* was not too distant, and small craft could use the river. An abundant water supply and good farming land were other factors in the town's prosperity, though the agricultural economy may have changed, from sheep to grain, during the period. Evidence suggesting this is provided by a fourth-century list of Roman officers within the Empire which includes an individual described as the procurator of the Imperial weaving works at *Venta*, a building not yet located.[5] It is easy enough to believe that the town was important; it is much more difficult to attempt to describe it, except by reference to other Roman towns.

Within the walled area there were streets laid out on a grid plan, houses, temples and other public buildings. The legends of the Middle Ages, perpetuated by Milner, described the Christian community of Roman Winchester in convincing terms and, though a church has not yet been found, *Venta* certainly had large buildings of a public nature. A fragment of an inscription found in Middle Brook Street bears letters one Roman foot in height (11½ inches), the largest lettering yet found on any Roman inscription in England.[6] Only two other inscriptions have ever been found. In 1854, when the old county prison in Jewry Street was being demolished, a blue sandstone altar was discovered in the foundations of a wall. It was inscribed to the Italian, German, Gallic and British Mothers, a group of early goddesses much worshipped by soldiers, and had been dedicated by Lucretianus, perhaps the first inhabitant of the city whose personal name has survived.[7] The third inscription was found when the south wall of the cathedral was being cleaned, but is too fragmentary to provide any useful information.

The street plan of the Roman town has not yet emerged, though there is evidence that the present High Street follows much the same line as the Roman road which must have linked West and East Gates. A north-to-south road approximately on the Middle Brook Street line has been identified in several places, along with houses on either side of it. This road would continue to Kingsgate, which could thus have a Roman origin.[8]

Within the town there were many spacious houses, and life was clearly comfortable and civilised for the more prosperous inhabitants. Mosaic pavements have been discovered in several areas, including the eastern end of St Clement's

Street near Hammond's Passage; a splendid dolphin mosaic was revealed in 1878 at the junction of the Minster Streets; plainer floors have been found in parts of the close (Dome Alley in 1880, now moved to the outer vestibule of the Deanery) and in the garden of 10 The Close (in 1952, left *in situ*). Other areas of mosaics were located in the Brook Street excavations of 1953, when the widening of St George's Street revealed, four feet under present ground level, the remains of unidentified Roman buildings, including a long mosaic corridor in brown and cream *tesserae*. Houses owed much to their Italian models; a stone baluster, found in 1957, is perhaps part of a courtyard veranda, and there are fascinating fragments of decorated wall plaster such as that found in 1958 in a house in St

2. Romano-British bronze head from Otterbourne.

George's Street, which depicts a dahlia-like flower in blue-white, with greenish-blue leaves. Another example has a repetitive branching design of flowers and leaves, with a strident border in stripes of blue and green and a striking background of Pompeiian red.

Something of the old pre-Roman skills and crafts continued to survive. A little box made of bronze, and originally intended to contain a seal, has a design of Celtic character in blue enamel, and must have been made by a craftsman who was either a Briton or much influenced by native examples. A storage jar found under *The George Hotel* in 1955 is of native type, and the same find included a jar, bowl and plate of the same period (A.D. 40-60). Trade with the continent, which had always existed, was encouraged; the inhabitants were able to use imported decorated bowls from Gaul, to cook with oil from Spain, and to drink Spanish wine, which they could quaff in beakers of glass imported from the Rhineland.[9] Glass beakers and an assortment of jewellery have been found in a large cemetery, recently excavated in the grounds of Lankhills School, which appears to have been in use from *c.* A.D. 320 to the end of the Roman occupation.[10] Some of the burials seem to have been of Saxon soldiers, perhaps the defenders of *Venta* at the end of the Roman era, although there is no evidence of any widespread fighting at that time. In the autumn of 1989 a further cemetery was excavated in Stable Gardens, within the city walls. In the mysterious years from *c.* A.D. 400-50 the city lingered on, perhaps with a slowly declining population, and with a constant fear of the new invaders.

These invaders were pagan warriors, in wandering raiding parties, and since the days of Bede they have been classified as Angles, Saxons and Jutes. Popular legends graphically describe how Winchester became a centre of fantastic Romano-British resistance to these warriors, that the town was in fact Camelot, Caer Gwent, and that the leader of the resistance was Arthur. Here history must part company from myth, though the Arthurian legend in Winchester has flourished for many hundreds of years. Thomas Rudborne could not accept it, but early writers liked to think that the Round Table in the Great Hall of the castle was part of the legend, and Arthur was credited with having built the castle in A.D. 523.[11] Arthur, as far as Winchester is concerned, may indeed represent some Romano-British chieftain who rallied his countrymen for a short while against the invaders after the Roman withdrawal, but 'the brave equals round th'encircled board, with blood red wine and British viands stored'[12] are, alas, only part of tradition's fairy tale, and not the true stuff of Winchester's history.

Heroic resistance there may well have been, but in the once flourishing city all that eventually survived was a memory of the importance of the site and its significance as a road centre, the great containing walls, and the buildings which began to crumble and decay. Swamp and marsh began to spread again and walls collapsed. The fate of the inhabitants is uncertain.

Chapter Two

Wintanceaster

It would be wrong to imagine that one concentrated attack was made on the Romano-British city. Indeed, there may have been those who were prepared to welcome the invaders, men whose trading contacts with the continent encouraged them to think that life would continue within the walls. Some Roman streets were cobbled, and rough timber buildings were erected, poor indeed compared with the public buildings of the Roman city but an indication that Winchester was not wholly deserted after the departure of the Romans.

The most influential of the new leaders were the chiefs who belonged to the family of Cerdic and his son (or grandson) Cynric, successful warriors who, in the words of the *Anglo-Saxon Chronicle*, 'succeeded to the Kingdom' in A.D. 519.[1] The activities of this royal line were important, recorded in oral tradition and eventually committed to writing in the *Anglo-Saxon Chronicle*. This is not an impartial account, as it was designed to record the successes and not the failures of the West Saxon kings; moreover, Winchester (Wintanceaster) was not of much importance to the pagan Saxons.[2] Cerdic was the founder of a great dynasty. Cynegils, King of Wessex A.D. 611-41, perhaps Cerdic's great-great-grandson, assured his family's place in history by becoming a convert to Christianity in A.D. 635, as a result of the great missionary journey of an Italian priest, Birinus, who had been sent in A.D. 634 to preach the Gospel to the heathen in England.[3] Cynegils was baptised at Dorchester-on-Thames, and it was this little town which became the centre of the first bishopric of the West Saxons. Cynegils' successor, his second son, Cenwealh, was also eventually baptised, and he built a minster church in Winchester. The exact date is unimportant; what matters is the decision to build this large church for, by the very nature of the royal patronage which established it, the Church was associated with the dynasty of the West Saxon kings. The Old Minster, as it was eventually called to distinguish it from later foundations, became the very heart of the civilisation of Wessex, of England, and of Western Europe. In the course of time its dedication came to include St Paul as well as St Peter, the Holy Trinity, and a local saint, St Swithun; it was built and rebuilt, suffered both additions and demolitions, was served by secular canons and by Benedictine monks, became the cathedral church of the diocesan bishop, and the burial place of the long dynasty of West Saxon kings. Its presence in Winchester has always been a determining factor in the city's history, and archaeological work in recent times has revealed the site of this important first building on the north side of the present cathedral.[4]

Saxon Winchester thus became a holy city and a royal town, as the mortuary chests in the choir of the present cathedral explain vividly. Though none of the chests are earlier than the time of Bishop Fox (d. 1528), they continue the traditions of earlier reliquaries, containing the bones of some of the most famous personages of Anglo-Saxon England who chose to be buried in Winchester, with the curious alleged addition of William Rufus.

Traditionally it is said to have been Bishop Haeddi, Bishop of Wessex from A.D. 676, who moved his throne, his *cathedra*, to the Old Minster from Dorchester. As a cathedral church, Old Minster was not only a natural centre for important meetings and a place where bishops and kings were buried: trade and commerce were encouraged by its presence, and liberal studies and the arts were patronised by those who were connected with it. The Minster's bishops were often statesmen, who came to be associated with successive kings as spiritual advisers and as politicians, and who encouraged the growth of law and order. Under Egbert, the kingdom of Wessex became the effective centre of a united England, at least of an England prepared to recognise the king of Wessex as *Bretwalda*, a title which may mean that he was deemed to be ruler of Britain.

Amongst the bishops buried in the precinct of Old Minster was St Swithun, who died in A.D. 861. By this time, Wessex was being subjected once more to a series of damaging raids from new invaders – the Vikings. The *Chronicle* records that a great horde came inland and stormed the city, though the invaders were eventually put to flight by the men of Hampshire and Berkshire under their aldermen. The civilisation which Church and king had encouraged could still succumb all too easily to foreign invaders. Swithun is credited with having built a wall round at least part of Winchester, perhaps the predecessor of the close wall, and also with building a bridge across the Itchen at the east end of the town; but after his death the Viking raids continued. When King Ethelred died, in A.D. 871, he was buried in Wimborne rather than Winchester. The revival associated with his brother and successor, Alfred, was relevant not just to Winchester and its interests. Alfred defeated the Danes, revived the Church, and recreated a Wessex where law, order and civilisation might once more flourish.

Alfred was fully aware of the importance of the Church once peace with the Danes seemed reasonably certain. Monasteries were a source of inspiration, and Alfred's determination to reinforce the Church in Winchester was most successful. He prepared the way for the foundation of two new religious houses (an abbey for nuns and a new community for monks) and two additional churches on the south side of the High Street, which proved to be determining factors in the eventual topography of the town.

Nunnaminster, the nuns' minster, can perhaps be more properly described as

EN HAC ET ALTERA E REGIONE
CISTA RELIQVIA SVNT CANVTE
ET RVFE REGVM EMMÆ REGINÆ
WINDE ET ALWINE EPISCPORVM.

SIT LAVS

CONFIDO

3. & 4. Details of the mortuary chest in the cathedral, which is reputed to contain the remains of Canute, William Rufus, Queen Emma and two Saxon bishops.

HIC · REX · EGBERTVS · PAV
SAT · CV · REGE · KENVLPhO
NOBIS · EGREGIA · MNNERA · VIO · TV

the joint foundation of Alfred and his wife, Queen Alswitha. Only a fraction of its site has been excavated, though the area of its precinct is reasonably well established. It lay at the south-eastern end of the High Street, included much of what is now the Broadway and almost certainly reached as far south as the wall of Wolvesey Castle. The abbey was a community of nuns following the Benedictine rule, and was closely connected with its royal patron. After Alfred's death, his Queen lived in the convent, dying there in A.D. 902. She may even have acted as abbess but, despite patronage, it was not a wealthy house; William of Malmesbury calls it the little monastery, *Monasteriolum.* When its boundaries were adjusted in the ninth century by King Edgar it acquired Abbey Mill, one of its great economic advantages, which remains in a much more modern form as one of the principal features of central Winchester.[5]

The foundation called New Minster is also associated with Alfred, though only very preliminary work, perhaps the mere suggestion of its foundation, occurred in his lifetime. His son, Edward the Elder, was the real founder, assisted by St Grimbold, a Frenchman who was one of the scholars who had helped King Alfred. The New Minster was built in the heart of the city on land obtained from the Old Minster through the good offices of Bishop Denewulf, *c.* A.D. 904.[6] At best it was a cramped and inconvenient arrangement, which left the ordinary townsfolk little room in which to develop their own activities on the south side of the 'Cyp', or High Street. The charter relating to the site also refers to a number of Winchester churches, and names several streets. Part of the new foundation was to be on the site of the 'Wind' or Wicker church, and it is tantalising to consider what this could mean; perhaps some very early building is indicated. There are also references to other, presumably small, churches of St Gregory and St Andrew, and to North, South, East and West Streets. New Minster, thus established under royal patronage, eventually became the burial place of Alfred and his wife, whose bodies were first placed in Old Minster. Alfred's ghost is said to have haunted that church until his new resting place was ready. In New Minster the great king was buried 'to the right of the High Altar'; with him his wife, Edward his second son and two grandsons. Only a small later stone, now in the city museum and engraved with the word Aelfred and the date 871, survives as a possible remnant of the burial place of 'England's darling'.[7] New Minster was famous for its many relics, brought from all over Europe. Under royal patronage it was soon a serious rival to the older foundation, and a serious nuisance too, in that its situation cramped and hemmed-in the older community. Little is known of the extent of the church or the nature of its monastic buildings.[8]

Both Old and New Minsters soon entered a period of decline, until the activities of three men who had close connections with Winchester brought about a great revival in the mid-10th century. Dunstan, Ethelwold and Oswald, contemporary figures, reorganised the Church in England during the reign of Edgar,

5. The minster plan from the north transept.

their patron, with such a marked degree of success that England became the centre of a highly specialised civilisation and culture. Winchester formed the very heart of this revival.

A native of Winchester, Ethelwold was devout, learned and apparently designed from his youth upwards for the service of the Church. He had gone to Abingdon, and became Archbishop of Canterbury after Dunstan. In A.D. 963 he was appointed to Winchester as a reforming bishop, bringing monks from Abingdon with him. They entered the Old Minster and turned out the secular priests there. It is arguable whether this was a necessary reform, or whether it was accompanied by violent action, but it was successful, and was followed by similar change at New Minster. The cathedral church was now in the care of monks, unusual when compared with most other European cathedrals. Ethelwold's revival of religious life in these two monasteries eventually included major architectural changes to their churches. An important charter of King Edgar affected the boundaries of all three Winchester houses; apparently the small dwellings of townsfolk were pulled down to make a larger monastic enclosure.

Old Minster was rebuilt, a reconstruction perhaps primarily intended to rehouse St Swithun's bones with suitable dignity, for the cult of that saintly bishop was becoming important in English religious circles. In A.D. 971, Ethelwold moved Swithun's bones from his tomb outside the Old Minster to a more honoured place within the church, where the great work of reconstruction was finished in A.D. 980, four years before Ethelwold died. Ten years later, under Bishop Alphege, further change or restoration was undertaken at the eastern end and a crypt and tower added, perhaps intended to rival the great new tower of New Minster. The sanctity of the older foundation was further confirmed by the addition of another special shrine or tomb for the relics of St Ethelwold.

In the 100 years before the Norman Conquest, Winchester thus had three eminent monastic foundations, with churches of high quality, whose communities made an important contribution to the cultural life of England. The monks' life was full, and subjected to the discipline of the *Regularis Concordia* of *c.* A.D. 970 which had been drawn up by Ethelwold and approved by a gathering of monks and nuns in the cathedral church. Not only architecture, but metalworking, weaving, and bone and ivory carving flourished under church patronage. The most splendid product of these reformed churches was the series of manuscripts in the style now known as the 'Winchester School' of illumination, which were products of their *scriptoria*. The earliest complete book in Winchester today is the Latin copy of Bede's Church history in the cathedral library, copied in about A.D. 960, apparently from an Irish manuscript, and a reminder of what the cathedral and the New Minster once possessed and were able to produce. It is not always easy to decide which 'Winchester books' were in fact written and illustrated in Winchester, for the style and manner of the artists were admirably reproduced in other monasteries. However, Winchester-style manuscripts are to be distinguished by the quality of the workmanship and by the framework of foliage which usually decorates each main design in a multitude of twists and turns. It is work which can be seen at its most splendid in the Benedictional of St Ethelwold and in the brilliant and vigorous representation of King Edgar offering New Minster its charter of refoundation. In the so-called *St Grimbold's Gospel* of the early 11th century, the framework has been filled in with angels not unlike those in an ivory carving in the city museum. At a later date, but still before the Norman Conquest, a further development took place, when some illustrations took the form of line drawings in a reddish-brown ink, with colour added, and of which the well-known picture of Canute and Emma offering a cross to New Minster is an example.[9]

Winchester monasteries were famous for other skills. The convent for nuns, St Mary's, has been credited with the making of fine needlework; St Cuthbert's stole, in far-away Durham, may have been sewn in Winchester. Music, too, was another product of the monasteries. Old Minster had a famous organ which produced a tremendous noise, hardly surprising since it had to be worked by 70 men. Scholars like Aelfric, called the Grammarian, and Wulfstan, the poet, who described the procession when St Swithun's bones were moved into the new cathedral, were monks whose place in history is secure.

The kings who made Winchester their capital may have lived in the High Street near the precinct of the three monasteries, though there were palaces and royal halls in other parts of Hampshire. The wall of Winchester secured the town from the ever-present threat of invading armies, though the defences were breached on several occasions. In Alfred's time and in the reign of his son, Edward the Elder, the defence system of southern England, in which Winchester was a vital link, was improved. An important document, the so-called Burghal Hidage, indicates the city's rôle.[10] Thirty towns within this system were fortified boroughs, Winchester and Wallingford being the two largest, each with an estimated 2,400 men manning the defences; calculation shows that the standard number required would be able to defend almost the exact length of the known medieval walls.

Another significant feature which brought prosperity to the late Anglo-Saxon city, once Alfred had secured peace with the Danes, was the presence of a revived mint, or mints, to manufacture the coin of the realm.[11] Pennies were coined bearing the inscription 'Win', and silver halfpennies also made, though none have survived. Alfred has been called the inventor of the halfpenny. Later kings did not order the name of the mint to be included as part of the design, but it seems likely that a mint continued to work in Winchester. By the time of Athelstan there were six moneyers in the city, and at the heyday of the revival associated with Ethelwold the number had increased to nine; they produced an attractive small silver coin, with the king's head on one side, and a cross and the moneyer's name and mint on the reverse. Name and place, both abbreviated,

6. Statue of King Alfred.

are separated by the word *On*, meaning 'at'. The political troubles of Ethelred the Unready's reign produced a need for vast quantities of coin for Danegeld, and the number of moneyers working in Winchester rose to forty. Considerable numbers of their coins have been found in Scandinavia.

The moneyers were soon in a class of their own, men of substance following a risky profession. The name of Godwin Socche, a master moneyer in the High Street, is found on coins of four kings, including those of Edward the Confessor. A small lead trial-piece, a rare example of its kind, and used by a moneyer called Aestan in the same reign, was found in an excavation in Middle Brook Street in 1953.

As well as standard coinage, standard weights and measures were a sign of the stability of the late Anglo-Saxon kingdom. Winchester, like London, kept the necessary standard measures in weight and in length. In Edgar's reign the ordinance of the Hundred required that one money only should pass through the king's dominion, and let one measure and one weight pass such as is observed in London and at Winchester'.[12]

A survey made for Henry I in 1110 comparing the contemporary city with Winchester in the days of Edward the Confessor shows that most of the essential features of its topography are to be found in the last 50 years before the Norman Conquest.[13] The main street (High Street, *Altus Vicus* or 'Cyp') was occupied in part on the south side by an enclosure surrounding the three great monastic churches. Further west, and still on the south side, there was probably a royal hall, the king's residence, and beyond this, towards Westgate, there seem to have been about seventeen other properties of which the king was lord, though the occupants were not particularly connected with his household. On the other side of the road, High Street north, the king was again the chief owner: at the east end stood the Chenictehall, 'held freely from King Edward'; at the west end another knights' hall was similarly held. Whatever their function, the title must suggest a group of soldiers (chenictes) and the situation of these two halls suggests that their function was connected with the defence of the city. Possibly they were the knights who guarded the Anglo-Saxon treasures when they had to be moved, just as the chamberlains' knights did in the early Norman period. There is little indication of variation in the size and nature of buildings, though some variety is indicated by sums paid in *gablum,* the rent paid to the Crown. In the High Street there were houses, land, stalls, shops (escheopes) and a baulk prison house on the north side, east of God-begot, apparently in the charge of a knight called Ailward. The inhabitants singled out for description were usually either priests, moneyers, or local officers – provosts or bedells. Amongst the named priests, Elsi appears to be associated with a large multiple holding, including a church, on the north side of the High Street towards the east, and this is perhaps the property which later became the Linenselde or Cloth Hall. In the time of King Edward the Crown had 63 burgesses in the High Street.

There was a substantial suburb outside Westgate, and there were houses outside Northgate, 'nine above the ditch', and nine at Pallies Putte, not yet identified. On the northern side of the High Street most of the street pattern as it was in the 18th century, if not all of it, was already in existence. Snithelinge Street (Tower Street) had comparatively few houses, but Bredene Street (Staple Gardens) was a substantial area with a large number of royal holdings, including several houses each distinguished as a *Mansio.* The king also had property which paid *gablum* in Scowertenstreat (Jewry Street), Alware Street and Fleshmonger Street (St Peter Street). Edward the Confessor's treasurer, Henry, lived in a *mansio* in 'Wengenestret', later Middle Brook Street. Tannerstret (Lower Brook) contained much royal property, as did Bucchestreet, which has disappeared except for its eastern entry, Busket or Buck Street. Off the south side of the High Street, Caple Street (St Thomas), Gold Street (Southgate), and Gerestret (Trafalgar Street) were also in existence. Exactly how old the Winchester street pattern is remains uncertain; recent archaeological evidence suggests that Gar Street dates perhaps from the period of the Burghal Hidage; Fleshmonger Street, Sheildwright Street (Upper Brook), Tanner Street and the High Street also date from the Anglo-Saxon period. The Brook Streets perhaps originated with Ethelwold's 'making of the conduits'; High Street and Middle Brook follow, at least in part, the lines of Roman roads.

Pre-Conquest Winchester thus contained many of the elements of its later prosperity. It was a strong town, with a dependable wall and a garrison; its mints and its churches were closely linked with the royal presence. Though the majority of its inhabitants were humble people, living in small and unsophisticated dwellings, there were many prosperous burgesses, subjected in theory to the king as lord of the land on which their houses were built, but free from the tiresome restrictions of a manorial overlord. There were local officials and a court where the customs of Winchester were made and upheld. Above all, pre-Conquest Winchester was a royal city, a city of churches and the capital of England, where the crowning of Edward the Confessor on Easter Day (3 April) 1043 was a ceremony of much pomp and magnificence, carried out by Archbishop Eadsige of Canterbury, assisted by other bishops, and followed by the arrival in Winchester of ambassadors from Germany, France and Norway, with messages of congratulation and with varied gifts. It was the last splendid royal occasion of Anglo-Saxon Winchester.

Chapter Three

The Struggle for Freedom, 1066-1215

The realm would never have been subdued had Winchester remained a stronghold for Englishmen; it was vitally important that the stamp of the Norman Conquest should be firmly impressed on the capital of England. The city was surrendered to Duke William by Edward's widow, Edith, in November 1066. There was no fighting; there had been a pro-Norman party since the days of Emma and Canute, and it has been suggested that the generosity of the Anglo-Saxon kings towards the Church had created amongst laymen a feeling of unwillingness to support the native royal dynasty.[1] Long before 1066, substantial parts of modern Winchester had been secured by the Church, the most important landowner being the Bishop of Winchester. He was lord of much land outside the southern and eastern walls, which was divided by the River Itchen into east and west sokes. The west soke was still electing its own mayors as late as 1838, and the bishop's jurisdiction was exercised until 1851 through his Cheyney court, to which all his tenants owed suit.[2] Within the walls, lesser holdings owned by ecclesiastical landlords were sometimes linked with specific manors. These 'haws' were part of the defence of the county: the abbeys of Wherwell and Romsey owned city property, as did the Archbishop of York.[3]

The Conquest in general left these ecclesiastical landowners undisturbed: it was the conquered Saxon laity who were dispossessed. For example, Alwin of Corhampton's Winchester house was handed over to Hugh de Port, the greatest layman of Norman Hampshire and a contemporary of Ralph de Mortimer, who took over the eight haws of the Saxon cheping of Headbourne Worthy. Some holdings were taken by the new king himself, namely the seven haws of the thegn Saxi, and two which had belonged to the Countess Gytha, Harold Godwinson's mother. The widowed Queen Edith, Harold's sister, was left in peace in her house on the north side of the High Street; her chaplain and adviser, Bishop Stigand, was not so fortunate. He was eventually thrown into prison on various charges, including that of holding the see in plurality with the archbishopric of Canterbury since 1052. He died in custody in 1072, but was given an honourable burial in his own cathedral. Edith died in 1075 and the Conqueror 'brought her to Westminster' with great honour. There was a different sort of death in 1076, when Earl Waltheof was beheaded 'outside of Winchester' for plotting against the king.

If there was a resistance movement of any kind in Norman Winchester it is difficult to determine its strength or its supporters. Certainly 1066 was a disastrous year for New Minster, that great stronghold of the English kingdom. On St George's Day some of its monastic buildings had been burnt down, the abbot (Godwin's brother) and a number of his monks had been killed at Hastings, and the monastery was left without an abbot for many years. Though there is no evidence that William I pursued a policy of revenge against the community, he drove a hard bargain with New Minster. The monks gave him the entire site of their burnt-out offices so that, in the words of their register, 'the king could construct his palace with his wall ... and in the fourth year of his reign the most noble King built his hall and his palace on this land'.[4] There was compensatory land given at Alton and churches at Kingsclere, a poor exchange for the loss of the Winchester precinct.

7. The west front of the cathedral.

Bishop Giffard's great contribution to the topography of Winchester was the removal of New Minster in 1110 from its cramped site near the cathedral to a comparatively undeveloped area on the north side of the city at Hyde; henceforth, the monastery was usually called Hyde Abbey. The whole of New Minster was destroyed, and the site was incorporated into the cathedral churchyard. According to New Minster historians, William I's palace with its great royal hall was constructed in 1069-70. From the survey of Winchester made in 1110 for Henry I, it is clear that the monastic site was not large enough and that burgesses' houses were demolished to make room for the Conqueror's palace. Twelve Saxon householders were deprived of their homes: 'they held houses and they were burgesses'; 'part of the site was the King's, part the Abbot's; now it is all occupied by the King's house'.[5]

Though the Norman palace was not nearly as large as the cathedral, it included a great hall, and the new building must have been a dominant feature within the High Street. Nothing now remains above ground, except perhaps some small patterned stones of a horseshoe design re-used in the rebuilt chimney-breast in St Lawrence's Passage. Tradition associates St Lawrence's church with the palace, which consisted of a group of buildings of various kinds within the jurisdiction of an important royal official, the constable. Residents in the constabulary owed suit to his court rather than to any court presided over by a city official. In 1212 the bailiffs were still paying a rent to the constable of the castle for a tenement which belonged to the king, 'where anciently was his hall'; a site between the two Minster Street entrances from the High Street is indicated.[6] The area behind, stretching south along what is now Great Minster Street, was also part of the constabulary. Houses on the western boundary of the cathedral churchyard were described as being 'in the Constabulary' years after the palace had disappeared, and are still occasionally referred to in this way. The area of the Pentice and the Square, or at least the northern side of the Square, was occupied by forges and by the royal mint. One roadway had been stopped up 'by the King's kitchen', and in the High Street the block called 'Mewenhaia', containing the royal mews, remained for many years after the palace had disappeared. William I may have constructed an entirely new group of buildings, or merely extended the existing Anglo-Saxon palace.

The Conquest, therefore, did not mean a sudden royal withdrawal. Winchester remained a royal headquarters, the centre of an expanding civil service, and enjoyed many financial and trading advantages from the presence of the Norman kings. Despite the rise of London it was to Winchester that the returns of the Domesday Survey were sent, and the development of the royal treasury was one reason why Winchester could still claim to be the capital of England.[7] Winchester under the Normans was a prosperous city, whose French- and English-speaking inhabitants were slowly learning to live as one community. It is not known how many men could read and write. There must have been an increasing number of bilingual Wintonians speaking French and English, while Latin remained the language of official record. By the time of John's reign a high grammar school, in what is now Symonds Street, was well established.[8]

The decision to pull down Old Minster was not surprising, because of its associations with the Saxon dynasty. Stigand's successor, the Norman Walkelin, was determined at first to replace its monks with a community of canons, a proposal prevented by the pope.[9] The new Norman building, south of the old complex and built over part of it, was deliberately designed to impress by mere size alone, but the quality of the surviving early Norman workmanship in the north and south ends of the two transepts is not high and suggests a building constructed by reluctant or inexperienced hands. It contrasts strongly with the impressive quality of the later tower, rebuilt under the second Norman bishop, William Giffard, when the central tower of the new church fell. It was said that the tower had fallen because Rufus had been buried beneath it, but architectural reasons can be advanced for its collapse; early Norman towers elsewhere met a similar fate. Sometimes called Walkelin's tower, it may have been rebuilt with that bishop's money; it was not his building. The tower's fine stonework, carefully set out and beautifully faced, is of a high standard, a credit to the generation of masons who constructed it. Soon after its completion, the relics of St Ethelwold were transferred to a new shrine in the cathedral. The original Norman east end was altered in the late 12th and early 13th centuries, and the western front, with two towers, was also rebuilt at a later date. The overall length of the Norman church was vast, and the west front extended far beyond its present boundary, to a line marked by the inscribed stone set in the wall of 11 The Close.

Nothing is known with any exactitude of the men who created this new building, which needed a great task force of manual labourers, and little is known of its monks. Walkelin appointed his own brother, Simeon, as the first Norman prior. It is not possible to suggest exact dates for every stage of the new Norman architecture of the cathedral or of the new close on the southern side of the great church but, according to the Winchester annalist, work on the cathedral began in 1079. In 1093 a solemn procession carried the shrine of St Swithun from the Old Minster to the new cathedral, and on the same day the demolition of the Old Minster was begun. Nothing was left except the high altar and one *porticus*: the altar was demolished in 1094, when relics of St Swithun and other saints were found beneath it.

Prior Simeon died in 1082, and the next prior after the Conquest was another Norman, Geoffrey, known as a literary wit, but good and holy. He died in 1107 after a protracted illness in which he gained the reputation of being almost a saint, and miracles were reported at his tomb. Perhaps Winchester needed a famous saint: there was as yet no indication that the cult of St Swithun or visits to his tomb were major features of the life of the reformed community. In any case, St Swithun was an English saint, and Englishmen were not always popular.

8. The south transept of the cathedral.

These impressive buildings, the new cathedral and the royal palace, were the
outward signs of the continued presence of royal administrators and flourishing
monasteries under royal patronage. Winchester was still the capital despite the
steady rise of London. Even the civil war of Stephen's reign proved to be only a
temporary set-back in the growth of Winchester's commercial prosperity. Bishop
Henry de Blois took a leading and varied part in the campaign of his brother,
King Stephen, against their cousin, the Empress Matilda. During this conflict he
was responsible for burning part of the city, including the palace in the High
Street. He fortified his own castle at Wolvesey, but he also collected antiques,
patronised goldsmiths, manuscript writers and illuminators, and founded the
Hospital of St Cross in his vill of Sparkford as a place of refuge for the sick and
poor, casualties of the times. His episcopate, for all its troubles, saw Winchester
taking its full part in what has sometimes been called the Romanesque revival,
and the survey of the town which he ordered in 1148 is an important source of
information which shows how quickly Winchester had recovered from the disasters of the civil war. De Blois was an outstanding European figure whose mark is
still on his cathedral, on Wolvesey and St Cross. He had once hoped that Winchester might be the seat of England's third archbishopric; but a city dominated
by a politically-minded bishop might well have found it impossible to achieve
the degree of local independence which was such a feature of Winchester's early
constitution. The Treaty of Winchester, agreed in 1153, settled the succession to
the English throne on Henry Plantagenet, and the city soon took its place
amongst those urban groups striving for local independence. With the accession
of Henry II, de Blois left England for a temporary exile in Cluny; henceforth
there were to be no more bishops who could be described as 'the leader of the
citizens'.[10]

Significantly, Winchester's first two surviving royal charters were obtained
whilst the bishop was in exile. Norman townsmen resented the bureaucrats who
regarded them as merely part of the shire, and it was the aim of Winchester not
to throw off the royal authority, but to establish direct contact with it by excluding the sheriff and his officials. The most important financial privilege which
could be gained was the right of returning its own farm (taxes) to the exchequer; that is, to send up the farm monies collected for the king direct instead of
paying via the sheriff. When this right had been secured in perpetuity, for a
fixed sum as a fee farm, an important stage had been reached. Winchester, however, did not gain this measure of independence until 1327. The desire for independence was counterbalanced by economic factors, the most important of
these being the prosperity which the city gained from being a royal centre.

Winchester was not cramped by manorial custom and manorial lords. Most of
the inhabitants were burgesses, holding a house in the borough and paying a
variety of local customs for the privilege. Perhaps the most important feature of
their tenure was the right to sell or devise real estate: houses and other prop-

erties could be let, sold or bequeathed by will, provided notice of the change was given. Private charters giving details of these changes had to be read in the city court and entered on the court roll, and in due course the change was legally established. Much can be discovered about the topography of medieval Winchester and the descent of properties from one generation to another, either in a variety of private charters, in the enrolment of those charters on the city court rolls, or the later books of enrolments.

Firm evidence for the existence of guilds in Winchester can be found from the reign of Henry I onwards. The Guild Merchant played an important part in the constitutional progress of the city. From the evidence of the only surviving pipe roll (1129-30) from the reign of Henry I, it is clear that craft guilds of weavers and fullers were already in existence.[11] The charter which Henry I gave to Wilton between 1121 and 1133 granted 'to my burgesses of Wilton to the Gild Merchant (all those liberties) which my burgesses of London and Winchester have'. The real beginning of Winchester's advance towards freedom in local government was almost certainly a charter of Henry I, now lost, perhaps burnt in the civil war of Stephen's reign – a charter to guildsmen, worthy men, or burgesses. This charter, in general terms, was accepted into the Middle Ages as the foundation stone of Winchester's local liberties, and referred to in the charter of Henry II which confirms on the citizens 'all liberties and customs which they used to have in the time of King Henry my ancestor'. In the early 15th century it became necessary to make a new tarrage, or list of properties paying a proportion of the fee farm rent, and the roll, made in or soon after 1417, contains a copy of the alleged contents of Henry I's charter. That a degree of corporate action other than by members of the Guild Merchant was possible can be implied from other sources.

Moreover, the 'men of Winchester', not the guildsmen, accounted to the sheriff for all their financial payments owing to the king from the city, and then the sheriff 'returned' the farm to the exchequer. The question of who was responsible for collecting the king's money is not one of mere pedantic constitutional or financial history, but a vital matter which concerned the development of the city. In the years 1155-7 the return for Winchester was made by a certain Stigand. When the late Professor Tait's outstanding book on the medieval English borough was published in 1936, he described Stigand as perhaps the reeve (*praepositus*) of the city, and an enrolment in the cartulary of St Denis' Priory makes this certain.[12] Stigand may have died in office, for the pipe roll of the next year shows that his son, Gervase, accounted for 160 marks, 'his father's money', and in 1158 the farm of the city reverted to the sheriff of the county. As the most likely date for Henry II's two Winchester charters is 1155, it is difficult not to think that Stigand as reeve played a prominent part in their negotiation. That the city returned to its own farm in the reign of Henry II was known to a 15th-century town clerk; under Henry's name he wrote, 'in his time the city of Winchester was handed over to the citizens whilst it pleased him'.

9.   Portico frieze on the Guildhall.

10.   Charter of Henry II, 1155.

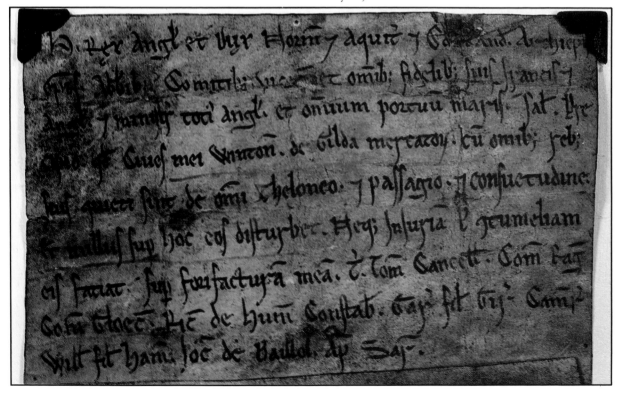

Henry II granted one charter for the benefit of the Winchester Guild Merchant and one to 'my citizens'; that is, there were two local groups able to negotiate with the Crown. The grant to the Guild Merchant is endorsed 'Prima Carta' in a 14th-century hand, and it has always been called the first charter. In brief, it is a royal command addressed to the king's officers and subjects, French and English, requiring that those citizens of Winchester who are of the Guild Merchant are to be quit of all tolls and customs, and that 'no-one disturb them'. The Winchester Guild at this time was in a strong position.[13] The charter for the citizens was also given at Salisbury and has the same witnesses with two additions. It confirms the privileges enjoyed by citizens in Henry I's reign, including the right of holding property according to the custom of Winchester.[14] The same considerations apply to its dating, and the evidence of the handwriting of the two chancery scribes who wrote out the two grants confirms this date; it seems probable that both charters were obtained in 1155 on the same occasion.

Between the years 1158 and 1190 the power of the Winchester Guild grew, and it was the Guild Merchant which obtained the next charter, from Richard I, when the king was at Nonancourt on his way to join the crusade.[15] His charter confirms the rights which the guildsmen had in the days of Henry I, including the right to hold tenements according to the custom of the city and also the rights of making purchases and mortgages according to Winchester practice. Illegal customs levied at the time of the Civil War were quashed, the citizens were to have the king's firm peace, merchants travelling to Winchester were to come and go in peace, and the citizens of the Guild Merchant were exempted from pleading outside the walls of Winchester. By 1190 the Guild Merchant was well established, and its privileges were highly valued in other English towns whose guildsmen sought similar treatment. It is hardly surprising that Winchester became known as the mother of cities.

It is difficult to believe that by 1190 the borough community in Winchester and the Guild Merchant were only two aspects of the same body, for the charter of Richard I specifically exempted a most important group of inhabitants, 'our moneyers and our officers'. That is, in 1190 there was living in Winchester an influential group of men to whom the fundamental rights had not been given, particularly the right of trial in a local court. When it becomes possible to compile a list of mayors and bailiffs from the early years of Henry III's reign onwards, it is often these royal officers excluded from the charter of 1190 who are also named as city officials. The evidence would seem to suggest that the developments which took place next were the result of movements for independence inaugurated by citizens to whom the privileges of the charter of 1190 did not apply.

The success of that movement resulted in the decline of the Guild Merchant, though joining the guild and, therefore, becoming a freeman remained the normal method of taking up full citizenship until the passing of the 1835

Reform Act. Between 1190 and 1215, the date of John's charter to Winchester, the mayor emerged as the chief official of local government, rather than the aldermen of the Guild Merchant. In return for the payment of the farm the city was able to manage its own financial affairs and, in this respect at least, to exclude the sheriff. The king could revoke this freedom at will, or if payments fell into arrears. Not until 1327 was it granted in perpetuity as a fee farm.[16]

The first recorded mention of a mayor, unnamed, occurs on 5 April 1200 in an enrolment of Letters Patent preserved on the charter roll for the first year of John's reign.[17] He was probably Elias Westman, pardoned six marks by the king in December 1207 for the 'overselling' of wine and in 1215 given land in Cranborne. He held office in 1207, 1215, 1216, 1221, 1223 and perhaps also from 1227-8. A very early document relating to Hyde Abbey and now preserved amongst the muniments of Winchester College names Thomas Oisun as mayor and as he had died or left Winchester by 1207-8 he may have been Westman's predecessor. There is no foundation for the existence of the alleged mayor of 1184, the mythical Florence de Lunn, who was an invention of John Trussell.[18]

After 1234 the names of at least 20 other mayors can be distinguished before 1301 when the Book of Enrolments (now known as Stowe MS 846) begins, and from when it becomes possible to draw up an unbroken list. Few early mayors held office for only one year, and the existence of a mayor did not signify the absence of other officers.

The king's orders were addressed to a variety of local officials, apparently indiscriminately, at the time when the powers of the mayoralty were developing. Henry III was loyal to Winchester, and positions in his household were frequently filled by Winchester men. The early close rolls show the royal commands addressed to the mayor alone, to the mayor and bailiffs, to the bailiffs alone, and to the mayor and *praepositii*. Often the term 'worthy men' (*Probi Homines*) was a description used by the king when referring to Winchester's inhabitants in orders addressed to other authorities. In John's reign, at least, the royal concern was only to see that there were responsible local officials to whom commands might be addressed and who would carry them out. Few letters close related to anything other than the needs of the royal household, sent, for example, when the king wanted wine, corn, spices for the Easter feast, or some form of transport.

The mayor was the head of the commune, the incipient corporation of Winchester, and its official acts were given legal authority by its use of a common seal, which was also frequently added to private documents for greater authentication. The earliest surviving impression of this seal appears to be that on a deed preserved amongst the muniments of Selborne Priory at Magdalen College, Oxford, belonging to the period 1225-30, during the early part of Westman's mayoralty. Significantly perhaps there are deeds of an earlier date in this collection upon which the city seal has not been used, its place being taken by that of the Oisun family. The chief feature of the city seal is a large Norman castle on the obverse, apparently with donjon keep and side turrets, perhaps representing the castle of the western hill. The legend, rarely complete on surviving examples, reads *Sigill: Civium: Wintoniensium.* On the reverse are a small cross and fleur-de-lis separated by the legend *Confirmatio si'lis.*[19]

Thus in the early years of the 13th century a corporate body was developing: it was not yet incorporated, but it was recognised by the king and had the powers of using a common seal and choosing a mayor. In one further respect the reign of John marked another stage in local government. His charter of 1215, not addressed to the guildsmen but to the citizens at large, granted them the site of two mills at Coitbury. This was the first real

11. Winchester city seal on a document of 1407.

estate ever owned by the corporate body.[20] Of less practical value was the confirmation of the mint and exchange at Winchester, for these hallowed features of the city's economic life were already in decline.

The mint had continued to be an important feature of post-Conquest Winchester, and associated with it was the exchange, which issued bullion to the moneyer and coins to the public. Between 1141 (when much of Winchester was burnt down) and 1152, there are no known examples of coins made in the city, but there was a revival in Henry II's time. The exchange was reorganised and rebuilt in about 1180 as a result of reforms initiated by the then bishop, Richard of Ilchester. In June 1215 there was a crisis when John gave the Winchester mint house to William de Pavilly, an ex-mayor of Rouen, who was in need of compensation for the losses which he had incurred as a result of the English defeats in Normandy. But the citizens stood firm, and soon John sent formal notification to the barons of the exchequer that there was always to be a mint in Winchester.[21] The citizens wanted to retain what had always been a sign of their prosperity and of royal patronage.

Pavilly seems to have made little use of his grant. After his death the old mint was leased to the city by Henry III at a rent of £6 a year and used as a drapery. In the Tarrage Roll of 1417 the Pentice is described as 'the pentice the which is now called in the King's Exchequer the drapery, formerly the King's mint'; the site of the old mint becomes obvious. It consisted of a large building (*Magna Domus*) to the south of the present Pentice and perhaps with a frontage to the north, but entered also from the west. The earliest Pentice buildings proper were probably a row of shanties or very small buildings, even stalls, *sub pentice*, put up in an attempt not to waste the valuable strip of frontage in the High Street. When Edward I instituted further reform and a new coinage in 1279, the Winchester mint shut and was never reopened. By 1298 the drapery building was already divided into separate holdings, some of which soon merged with the Pentice row in front, and there are later references, in 1359, to the pulling down of the Wol-selde and the receiving of its materials elsewhere in the city.

Mint and exchange were separated physically from the new royal head-quarters, the castle on the western hill for which there is documentary evidence from 1155.[22] Within its walls there were houses belonging to the king, a gaol, quarters for the queen, and the treasury of the realm. The main building was the king's great hall, and the castle was an integral part of the military power which backed the Norman and Angevin kings. It was a strong point from which to control the roads radiating from Winchester, along which slowly travelled the heavy carts containing the king's money.

It was the duty of several royal departments to see that the king was supplied with money, which might be stored in the wardrobe, soon an administrative unit in its own right. The need for a travelling treasury became apparent in John's reign, when the king frequently moved from place to place. This was a factor that contributed to Winchester's decline as a royal town, and thus the eventual triumph of London. When a French invasion of England occurred in the months of crisis which followed Magna Carta, moreover, the defences of Win-chester Castle did not prove effective. Castle and town surrendered to Louis of France in 1215 after only a short siege.

The innovations of Henry I and Henry II in law administration proved to be more lasting, and Winchester was an assize town until the reforms of 1974. Judges sat at the castle, were given presents by the corporation, and were enter-tained by the Hampshire gentry. Lawyers inevitably accompanied the retinue on circuit and Winchester became a good headquarters for the legal profession. A county prison was necessary, although imprisonment before trial was more usual than imprisonment after a conviction: the penalties of death and mutila-tion were short and sharp. There has been a county gaol in Winchester for hundreds of years.[23] In Edward the Confessor's time felons were kept in the prison in the High Street, and under the Angevin kings there was a gaol in the castle, maintained by successive sheriffs of Hampshire. An order of 1228 forbade

12. An early 19th-century painting by T. Hart, a friend of Turner, of the outer side of the West Gate.

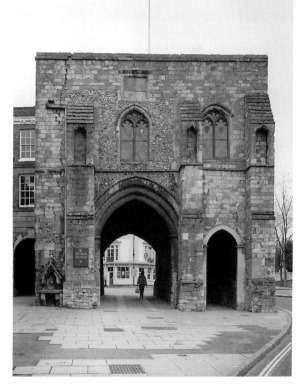

13. A modern view of Westgate.

the sheriff to keep prisoners there, and the county gaol was removed to the site between Staple Gardens and Jewry Street, where it occurs in the tarrage of *c.*1417; it is also depicted in Speed's map of 1611, and was rebuilt in 1788. Political prisoners and some breakers of forest law were kept in the castle, while Wintonians were put into the Westgate, a city prison maintained by city funds.

Henry III loved Winchester and its castle, where he had been born on 1 October 1207, and spent much time there. A major building operation, the creation of a new hall, was begun in 1222 under the direction of a number of 'keepers' including the mayor of Winchester, and the work went on for several years. Much of the later work was superintended by Elias of Dereham, and the decorations included a 'wheel of fortune' which may have been the predecessor of the Round Table. The fortifications were strengthened and a great new don-jon keep was added in 1259-68. It is tempting to think that this is the massive building which appears in the first 'view' of Winchester, a 14th-century drawing, discussed by J. Harvey in *C.R.*, 1958.

The great hall survives as Henry III's contribution to Winchester, but in other respects his reign was a disastrous period in the city's history. A few early parliaments were held in the castle hall, and in 1270 Winchester was the scene of a brilliant military assembly, when the Lord Edward, Henry III's heir, assembled his fellow crusaders before going off to the Holy Land. When the king died in 1272 the young prince was still abroad, and the Winchester annalist recorded the death of Henry of Winchester in a brief factual manner without encomium. Much of Henry III's work was destroyed by fire in 1302, when Edward I and his second wife, Margaret of France, had a fortunate escape. The castle never recovered its former glory, and though there were later royal visits the increasing use of gunpowder soon made its future uncertain.

Another important result of the coming of the Normans was the establishment in Winchester of a Jewish colony, an extremely influential group until their expulsion by Edward I in 1290. They settled in an area bounded on the west by *Vicus Judeorum*, the street of the Jews, being, as in other towns, sufficiently near the castle to ensure royal protection. Winchester Jews were moneylenders, but it is clear that there were also Jewish traders engaged in a variety of operations. Nor, despite the canon law of the Church, was money-lending confined to Jews.

The first mention of Winchester Jews appears to be in the survey of 1148. Perhaps their arrival should be regarded as part of the revival and new prosperity which followed the calamities of the civil war. A synagogue and a school were built in the area between Jewry Street and the present Royal Oak Passage; a separate Jewish cemetery was permitted on the western hill, significantly on land within a manor of the Priory of St Swithun, though the landlord was the Hospital of St John. The Jewish colony escaped the dreadful pogroms which marred the years 1189-90 in other parts of England. 'Winchester alone spared

14. The Round Table.

her vermin', wrote a critical contemporary and, in fact, the Winchester Jews were not only tolerated but were positively welcomed by some Wintonians. In 1194, when Jewish registries were set up in certain English towns, Winchester was included. In these centres single copies of the tripartite chirographs that recorded each financial transaction were kept in *archae* (chests), which were often looted or burned in times of unrest. Chests were under the care of four local chirographers, two Christians and two Jews.

In 1226, the Jewish community in Winchester obtained permission to leave off that distinguishing sign, the badge or *tabula*. Its members prospered, but Jews were always at risk, if not from the citizens then certainly from their patrons, the kings of England, who could tax Jews at will whenever the royal treasury needed replenishing. In 1211 Isaac the Chirographer, a Winchester Jew, his wife, Chera, and their children were taxed at 5,100 marks, and actually paid off £1,336 9s. 6½d., the largest sum of its kind on the roll of 1212. Jewish women played a leading part in the life of the community, and Chera was an important financier: her transactions had extended to Essex and Bedford. After her death, the best-known Winchester Jewess was Licorcia, who settled in the city after the death of her husband, David of Oxford. She was one of the sufferers in 1264 when the followers of Simon de Montfort the younger sacked Winchester, and the Jewish community was at grave risk. Hers was a family which made enemies: Licorcia herself was murdered, either in Winchester or King's Worthy, in 1276 or 1277, and at the same time her Christian maid was also killed. By this time anti-Jewish feeling was once more rampant in many English towns, and in 1278 many Jews were flung into prison for coin clipping, amongst them Benedict the Chirographer, Licorcia's son. He was tried and hanged in Winchester. The pipe roll of 1285 contains an account of his property, and shows him to have been a jeweller and pawnbroker: his chattels include large numbers of silver cups, spoons and rings, peridots and garnets, as well as 'forty-nine books of the law of the Jews'. Part of his estate was purchased by a well-known Winchester goldsmith, John Moraunt, and it may have included Moraunt's Hall in St Clement's Street.

Other Jews managed to leave the city as fugitives, amongst them Benedict the Guildsman, who had owned houses in all the important streets of the city: his property was confiscated and regranted to his non-Jewish fellow citizens in 1279. He was the man who made history in 1268 when the then mayor, Simon the Draper, allowed him to be admitted to the Winchester Guild Merchant. The clients to whom he lent money included such prominent laymen as Adam de Gurdon, who can only be described as a Hampshire highwayman; Sir William de Lisle of the Thruxton and Isle of Wight family, which was always financially embarrassed; and heads of religious houses, such as Prior Valentine of Winchester Cathedral, whom Benedict successfully sued, and the Abbot of Beaulieu. A prominent Winchester citizen, Henry de Derngate, was arrested in 1279 for buying 'goods of Jews hanged for trespasses of the coinage ... clothes, furs, books of Christians and Jews, copper lamps and girdles of silk ... in order to sell them'. He was fined 1,000 marks.[24] The expulsion of 1290 marked a stage in the decline of the medieval city. The Jewish area, in parts, was not completely re-developed until the beginning of the 19th century, and Winchester citizens lost a valuable source of contact with a wider world. The Jews of Winchester had provided, too, the credit and the financial acumen which were essential aspects of the city's prosperity.

Chapter Four

Church and Society

Medieval Wintonians had no excuse whatsoever for not going to church, as there were parish churches everywhere – within the wall, on top of the city gates and in the early suburbs.[1] In 1990 only one parish church, St Lawrence, remains within the walls, wedged in tightly on a central site south of the High Street on the edge of the Square. It is a church which has had many a narrow escape, as its plain interior indicates. Part of the fabric is Norman but, significantly, the advowson used to belong to Hyde Abbey (New Minster).[2] It may well be that in origin it was what St Bartholomew's at Hyde became later, a small 'parish' church used by lay folk associated with New Minster rather than, as has been suggested, a chapel of the royal palace. In *c.*1477 the church was rebuilt through the generosity of a group of parishioners, whose names Wavell recorded from a document which he saw, but which is now lost.[3] Presumably the tower dates from this period, although it has been much altered. A blocked door in the northern wall represents the old way through from the High Street before the making of St Lawrence's Passage; the door looks Norman, but could be Jacobean, and can also be seen as an integral feature of 41 High Street.

In the paved area immediately north of the group of buildings now described as God-begot, the ground plan of one of Winchester's earliest churches can be seen marked out. This is a site which was excavated in 1957, and marks all that is now left of St Peter *in Macellis*, St Peter in the Flesh Shambles. Not only has excavation revealed much about the building, but documentary evidence shows that it had been founded before 1012 by a Wintonian named Athelwine, in memory of his parents. It is possible that other Winchester churches owe their origins to this sort of private piety. St Peter *in Macellis* was small, and in its earliest form of 1012 had a rectangular chancel built of flint and stone, with sarsen stones and one Roman baluster built into it. It was rebuilt in the 12th century, an apse added at the eastern end, and the northern aisle built. The western end, possibly the site of the church's bell tower, has not been recovered.

In the north-east corner of Winchester two churches dedicated to St John survive: St John in the Hospital, and St John in the Soke (*in Montibus*, or 'uppe doune') which, architecturally, is the most interesting of all the parish churches. Its tower, like that of St Peter Chesil, is a feature of the soke. That church is also a fine medieval building, but is redundant and has been converted into a

15. St Peter Chesil.

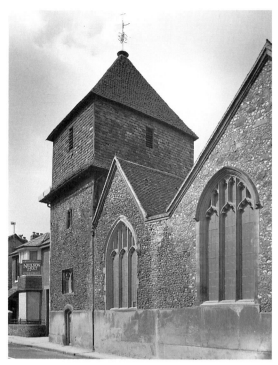

16. St Michael in the Soke,
now used by Winchester College.

17.   Kingsgate, with St Swithun's church above, incorporated into the city wall.

theatre. Further south there remains the church of St Michael, Norman in origin but with a new chapel added by Butterfield in the 19th century, now used as a chapel by Winchester College.

Eastgate and Northgate had churches over them, both dedicated to St Mary and serving small parishes, while St Swithun above Kingsgate is still to be seen. St Bartholomew is the surviving parish church at Hyde, where there used also to be a chapel dedicated to St Stephen. If the private chapels, royal chapels and the episcopal chapel at Wolvesey are also included, and allowance made for the men and women of the three great monastic churches, a considerable proportion of the population of medieval Winchester was dependent on Mother Church for sustenance.

The establishment of four friaries in Winchester poses some interesting social and economic questions. Friars were usually to be found in poverty-stricken districts ill-served by parish churches or by the relief work associated with monasteries.[4] The first order to be established appears to have been that of the Dominicans, also known as Black Friars or Friars-Preachers. In c.1231-4 a small group under the patronage of the bishop, Peter des Roches, established itself in buildings at the north-eastern end of the High Street, near St John's Hospital. The site occupied about two-and-a-half acres, and was bounded to the west by Busket Lane. They preached the crusade in Winchester and many well-known men, including the king's brother, Richard of Cornwall, took the cross. Their church was dedicated to St Catherine, a saint particularly associated with crusaders. Nearby were the Franciscans, also established under royal patronage at about the same time. Their church, dedicated to St Francis, occupied 'the whole northern part of the space between Middle Brook Street, North Walls, and Lower Brooks', but did not go as far as Cossack Lane. The two other friaries were on the southern side of the town, outside the walled area. The Austin Friars, or Friars Hermit, whose church was dedicated to St Mary, eventually settled on a site in Southgate Street; the boundary cannot be determined precisely, although part of the area is still covered by a house called The Friary. Further to the east, the Carmelite or White Friars built their friary on the east side of Kingsgate Street; their church, too, was dedicated to the Blessed Virgin.

An unusual addition to the ecclesiastical communities was made in 1301 by Bishop John de Pontissara, when he founded the College of St Elizabeth of Hungary. St Elizabeth's was really a large chantry, for secular priests, with a substantial church, a belfry, and a staff of clerics and choristers under a provost. Its site, outside Wolvesey, was to the east of the later buildings of Winchester College in what was called St Stephen's Mead. It was the community's duty to pray for the souls of the quick and the dead, particularly for the royal family and bishops of Winchester.

Besides all the parish churches, friaries and the royal chapels, some wealthy Wintonians had their own private oratories and there were also the churches of the three Benedictine foundations. These communities made a particular and significant contribution to the life of medieval Winchester. The heads of the houses were great people, usually revered and respected. They lived in state, attending the conferences of the realm, going to parliament, advising kings, and opening a Winchester window to a wider world. Their buildings set a standard of architectural merit, and they had distinguished visitors. There were educational opportunities too, though these were limited in their scope. Trade and commerce were stimulated, but the priory was frequently insolvent. Almost every shrine in England sold small base-metal badges to its pilgrim visitors; many examples are known, but surprisingly not one specimen has been found to indicate that its wearer had been on a pilgrimage to Winchester. The alterations at the east end of the cathedral in Bishop de Lucy's time are in fact the main evidence for believing that a large concourse of pilgrims visited St Swithun's shrine. Indeed, Pilgrims' Hall owes its name solely to a suggestion of Milner's, developed in the 19th century. The 'site' of St Swithun's shrine was marked out in 1936, although this was described as an act of faith rather than knowledge.

Despite the high reputation which the monastery had gained in the 12th century, the medieval priory was not famous for the making of manuscripts nor the writing of history.[5] The Annals were kept after Richard of Devizes died, but the

record ends in 1277, and is only a record, not distinguished by brilliant or pene-
trating description. A brief revival in the 15th century produced the historical
works of Thomas Rudborne, a scholar who made good use of earlier
manuscripts, now lost. Of illumination little has survived, though there are
many examples of beautiful handwriting amongst the various records of priory
business. It is the cathedral fabric which provides the best evidence of the artistic standard which the priory of St Swithun was able to ensure for future generations to enjoy. For example, the oak choir stalls, of c.1308, are the best of their
kind in England with a standard of artistic perfection which can hardly be sur-
passed: the decorations include over 500 heads, each carved with meticulous
care, and many of them clearly representations of living individuals. In the same
splendid tradition is the line of small decorated gables behind the feretory, a
series which once contained the statues of the benefactors and saints whose
names are recorded beneath them, a particular feature of this cathedral. The
scattered fragments of medieval sculpture which once adorned the place, and
which fell victim to reformers in the 16th and 17th centuries, are frequently of
unrivalled quality.

The priory precincts, which surrounded the cathedral on all sides, formed a
major part of the medieval city, and are still a vitally important part of the modern town. Access to the priory was by a great gate-house at the junction of Minster Street and Minster Lane. Traces of the building are visible in the extreme
north end of the close wall along the present Symonds Street, and the gate led
into a large flint-paved courtyard, behind the house now known as 10 The
Close, and other parts of the western range.

Until it was replaced in the mid-14th century by Bishop Edington, the west
front of the cathedral extended much further west than it does now. It was
partly obscured by a charnel chapel, the chapel of St Mary in the Forecourt.
The precinct wall on either side of the gate-house continued south along
Symonds Street, as it does today, and to the north contained buildings, some of
which were pulled down c.1853, although two survive (now 1 and 2 Great
Minster Street). The great churchyard, the main burial ground of generations
of Winchester citizens, lay to the north of the cathedral; the boundary of the
area which had once belonged to New Minster is said to have been marked by
a wall called Paradise Wall which ran parallel to and north of the nave of
the cathedral, about forty yards away from it, as shown on Godson's map of
Winchester in 1750.

The monastic buildings were on the south side of the church, as in the
arrangement found in other Benedictine houses.[6] Immediately south was the
cloister, entered by east and west doors, traces of which can still be seen: the present south doorway only dates from the early 19th century, although the
wooden door itself is much earlier. The cloister garth has lost its original shape
but still gives some idea of the effect of monastic enclosure. The western range

of buildings, often put to varied use in Benedictine communities, continued up to the church in a line from the house now numbered 10 The Close, and probably contained the main guest hall of the monastery, over a vaulted undercroft used by the cellarer. A considerable proportion of this undercroft, apparently Norman in origin with a later vault of *c*.1240, still remains, as well as the remnant of a large window at the south end of the upper floor. The south side of the cloister has gone, along with the monastic buildings on this side, though part of 10 The Close contains remnants of other early vaulted rooms. These were probably the kitchen and butteries of the monastic refectory which is known to have been here, a first-floor building which was entered by an external stairway. The eastern range of the cloister was separated from the church by a slype, the present dark tunnel now leading to 1 The Close, and to the infirmary of monastic times. Next to and south of the slype was the Norman chapter-house, with a fine colonnaded entrance off the cloister. Some arcading and the monolith columns of the entrance are all that remain of this important building. Stone columns of this kind are unusual in Norman or medieval work, and it has been suggested that the pillars are the reused remnants of some Roman building. The Norman and medieval arrangement of other monastic buildings on this side of the cloister remains uncertain, though the dormitory must have been here.

On the other side of the south cloister a much larger area contained the prior's house, including his hall (or halls) and his kitchen: one hall, a long 15th-century building, adjoined the south-east corner of the cloister and now forms part of the Deanery. There appears to have been some sort of office, an audit room perhaps, at the southern end of the hall, and further east the attractive porch used to lead into an open courtyard. There were other monastic buildings adjoining it and stretching eastwards. This eastern section of the Prior's Lodging, whatever it was, now more or less replaced by the 17th-century long gallery, looked out onto an area called the Green Court. Most of the close on this side was open space, a great garden on the site of the present Dome Alley and Mirabel Close, surrounding the mysterious building now known as Pilgrims' Hall.[7] Entry to the southern close was via the existing Prior's Gate and its predecessors, but there was another way in through the south wall along St Swithun's Street. This has been marked out in brick fairly recently, and the old opening partly renewed. The eastern half of the southern close was bounded by a branch of the River Itchen and by Wolvesey Wall. On its southern section along what is now College Street, formerly 'the road leading to Floodstock', the close wall is also the city wall, on the city ditch. Just before the place where the river now goes under the street, the prior had a small overhead gallery which enabled the community to pass into one of their outer gardens on the south side of College Street.

The entire precinct was well served by a water-borne sewage system. This was the monastic Lockbourne, traditionally associated with Bishop Ethelwold and

18. Excavation at St Mary's Abbey.

watering every part of the monastery. Much of it still survives unaltered. Drinking water was supplied from a conduit house at Easton, and was carried in lead piping into the close via the appropriately named Water Lane and Water Close, the small entry from Colebrook Street. The extent and nature of the buildings at this, the east close end of the precinct, is uncertain, as the monks' cemetery does not appear to have gone completely round the east end of the cathedral. The use of the present burial ground there has not revealed any medieval or later burials.

In contrast to St Swithun's, which survived the Dissolution, little is known of the layout of the once famous St Mary's Abbey despite the comparatively large area of Winchester which it occupied. In 1317, Roger de Inkepen, a Winchester citizen, endowed a charnel chapel dedicated to the Holy Trinity, which lay in the present Broadway. The abbey church was a fine building, with a spire which must have been a local landmark. The nuns were popular in Winchester; local girls were educated in the abbey school, the poor were nursed in the sisters' hospital (near the Charnel) and in the south-east corner of Winchester a substantial number of humble citizens depended on the convent for some proportion of their livelihood. The nuns' most useful local privilege, also a burden, was the responsibility of maintaining Eastgate, and the right to collect tolls on certain goods entering the city there.

Little is known of the extent and layout of the abbey buildings at Hyde, save that New Minster housed the treasures of the foundation, including the bones

19. Hyde Abbey gateway.

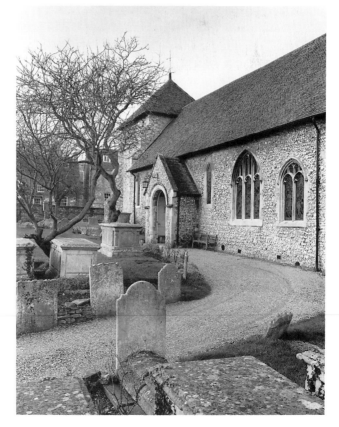

20. St Bartholomew in the Soke.

of Alfred, his queen and St Grimbold, and the cross of Canute and Emma. In 1141, the new church was burnt out during the civil war between the forces of Matilda and the bishop, Henry de Blois; many of the relics were destroyed. De Blois eventually made some restitution and, according to Rudborne, the church was rebuilt in 1196. It is presumably to this rebuilding that the surviving Romanesque capitals belong, those superbly carved fragments which are now in the parish church of St Bartholomew. The repairing of the monastery went on very slowly, and in 1311 Bishop Woodlock recommended that collections should be made throughout his diocese, the money obtained being given to Hyde for the completion of its monastery.[8] Any new prosperity was not to endure, for the monastery was much affected by the Black Death. In 1352 it was surrendered to Bishop Edington, on account of its 'need, indigence and misery'. It was an unfortunate community. In the early 15th century there were quarrels with the bishops and corporation of Winchester over the vexed question of the abbey tenants in the Hyde Street area outside Northgate. In 1445 a fire broke out in the abbey church, and the bell-tower, with its eight bells, was destroyed. Cardinal Beaufort left £200 for its restoration. A number of stone coffins broken and destroyed in 1788 were apparently contained in the nave, and a few surviving medieval documents refer to numerous altars within the church, including those of St Andrew, St Katherine and St Blaize. There was a lady chapel and perhaps also a chapel dedicated to St Thomas the Martyr.

The monastery had large estates, including much Winchester property. A few isolated Hyde documents which have survived relate to the area north of the abbey, Abbot's Barton, and Abbot's Worthy.[9] The mill there was farmed out. Abbot's Barton, as its name suggests, was kept in hand and contributed direct to the 'portion' of the abbot, and the revenue from Abbot's Worthy was apportioned in the same way.[10] In a community with such a large proportion of monks, nuns and parish priests, and being a city of active Christian belief, great care was taken to provide for the poor and needy, the old and infirm, and the indigent traveller. There were five hospitals for these varying purposes.

Early in the 12th century Bishop de Blois founded a hospital at Sparkford, a small tithing on the main Southampton-Winchester road about three miles from the city centre. Its chapel, in the parish of St Faith, was dedicated to the Holy Cross and the adjacent buildings were to be a home for 'thirteen poor men, feeble and so reduced in strength that they can scarcely, or not at all, support themselves without other aid'. They were to 'be housed, clothed, and fed with a daily loaf of wheaten bread, three dishes at dinner, and one for supper, and drink in sufficient quantity'. In addition, 100 poor men were to be given a daily meal. The endowment was substantial, chiefly in land throughout the county. In 1187 Pope Clement II added the considerable privilege of sanctuary: 'You may also receive clerks or laymen fleeing from the secular power, freely and deliberately, and retain them ... without contradiction from anyone'.[11] After

21. The Hospital of St Cross.

about 1303, the right of the bishops of Winchester to control the hospital was never questioned, although the masters appointed by some bishops were often unpopular choices, whose actions laid them open to criticism. It was a large establishment, made up of the master, four priests, 13 secular clerks and a number of choristers, whose chief task was to sing daily services in the magnificent chapel. This was such a striking feature that men ceased to call the small collection of houses along the main road, and what is now Cripstead Lane and Back Street, anything else but 'St Cross'.

Long before de Blois' famous foundation there was another hospital on the outskirts of Winchester, that dedicated to St Mary Magdalene on the eastern hill. Nothing now remains of it save the name Morn Hill, a doorway rebuilt into the Catholic church in Jewry Street and a splendid series of drawings made for the Society of Antiquaries in the 18th century by J. Schnebbelie, when the build-ings were in decay. As a foundation, however, it has survived as the small group of St Mary Magdalene almshouses on the Weirs, which can be approached via Mant's Passage from the eastern arm of Colebrook Street. These were built *c*.1926 to the design of a local surveyor, Harold Sawyer. The group now forms part of St John's Winchester Charity.

The foundation must have dated from 1155 at the latest, and the origin of the hospital is probably earlier. Plantagenet kings supported it by gifts of alms for the sick and the lepers on the hill. Since an inquiry had to be held in 1333 to try to establish the origin and functions of this particular hospital, it would seem that its earliest foundation documents had been lost by that date. Responsibility for supervision lay with a master, or *custos*, as at St Cross, and the most distin-guished master was undoubtedly William Wayneflete, later Bishop of Winch-ester and founder of Magdalen College, Oxford. In his time the hospital pro-vided for seven poor men and seven poor women, who were maintained by small sums of money and gifts in kind, including old clothes and flitches of bacon. The chapel was already the main feature, and was provided with a cer-tain number of books and a 'green carpet patterned with birds and with roses'. It stood south of the master's lodging, was 77 ft. long by 36 ft. wide, and had a nave with two aisles. In general, the style was late Norman Transitional, with characteristic pointed arches and perhaps earlier pillars. The arches were deco-rated with bold geometric designs, and the interior walls were covered in a vari-ety of wall paintings, depicting St Peter with his keys and the martyrdom of St Thomas à Becket. It could well have been a stopping place for those indefati-gable travellers who wished to visit both St Swithun and St Thomas of Canter-bury, but it was a hospital originally intended for those suffering from the variety of infectious diseases described as leprosy.[12]

The nuns of St Mary's maintained a much smaller hospital, on a site near the statue of King Alfred. This 'spital' building seems to have been used for poor women only. It was still in active use at the time of the Dissolution, when poor sisters were being maintained there, and the actual building remained until *c*.1798.

The monks of the cathedral priory maintained another hospital, in College Street. This venture originated as a home for the aged and impoverished par-ents of monks. It was a substantial building, south of the present College Street frontage, with a large chapel on the street.[13] In a painting of *c*.1690 the chapel appears as a flint building, about sixty-six feet long and twenty-seven feet broad, reaching from the present east end of the old brewery (library) to just beyond the porch of the headmaster's present house. On its western side was the gate which led into the hospital, and it seems unlikely that the chapel had an eastern window, since Wykeham built the college brewery right up against it. The hospi-tal itself contained a great hall and a group of small rooms; next to it was a sepa-

22. St John's Hospital.

rate kitchen with a thatched roof. All these buildings probably dated from the
first quarter of the 14th century. They were regularly maintained by the priory,
and part of the precinct was repaired in 1396 with stone and flint from the old
Norman front of the cathedral. There are only tantalising glimpses of the work
done by this particular institution, but its ancient origin is suggested in the
famous attack made on Prior Alexander in 1331 when one of his monks, Peter
Basing, accused him of various offences against the order and good government
of the priory. One of his misdeeds was stated to be the selling to outsiders of
portions due to the destitute parents of monks 'anciently maintained in a small
hospital'. But the prior was able to prove his good intentions, and the monk
Peter was described as a man who had stolen away from the monastery with
large sums of gold and silver and later appeared at the Papal Court 'not merely

as an erring sheep ... but as a stinking he-goat, trying to butt the Prior and convent with his horns'. In 1400 there were 16 sisters in the hospital, each receiving a yearly stipend of 15s. 2d. There was certainly a similar kind of hospital at Hyde, to care for the parents of monks who could not be expected to support their aged parents themselves, a normal obligation of medieval life.

St John's was the most important and the oldest of the five hospitals in the city. It is not certain when St John's was founded, but the monks at Hyde Abbey commemorated Bishop Brinstan (d. 934) as its founder each year, and when Leland came to Winchester he wrote 'there is an image of St Brinstan ... [in the Chapel] and I have read that St Brinstan founded a Hospital in Winchester'.[14] The foundation may well be of Anglo-Saxon origin, and the site on the north side of the High Street has been used since at least the early 13th century. At St John's, unlike St Cross, there were inmates of both sexes, but like St Cross it was a wealthy foundation. Its archives begin when it consisted of a chapel dedicated to St John the Baptist and a large building known as St John's House, presumably divided internally. Here the poor and needy were succoured and nursed, the Fraternity of St John met, and here the Corpus Christi Day procession began every year. The mayor was elected and other officers were chosen, or reprimanded when necessary, each autumn at St John's. The corporation's regular meetings were held there, and its records kept there in the common chest of the city. When 'Common Convocation' was held for the purpose of taking note of the transfer of private property, the charters recording these transfers were 'sealed' at St John's. The head of the hospital was usually described in early documents as *magister* (master) or *custos* (keeper or warden). By the end of the 14th century the master was sometimes, not always, the chief chaplain, but long before this it had become accepted practice for matters relating to the hospital's property to have 'the assent of the Mayor and Commonalty'. Not only the hospital seal, but the seal of the corporation had to be appended to such transactions, while every mayor had to check the inventory of St John's goods. Appointment as *custos* was sometimes regarded as equivalent to holding civic office.

The hospital's great rental roll of 1294 displays its many individual benefactors and shows an income derived largely from ground rents. In Winchester, many tenements and some shops in the High Street paid these rents; in every street the foundation could claim financial connection with at least one property. Some of the most profitable investments were the shops on St Giles' Hill, including a 'great shop in the Mercery opposite the Goldsmiths'; the hospital also owned other shops there which sold skins, garlic, wool, fish, cutlery and second-hand clothes.[15] The custos received 40s. a year. There were also two chaplains, male and female nurses, a collector of grain in the market and a hospital cook. In practice the permanent residents were generally men and women recommended by the corporation. The community of Christians who formed the medieval city had clear ideas about the rule of law and the maintenance of an ordered society.

Chapter Five

Aspects of the Medieval Economy

The river and its tributary streams formed an essential part of Winchester's economic life. A good water supply was necessary for many of the processes of the cloth industry, and the river could be used for transport, especially for the carrying of non-perishable, heavy goods, such as building materials. It also provided both drinking water and drainage. The Bishop of Winchester was considered to be the suzerain of the river and was the chief riparian owner, since the Itchen went through his soke, and the road along most of the eastern bank was the Chesil or Strand Street. From the time of Bishop Godfrey de Lucy (1189-1204) the bishops were entitled to levy toll on all hides, leather and certain other goods entering the river 'by the trench', that is, by the canal. Though there are scattered references, chiefly in the later medieval Brokage Books of Southampton Corporation, to goods travelling from Southampton to Winchester by water, the main method of transport between the two towns was by wheeled cart along the main Southampton-Winchester road. It is, however, practical to consider how the earlier bishops brought their building materials to Winchester, and it seems likely that de Lucy used his canal to transport the Caen stone employed in the rebuilding of the east end of the cathedral. In this respect he was following the example of earlier builders who had used Binsted stone, and anticipating Edington and Wykeham, whose supplies of Caen and Beer stone must surely have travelled in the same way. Other building materials which were not likely to have come by road include the blue Cornish slates used for roofing the chapel on St Catherine's Hill and the so-called Pilgrims' Hall.

Water mills were important to the local economy. There were fulling mills, corn-grinding mills, and at least one tawing mill where leather was made supple so that it could be used for shoes and sandals. Amongst those surviving, the City Mill at Eastgate Bridge appears in Domesday as the mill of the Abbess of Wherwell; it passed to the corporation in 1554.[1] The little mill which was once owned by the Cistercian nuns of Wintney has a confused history; it was called Posterne Mill, deriving its name from its situation near a postern gate at the west end of the south side of Colebrook Street, adjacent to the close wall. Its mill stream was indicated on Godson's map of 1750 as running round the east end of the cathedral to the west of the stream of St Mary's Abbey, and is still to be heard running underground.[2] The Abbess of Winchester's mill, Abbey Mill, existed in Anglo-

23. City Mill, now in the care of the National Trust.

24. Wharf Mill.

Saxon times, but its medieval history is virtually lost. It paid a water rate to the Bishop of Winchester, and the variety of control which the bishop was able to exercise over the Winchester mills is clearly delineated in the pipe rolls.

The rolls distinguish between the mills 'of the separate account', let on leases, and a second group which paid *aquagium*, a sort of water rate for the right to make use of the bishop's water. The mills 'of the separate account' were the *Molendium de Fonte Segrim*, the mill of Segrim's Fount, known now as Wharf Mill; the mill called Floodstock, at the east end of College Street; and a group of mills under the main heading *Bartona*, where there were at least two mills, one or more called Barton, the other Crepestre. Since the accountant who wrote up the pipe rolls was concerned with the bishop's property, it might be mentioned that the actual barton (or grange) which belonged to the bishop was in the north-east end of Water Lane, towards Winnall.[3] Bishop's Barton, as it was called, survived for years, and is not to be confused with its better-known Winchester neighbours – Prior's Barton of St Swithun's Priory, and Abbot's Barton of Hyde Abbey. It is probable, therefore, that early pipe roll references to the Barton mills may include a mill or mills at Durngate. The fifth mill 'of separate account' was the mill at Sparkford, to be distinguished from the mill of St Cross Hospital. The bishop's mill at Durngate was probably on or very near the site of a recently demolished 18th-century building, a mill still used for grinding in 1946; it is possible that a second mill occupied the site near *The Willow Tree Inn*.

Just below Durngate, a branch of the river goes off to the west to form the stream called Coitbury. Here were medieval mills whose history is quite distinct from those owned by the Bishop of Winchester. The mills were fulling mills, and they formed the first piece of real estate owned by the mayor and corporation. The site of one of them can be identified on the east side of Tanner Street (Lower Brook) with Coitbury water on its east and the millpond in it.[4] The second mill may have been on the triangular island now partly occupied by the new health clinic. Coitbury appears to have been the name given to this small island, and the name was also applied to a lane, the river, and 'the place called Coitbury'.

The fair on St Giles' Hill was another feature of the local economy controlled by the bishops.[5] The right to hold a fair there was first granted to Bishop Walkelin by William Rufus; it was to last for the three days of the Vigil, Feast and day after St Giles' Day, and the hill was named from the fair, not vice versa. Later kings extended the fair's length to 16 days and it soon became known all over England and the trading world. At the height of its success, the fair brought in the huge sum of nearly £150 a year to the bishopric. A vast number of people, English and European, visited it; other business had to stop whilst it was on, and even the city courts were forbidden to sit. Instead, a special court, naturally belonging to the bishop, administered merchant law to those who sought to have their actions settled in that way: this Pie Powder Court, quite distinct from

the city's own court of the same name, met in a temporary pavilion, and was
called 'Pavillion Court' (by corruption, Palm Court, held in Palm Hall; there is
still a house of this name on the hill). Merchants came from all over England,
and even from Ireland, most of them trading in wool or cloth. Perhaps this is
how the city acquired its Irish mayor, Richard Le Iries (Richard Iberniensis), in
*c.*1240. There were Frenchmen, Spaniards and men from the Low Countries.
They brought in wine, spices, silks and the other luxuries of medieval life, for
this was one of the four most important fairs in England. Though there were
some temporary stalls, the hill had a permanent layout of streets and shops,
named after the nationality of the merchants who used them, and there is some
indication that the area spread westwards, over the hill towards Chesil, in the
soke. St Giles' chapel was the most permanent feature, although it was once
badly burnt. In some ways the fair was a nuisance. Travellers were required to
pay toll to the bishop at Redbridge, Romsey, Crawley, Cheriton, Alresford and
Alton, and some of his tenants far away from the city were required to help at
fair time. There were frequent disputes between citizens and bishops, quarrels
at fair time, and arguments about the river. Moreover, the corporation's restrictions on trade and industry positively encouraged men to leave the centre of the
city and live in the soke where these regulations did not apply, despite the fact
that this could mean prosecution.

The inhabitants of early medieval Winchester were able to pursue a wide variety of occupations, and there were early craft guilds of fullers and weavers
whose struggles for independence appear in the payments which they made to
the king.[6] From the very nature of Winchester's natural resources, many of its
inhabitants were engaged in the woollen and cloth trades, and the fluctuating
fortunes of these industries are reflected in the varied economic prosperity of
the town. Through its regulations, the corporation was instrumental in hamper-
ing the manufacture of cloth. In the Usages of *c.*1276, looms and weavers were
strictly regulated.[7] No work was to be done outside the walls of Winchester and
every loom within had to pay 5s. a year. Every master weaver had to be a member of the guild, and wages of journeymen were fixed at 18d. per week in winter
and 2s. in summer when a longer working day was possible. Journeymen could
not be hired except on St Andrew's Day and yarn had to be bought only in the
Wolselde. The size of the pieces of cloth woven was also closely regulated to the
Winchester standard measure of 24 or 27 yards. Nightwork was not allowed,
except for very particular reasons at times of special difficulty. Not surprisingly
many men preferred to work in the soke, although that meant the risk of prosecution in the city courts or even in the court of the king's bench. It is clear that
the Usages were, in fact, echoing earlier restrictions; 50 or 60 years before the
Usages, weavers and fullers had not been allowed to sell cloth to foreigners, to
go outside the town or dip or dry cloth. If illicit trading was discovered, the
goods of the unfortunate craftsmen could be forfeited.

King John's grant of the Coitbury fulling mills to the corporation encouraged local government in its restrictions, for weavers tended to concentrate in the Brooks area near the Coitbury Mills, and lengths of cloth were dried on racks in the same districts. Amongst the earliest merchants trading in the export of wool (*c.*1272-81), Roger de Dunstaple, Hugh de Fulflood, and Thomas de Michel-dever were important citizens, men who could not be convicted in the city courts if the evidence against them was that of a fuller or weaver. Moreover, cloth-making was carried on by many men with 'un-English' names, and it may have been thought desirable to restrict them. Significantly, local cloth was described in the Usages as 'Chalones' after the town of Châlons-sur-Marne. Yet despite, or because of, the restrictions, men continued to work at the fulling and weaving trades 'outside of the walls' of the city; the bishop had at least one fulling mill, at Barton, and individual weavers paid sums into the episcopal trea-sury. One of the most prominent was Jordan Le Draper, who had property on St Giles' Hill and was perhaps the tenant of the bishop's fulling mill at Alresford. William de Dunstaple belonged to a family which traded in wool. When he died

at the beginning of Edward II's reign his estate included not only the Clothselde, held from the king, but also tenements in Gar Street, Gold Street, Buck Street, Jewry Street, Whitbread Lane, Colebrook Street, 25 shops in the soke and on St Giles' Hill, and a house and land at Sparkford.[8]

The great merchants of early medieval Winchester were not monopolists trading in only one particular product; there were specialists, but most merchants were general traders. Citizens who were commercially successful frequently became landed gentle-men, investing their money in real estate in the neighbouring Hampshire countryside. Another member of Jordan Le Draper's family, Simon, called the Draper and also 'de Winton', was an extensive landowner, having property in Lainston, Otter-bourne, Fulflood, Headbourne

25. Silver seal matrix (obverse), a royal seal used in the Winchester Court to register loans. The statute of Acton Burnell (1283) allowed contracts for loans and mortgages to be recognised in a few important boroughs, removing the need to use the central higher courts. This is the oldest piece of silver in the custody of the corporation. The smaller reverse matrix was lost in the early 14th century by Petronilla de Winton, wife of a local official.

Worthy, Weeke, and a mansion house at Soberton. He was knighted, may have gone on crusade, was Sheriff of Hampshire from 1283-5 and sat with the judges of assize, while his personal seal bore his coat of arms. He was mayor of Winchester on a number of occasions between 1266 and 1270, a substantial trader in wool and in wine, and a man who benefited from the advice of his Jewish friends.[9]

The detailed arrangements for the Corpus Christi Day procession reveal some of the other occupations. First came the carpenters and tilers, the smiths and barbers, then cooks and butchers. Cobblers, carrying two lights, marched next, then tanners and tapeners. Brothers of the Guild of St Thomas followed, and serjeants of the tailors, fishmongers, and skinners came seventh, vintners and brothers of St Anne next, then weavers carrying two lights, fullers and dyers likewise, candlemakers, masons and mercers. Round the Host walked four members of the Fraternity of St John, each carrying a lighted torch. Women also took part in the procession, apparently in the same order of precedence as their husbands.

Street names give some indication of the occupations of their inhabitants, and presumably in the period before the Norman Conquest the side streets were inhabited at least in part by tradesmen and manufacturers following specific occupations. Despite their names, however, individual streets had no monopoly in certain crafts, industries, or occupations. Goldsmiths' Row, the Mercery, Dubbers' Row, St Nicholas in the Fish, St Peter in the Flesh Shambles, indicate significant use at some time, as does Gold Street and probably Silver Hill. Among little-known prosperous early goldsmiths, John Morant (fl. 1314), alias Palmer, owned much property including the house called Morants Hall, and John Stul had a capital tenement within the aldermany of Wongar Street. Trade-names persisting down to the time of the Black Death include Le Canevasser, Gardiner, Fuller, Skinner, Le Breware, and Wyneman; Golfridus le Lyn'draper, Radulph le Spicer, Henry le Fischere, Philip le Hattere, Gilbert le Helier, and Stephen Hotecake.

Place-names used as personal surnames give some idea of movement to Winchester from other parts of southern England. William de Malmesbury, William de Bristowle, John de Wyght (a priest), Robert Bosyngton, William (de) Langeport (a priest), John Barbaton de Aulton, William de Bury, John Motesfonte, Robert Barbor de Romsey, Stephen Tysted, William de Wyke, Richard de Kilmeston, John Wynhale, John de Nutschullyng and John de Whitchurch are only a few of the men whose families must originally have come from areas outside Winchester. Adam de Northampton de Winton, a civil servant of the late 13th century, and the Berkshire family of Inkepens do not suggest a static population. One householder in Wongar Street in the early 14th century was described as John Parys de Micheldever, and sometimes names indicate possible occupation and place of origin, as was the case with William le Butiller de Candeuver.

Houses in the town were both large and small, ranging from capital tene-ments, which were substantial buildings, to cottages, either single or grouped 'under one roof'. Occasionally a house is described as *perinum*, stone built. La Peryne was the medieval building on part of the site of the present *Hampshire Chronicle* office. Shops were also single or 'under one roof'. Unusually large entrances to private houses were noted in the deeds or lease relating to the building concerned, such as 'with an entry by a great gate'. A similar entry marked the way to the *Red Lion*, an important property on the south side of the High Street. Presumably many small houses were thatched, but some were tiled, and fine examples of glazed ridge tiles have been found. It is not always possible to distinguish an inn from an ordinary dwelling house, since a private house might well be called by a particular sign. *The Moon*, on the north-eastern corner of Jewry Street and High Street, always seems to have been used as an inn, and was rebuilt early in the 15th century by Mark le Faire, and renamed *The George* at the time of Agincourt. *The Hart*, later *The White Hart* (just below the present Lloyds Bank in the High Street), and *The Chequers*, opposite, were also long-established hostelries, as was the inn called *The Bell* belonging to the prior and convent of St Swithun, within the area of the Linen Selde. The Abbess of Wherwell's inn, just inside Northgate, was also ancient and, since inns imply travellers, there were numerous smithies near the gates and at least one in the centre adjoining the ancient entry to New Minster called Thomasgate.[10]

Pedestrians could move quickly from one part of the town to another using small lanes, some called after the trade or the church which had brought about their original use. Velteres Lane, off Wongar Street, and nearby St Pancras' Lane, were in use over a long period. Other small passageways had temporary descriptions: 'the lane leading from William Beckhampton's house, with full entry into it', was a property boundary which must have meant much at the time. Silver Hill was almost a lane, and was sometimes described as 'the lane leading from Wongar Street to Tanner Street'. Hogheles Lane, from St Clement's Street, was perhaps named after a family, just as it is today after a later owner, Hammond.

Because there were many open brooks, pedestrian and wheeled traffic was restricted in some of the northern side streets, and even in the High Street itself, east of the Pentice, there were open streams. There were a few 'island' tenants; the Inkepen property at the end of Wongar Street, 'opposite Mewen-hay', was one which survived until the 19th century. At the eastern end of the High Street the substantial 'island' within the precincts of Nunnaminster con-tinued as a block until *c.*1798.[11]

There were no pavements for pedestrians but the bailiffs were supposed to take note of any encroachment on the highway. Offenders were required to remove obstructions or compound for them by paying a fine. The discovery of such encroachments, or purprestures, was one of the objects of the 'viewing' of the city, carried out periodically by representatives of the corporation, with the main purpose of checking up on those properties which had to pay the *gablum* rent to the bailiffs on behalf of the Crown. On these occasions, the state of repair of properties was often noted, and conversions from single large units to smaller groups (or vice versa) recorded. A note was made of 'pallices' or 'pallaces' (fences), or any other kind of purpresture. Special permission had to be obtained from the corporation in order to build over the highway. There were frequent but unavailing attempts to keep the brooks clean and fresh. Just behind the east entry of Middle Brook Street was a large public lavatory, the Maidens' Chamber, and there was at least one public latrine, on the other side of the High Street, near the north-east end of the cathedral. Fortunate citizens could draw their drinking water from their own private wells, of which there were many, and there was also a town well, later a town pump, near the city cross. The priory had a supply of conduited drinking water.

The walled town was crowded, and there were important suburbs outside all the city gates. Beyond Westgate an area of hilly undeveloped land still remains open, in part at least. Oram's Arbour is a place of much antiquity, which the citizens have the right to use for recreation, this privilege being of uncertain origin. The area is described in the custumal of St Swithun's Priory as part of the manor of St James, under the heading 'Fulflood' and 'St Maria de Valle'. Other documents refer to the king's ditch called 'Her' bur', and it seems clear that the name referred to the great embankment which is shown on Godson's map of 1750. The city tarrages distinguished between the arbour of the city and the arbour of the Abbot of Hyde, but in 1698 a lease of all the land to Alexander Oram, a stocking-maker, continuing to his son William in 1756, gave the place its present name.

Chapter Six

City of Alliances

In this community of alliances between laymen and Church, between citizens and kings and their courtiers, the prosperity of Winchester came to depend ultimately upon two important factors: on the strength of its economy and on the ability of local government to govern. Much depended on the goodwill of central government; even with this the mayor's orders had no authority in many parts of the city. Not surprisingly local government evolved slowly, and there were many set-backs.

In the last half of the 13th century the commune was rent by various disputes, and on many occasions the king took the city's government into his own hands in order to re-establish law and order. Personal rivalries within the corporation were made much more difficult by anti-Jewish feeling and by external difficulties arising from disputes with Southampton. By 1327 the citizens of Southampton were wealthier than those of Winchester, though not as secure from foreign invaders.[1]

At a famous meeting held in St Cross 'before many magnates', the two towns had agreed that the men of Southampton and Winchester should be exempt from each other's tolls. The Winchester party on this occasion was led by Stephen Fromond. His successor, Simon the Draper (mayor from 1266-70), was a peacemaker of a different kind; his action in admitting one of the leading Winchester Jews, Benedict, to the Guild Merchant eventually helped to precipitate a constitutional crisis in the city, and in 1274 the king's intervention was necessary to prevent local civil war.[2]

In 1287 the city again had its constitution suspended, but in 1290 Edward I confirmed the previous charters in the first of many *inspeximus* grants, giving no new privileges.[3] Three weeks later, on 18 July 1290, the general edict expelling the Jews from England was published. Within a few months the civic constitution was again suspended, and from 1291-5 the city remained in the king's hands. Another suspension of local officials occurred in 1305 and there appears to have been no mayor between 1305 and 1307, when the city was punished for the escape of one of the king's hostages from Bayonne. Undoubtedly local government was a risky business for men prepared, or sometimes forced, to undertake it. The dangers were not only personal: the accession of every new monarch put the liberties gained by previous generations at risk, and every privilege gained had to be renewed continually by *inspeximus* charters bought with money which the city could not always afford. The constitution as it emerged at the end of the Middle Ages was headed by the mayor, 'the principal sustainer of the Franchise', whose term of office was one year, and who was personally responsible to the king for his management of the city. John Edgar, described as late mayor in 1258, was fined 200 marks for trespasses during his mayoralty. In times of national crisis, or if the mayor was ill, it was not usual to remove him; instead, the king would name a group of citizens to help him, as in the autumn of 1338 when fear of French invasion ran high, following the French sacking of Southampton.[4] In 1343 the mayor, Nicholas de Exonia, 'so broken by age ... and impoverished by adversity', was given a royal writ of aid empowering other citizens, of whom six were specifically named, to help him 'in the rule of the city and the safe custody thereof in the eminent perils of the present war'.[5]

To help the mayor there was a council, the 'Twenty-four', leading citizens who in practice were usually ex-mayors or likely to become mayors in the future. Two bailiffs were chosen after a form of double election, the commonalty of the city choosing them from four men picked out by the mayor and Twenty-four. Their functions were particularly those having any connection with central government, but they were not always prompt in carrying out the royal commands. They collected the tarrage, were usually responsible for any work done on the walls, and with the mayor they presided over the city court and later over the pie powder court. The bailiffs were described as having the specific duty of 'doing right to all the Commonalty' but there is no evidence suggesting to what extent the oligarchy was influenced by public opinion. Amongst the minor officers were four staff-bearers, who were sergeants 'to execute the order of the mayor and bailiffs', and predecessors of the present mace-bearers.

The clerk became increasingly important for he wrote and kept the city's records. By 1353, when the city's surviving accounts begin, they were the work of the bailiffs, but by the end of the 14th century it had become increasingly usual to appoint a city chamberlain or chamberlains. The aldermen of the city had duties more humble than their title suggests, being personally responsible for their wards. They were the chief presenting officers at the borough moot. As time went on the number of officials increased, and by the reign of Richard II the corporate body was appointing not only the mayor, town clerk and aldermen, but also coroners, constables, four auditors of the Twenty-four, four auditors of the commonalty, cofferers, chamberlains, ponderors, and pesagers.[6]

The corporation met in St John's but it did have another meeting place, the hall of court of the city, where the mayor and the two bailiffs presided regularly over the city courts. Before *c*.1351, this was in a building on the site of 43 High Street. Significantly this court, 'the Court of our Lord the King' to give its full title, met in a building on part of the site of the King's Hall, where the Norman

26.   The Brooks.

27.   Middle Brook.

palace had stood. After the Black Death it was held on the first floor of a larger corner building on the eastern junction of St Thomas Street and the High Street. After *c.*1400 this hall of court was used more and more for the general business of the corporation, and the building in which it was held became increasingly described as 'the Guildhall', though this was just what it never had been. It is now Winchester's 'old' Guildhall, from which the curfew is rung each evening.

In this hall of court the city court met three times a week, presided over by the mayor and assisted by the two bailiffs. Justice was administered according to the ancient custom of Winchester and a wide variety of cases could be heard, subject always to the royal right of intervention by means of a writ – taking the case elsewhere if it required particular action. This court may have been of very ancient origin, and local custom confirmed by the series of royal charters was the main defence in matters of dispute.[7] A landlord who wished to recover his property had to follow the Winchester procedure of planting a stake: a stake was driven into the ground before the door of the property in dispute, and after a year and a day he was able to make a recovery. The earliest stake roll dates from 1296-7.

Much of the court's time was spent in civil business, the transfer of real property, the *de facto* registration of those transfers by enrolment of charters, and in proceedings for recovery of land. The court also dealt with a variety of other cases classifiable as trespass, damage to individuals or to their property, but those more serious matters took up less time than the hundreds of cases of debt. All these varied types of business could be brought to their own court by Wintonians who were citizens, as of right, though some preferred to strengthen their situation by obtaining a royal writ.

Important land matters were indeed frequently removed by writ to royal courts, either to the king's bench in London or to the travelling assizes. Gradually the amount of serious work carried out by the court diminished, and by the later Middle Ages it usually met only each Friday. There were alternatives open to citizens who resented its frequent delays and adjournments. Cases of debt could be heard in the city's pie powder court or the court of merchant law, and after 1344 the appointment of county justices made it possible for regular sessions of the peace to be held in Winchester, with some city members of the bench.

A considerable part of the working week of the mayor and the two bailiffs was thus consumed by legal business, and the records of the city court form a large proportion of the city's archives. The earliest surviving city court roll is a fragment for 1269, and the early rolls record not only the justice dispensed in the city court, but also wills and private charters brought before it. In about 1302 arrangements were made to improve the recording of those private charters relating to the transfer of property. Two huge parchment books of enrolments were put into regular use, recording the names of mayors and bailiffs and many important local events.[8]

The court rolls were also used to record the minutes of the corporate body, for in the late medieval period all important decisions were certainly being enrolled as ordinances. Ordinances seem usually to have been the result of a meeting of burghmoot, and in theory at least they were decisions of the mayor, his 'peers' and all the commonalty of the city. Burghmoot was held several times a year, and was summoned by horn. Everyone who owed suit at the city court was supposed to appear in person, and the mayor presided.

A citizen of medieval Winchester would also observe a number of other jurisdictions; indeed he might be a resident of what is now Winchester but find himself, because of the nature of his property, having to use other courts presided over by non-city officials. Little is known of the jurisdiction of the liberty of the cloth selde, and it seems to have been restricted to tenants who lived within the precinct of the buildings on the western junction of Middle Brook Street and the High Street. It is referred to in the Winchester Domesday as Chapman's Hall, and appears in the early pipe rolls under that name. In 1330, Robert de Bokyngham gave the cloth selde and certain other Winchester properties to the prior and the convent of the cathedral.[9] The grant of the cloth selde included the building and a fair called 'Lousfeyre' held on Tuesday and Wednesday every week in the precinct, 'with all its liberties and free customs'. A memorandum in the cathedral cartulary, where this important donation was recorded, defines the privileges of the lord of the cloth selde as including the right to hold a court every three weeks for all his tenants within its limits, and 'he shall have all fees and amerciments'. In addition to this court, the lord was also given the profits of 'Le Lousefayre'; these consisted of one halfpenny on each piece of cloth sold on Tuesday and Wednesday, when, according to custom, no linen cloth or canvas could be sold anywhere in Winchester except under licence from the owner of the cloth selde. It was an important precinct, which included not only the place where the cloth was sold but also the church, appropriately called St Mary in the Linen Webb, and eventually the *Bell Inn*, a hostelry which remained in existence until recent years.

God-begot, an ancient holding, had been bequeathed to the priory in 1052 by Queen Emma, and here too there were a number of buildings including a church; the tenants owed suit at the God-begot court. A sufficient number of court rolls (four from Edward III to Henry VIII) have survived to show the procedure and the profits arising from Emma's gift and its confirmation by her son, Edward the Confessor, including the right of 'excluding all other officers from the place'. The court was held irregularly, and was presided over by a steward.[10]

In 1291, in a general statement relating to the duties of the inhabitants of God-begot, the corporation under the mayor, John Spragg, agreed that anyone who was resident in the manor should not be able to claim rights as a citizen, and would have to pay at least 10 marks to gain the freedom of the city. Trade between citizens and the God-begotters was expressly forbidden, and citizens who entered God-begot to attack or arrest one of the inhabitants rendered themselves liable to excommunication. The last surviving court roll provides a number of interesting incidents, involving trespass by city officials and actions which would now be classified as assaults causing grievous bodily harm. The separate jurisdiction of this curious entity came to an end with the Dissolution, though the new Dean and Chapter retained their ownership of the property until 1866, and the altered remnant of the building is one of Winchester's best-known features. The eastern section has recently been demolished, but the western part, a restaurant, still contains much of its original timber-framing; the High Street gables are additions of 1908, by a local firm of architects, Cancellor and Hill.

God-begot and the cloth selde were small areas. A substantial part of modern Winchester formed the bishop's soke, a separate entity which continued until the 19th century; its court, Cheyney Court, followed old and archaic procedure.

The bishop's officers were many: some were styled aldermen, with wards of St John, Chesil, Kingsgate Street, and Hyde Street. Outside the built-up areas the chief officers were the tithing men of Sparkford and Milland, the area of the mills. When Cheyney Court met these officers had to report any changes and investigate complaints in their areas. Law and order were supposed to be preserved by two constables of the soke, and the court was presided over by the bishop's bailiff of the soke. He was often a resident of the city, with a yearly salary of £3 0s. 10d. If he was too busy or too distinguished to sit in person, he could appoint deputies to act for him, one of whom was usually a professional lawyer. Over the years the court continued to hear petty cases of trespass and debt brought by the bishop's tenants in Winchester and on his other Hampshire manors. It also acted as a court of property registration, rather as the city court did; new tenants were required to take an oath swearing fealty to the lord of the manor of the soke, and leases and variations in leases were supposed to be recorded in the court's records.

A year-by-year record of the bishop's expenditure and receipts for his Winchester soke was kept, and the return entered on the bishop's pipe rolls, a series which provides a clear picture of the continuing importance of the bishops in their cathedral city, both as landlords of soke tenants and as the overlords of Winchester's great economic assets – the river, the mills, and St Giles' Fair. Returns for the mills and fair, and the bishop's own palace of Wolvesey, are usually to be found on the same series of rolls. By August 1259 Wolvesey had become the centre of administration for the bishop's estates.[11]

The noisy bustle of city life contrasted strongly with the silence of the countryside around, the downs and water meadows which provided Wintonians with most of their grain and livestock as well as that basic ingredient of the economy, wool. In the century after the grant of Henry II's charters there was a great period of expansion in the rural economy: waste land was enclosed, markets multiplied, and the Bishop of Winchester created six new towns.[12] Rural prosperity was inevitably reflected in Winchester's wealth.

Yet the signs of reversal and decline were apparent after 1290 when the community lost its Jews. The prosperity of the medieval city had been the prosperity of a city with alliances between communities, each with its own sense of rights and duties. There were Christians and Jews, lay folk and clergy, rich and poor, city men and soke men, God-begotters and linenselders. There were king's men, officers of the realm and of the county, and proud and successful merchants – Wintonians, aliens from Europe, or 'foreigners' from other English towns. It was a rich and prosperous city with an increasing population, though its prosperity was almost constantly at risk from the commonplace disasters of the medieval world. Plague and pestilence could decimate man and beast, while famine and war could not be avoided.

Chapter Seven

The Years of Decline and Revival

The last half of the 14th century contained the splendid years of art and architecture when the English Gothic style reached new heights. The major renova-
tions of the cathedral by two successive bishops, Edington and Wykeham, speak
for themselves, but it was also a period of moral decline, political corruption
and religious doubts, made more acute by the great tragedy of the Black Death.

In Hampshire the Black Death spread rapidly and was at its height in the
winter of 1348-9, an attack spent by the end of 1349. There were later revivals,
though, in 1361-2 (when many children died), 1369 and 1379. Attempts to
calculate the mortality rates have produced varied results: one suggested statistic
indicates an overall immediate decline in the population of 20 per cent in
1348-9, and of 50 per cent by 1400. It is not possible to arrive at definite statistics
for Winchester, but the evidence for severe population decline is irrefutable.

As soon as the news of the outbreak reached Bishop Edington, he issued
emergency orders to his clergy. In October 1348 he warned the prior and convent of the cathedral of the dangers about to descend on the diocese. Mothers
had been 'deprived of their children in the abyss of an unheard of plague, cities
stripped of their population ... more cruel than any two edged sword ... we are
struck with the greatest fear lest foul disease ravages any part of our city and
diocese'. To avert this danger, the prior was ordered to hold additional services
every Wednesday and Friday in the cathedral choir, and to walk every Friday
through the market place of Winchester in a public procession, joined by the
other city clergy and the citizens, 'with heads bent down, with feet bare, and
with fasting', in silence but for the repetition of the Lord's Prayer and the Hail
Mary.[1] These prayers and hopes were in vain. The Black Death came to Winchester with devastating consequences, and perhaps three- quarters of the population of the city was dead by 1349.

The mortality in 1348-9 amongst all classes of society was great enough to produce a general shortage of graves in the only communal burying place, the
great churchyard of the cathedral priory. In January 1349 a burial there precipi-
tated a riot; the officiating priest, one of the cathedral monks, was attacked and
the ceremony broken up. There was an immediate reaction from Bishop Edington, who denounced the individuals concerned and reiterated the Church's
doctrine of the resurrection of the body, and the need for burials in conse-

crated ground. Amongst the local Winchester clergy who are known to have died were the prior of St Swithun's, Alexander Heriard, and the abbess of St Mary, Isabella Spine. The first parish vacancy appears to have been that of the living of St Faith's, but this may be too early in the year (May 1348) to have been the result of the plague. The rectories of St Pancras, St Martin's outside West-gate, and All Saints in the Vines were vacant by January 1349; the vicar of St Bartholomew's, Hyde, resigned in early February, and the rector of St George was dead by 2 March. In the first three months of 1349 there were at least six vacancies in city parishes, and at least 17 parish churches were eventually left to decay and ruin. The disappearance of the parish churches or their existence as no more than ruins is clearly indicated from many differing sources.[2]

Many churches are recorded as being in decay by 1417, when the city tarrage was rewritten. Among them was St Paul's in Staple Gardens, where the churches of St Saviour and Our Lady were 'downe' by 1452, if not earlier. The church of St Martin outside Westgate escaped immediate desolation, but by 1387 its parishioners were asking the bishop if they could pull it down and use the ma-terials to repair the nearby chapel of St Mary, soon itself to fall into decay. Lay-men took advantage of the situation to appropriate church buildings for secular uses. Even in March 1370, in Wykeham's time, the bishop was taking note of the sad state of the city parishes and threatening to excommunicate any laymen who took away stones, tiles or other materials from the decayed churches. In July 1372 the mayor and bailiffs were cited for wrongful use of St Petroc, St Martin-in-the-Wall and St Nicholas, the problems continuing for many years. In 1395 Wykeham was still concerned, and set up a special commission to inquire into the sites of city churches usurped by laymen.[3]

The decline of medieval Winchester brought about by the Black Death was a major disaster, the final crisis in a series of events which can be said to have begun with the expulsion of the Jews in 1290, and which then proceeded through the decline of the woollen industry, the moving of the national staple away from the city and the growth of foreign competition.[4]

In the reign of Edward III, just before the outbreak of the Hundred Years War, a number of weavers and dyers from France and Flanders settled in Winchester under royal protection. The Black Death was a considerable blow, but the cloth trade still lingered on in Winchester, perhaps because of its foreign reinforce-ments, and city merchants continued to sell cloth to France, Spain and the Low Countries. Ulnage, the tax on cloth, was collected 'in the city, suburbs, and soke', evidence enough that the old restrictions were breaking down.[5] A long list of names suggests a fairly substantial revival; amongst the cloth exporters were Hugh and John Cran as well as Mark le Faire and Robert Soper, but Soper's son, William, preferred to leave Winchester and make a large fortune as a naval con-tractor in Southampton.[6] In general terms the decline continued, and in 1415 a group of fullers, who had leased from the city its mills at Coitbury and King's

Mill at Prior's Barton, were allowed to have their leases cancelled.

By 1417, Winchester had declined so much that the old account of the fee farm was hopelessly out of date, and it became necessary to rewrite the assessment. A new tarrage was drawn up early in 1417 and formed a model for all later versions; it provides a survey of much of the city and a list of the inhabitants who were liable to pay.[7] Winchester had no general street numbering before the 19th century, and until then properties were described in terms of their inhabitants in 1417. It thus becomes possible, through the tarrages, to follow the descent of many properties over a period of about four hundred years. This descent begins even before 1417, for the newly-made roll of that year lists not only those who then held property but also gives the names of the previous owners. A Latin copy belonging to Winchester College is probably slightly earlier than the English version discovered by the present writer some years ago in the city archives; it had been described as a 17th-century roll because it was produced in a lawsuit in 1631-2. It is not a complete survey, since the 'view' did not include the bishop's soke or the precincts of the great monasteries. If the evidence is reliable, it must provide a fair idea of the general topography of Winchester in the years after the Black Death.

The compilers of the various tarrages surveyed the north side of the High Street first, from west to east, including the entries into the side streets. At the end of the 14th century there were at least 100 tenements, of which about one third had stalls for the selling of goods. Only a few real shops can be distinguished and, significantly, these were all associated with the inns – one next to *The White Horse*, below Bredene Street (shop and garden), one in *The George Inn* complex, and groups of three associated with both *The Chequers* and *The Tabard*, adjacent hostelries further east, above the entry of Parchment Street. Further east still *The Swan* and *The Star* (later *The King's Head*) did not have shops, while *The Bell*, near the corner of Wongar Street, had a shop next to it. Some tenements had porches and 'pallaces' in front, and gutters running near the road. On the south side of the High Street there was less room for the ordinary domestic householder because of the monasteries. There were fewer tenements, some under one landlord, but a much larger number of cottages – over 40, especially at the ends of the High Street. Some of these were in the 'precincts', not on the main frontage. There were not many stalls and only a few shops, including one next to the only inn, *The Hart*.

In the aldermany of Jewry Street, which reached as far as Northgate and included Staple Gardens (Bredene Street) and Jewry Street itself, there was comparatively little building. Most of Bredene Street was garden. There were only two or three tenements including 'Dorkyng' and, in this street, as in Jewry Street, a total of about twenty cottages, mostly in groups of two or three dwellings. There were only approximately fifteen tenements. In the area of Fleshmonger Street and Parchment Street there was again little building: there

28. The Old Chesil Rectory, built *c.*1450.

29. The Blue Boar, built *c.*1340, the oldest surviving home in Winchester.

were many gardens, most of them privately owned and used as allotments, some cottages, and only a few tenements, including one which had belonged to Philip Aubyn, Mayor of Winchester in 1312-13. Parchment Street had more houses in it towards the High Street, but its northern end was occupied by gardens, finishing with the large plot called St Mary's Garden, approached by the great gate on the west side of the street. On the east side there was a great tenement which had belonged to the prior of Hayling, which was a complex of a house and three cottages approached by a great gate. It eventually passed to the Coram family. In Upper Brook Street almost the same pattern was repeated, with a few houses near the High Street and gardens at the ends towards the wall – even a meadow at the north-eastern corner. Wongar Street, next surveyed, had apparently managed to retain many of its tenements and houses; there were only a few gardens, at the north-western end, and there were still many buildings in Tanner Street, about sixteen tenements and six cottages on the south side and, on the east, more tenements and a small garden area towards Durngate. Two cottages in Buck Street stood in the water 'upon pillars'.

The side streets to the south of the High Street were also surveyed but the aldermany of Colebrook Street included a section of the north part of the High Street at Newbridge (over the streams there) and Buck Street. The corner tenement at Newbridge was usually inhabited by the keeper of the Trinity Charnel Chapel, and the other buildings in this area were chiefly cottages. Calpe Street seems to have been a street of private houses and a few cottages, though on its western side there were many gardens and two churches, St Thomas and St Alphege, the latter almost at the corner of St Clement Street. 'Morantisshall' stood here, in the 'south part of the lane', that is St Clement Street; it had become a garden site only by 1416-17. In Gold Street, important because it was the main route from Winchester to Southampton, the built-up area on the eastern side virtually stopped at All Saints' church, or its site, though there was a property beyond on the corner of St Swithun Street, an ancestor of the present *Green Man*, belonging to St Cross Hospital. On the opposite side of the road beneath the castle there were tenements and more than 20 cottages. There were only gardens on the east side of Gar Street, the pasture called Bemond's and more gardens on the west.

After the Black Death the walled town appears to have had its retail and industrial centre in the High Street and also in the Brooks, particularly Wongar Street, not listed in the later petitions as in decay. A distinction was drawn between cottages, of which there were many, and tenements, which were in some decline. Many tenements were still fronted by stalls, and there were still only a few distinct shops. Any industrial activity which there might have been south of the High Street in the early medieval town seems to have given way to private dwellings, though the empty garden areas were concentrated at the north edge of the town, remaining undeveloped until the 19th century.

30. A drawing by an inmate of the Westgate when it was used as a prison, probably dating from the early 15th century.

It is against this background of economic decline and the disasters of the Hundred Years War that the corporation tried to obtain a series of charters providing some form of economic relief. On 30 November 1377 a series of orders was issued to many towns and cities instructing them to provide a certain number of balingers for the Royal Navy. The mayor of Winchester and 19 other named citizens were thus required to build 'one small barge ... with from fifty to forty oars with all speed to be built before 1 March next ... or the King will deservedly punish them'.[8] Despite this threat, by 1 February 1378, Winchester had not even begun the work, and the excuse put forward was accepted:

They are so burdened with building of the city walls, with payment of the two-tenths last granted to the King by the Commons of the realm and diverse other charges to which they are daily subjected that by reason of their narrow means they may not without grevious impoverishment [build] the same without other support.

This 'other support' was to come, by compulsion, from merchants of the soke, alleged to be richer than anyone dwelling within the walls. Winchester paid for a balinger, and the city's privileges were confirmed.

Soke men continued to be persecuted – a grocer who had dared to shop in Southgate Street, butchers 'selling in the Soke in a place called Seyntjonestrete against the liberty and customs of the aforesaid city', dyers who dared to practise their trade in the soke, fullers 'for using the artifice of fulling in the Soke and suburbs of Winchester to the great hurt of the city and the deterioration of the payment of the King's farm', and groups of weavers who had worked 'outside the walls'.[9]

There was much trouble in 1381, and what has been called a rising against the oligarchy.[10] In 1418, the city brought its plight to the king's notice by parliamentary petition. A third of Winchester was said to be desolate, and the bailiffs unable to pay the fee farm. The mayor and commonalty asked for permission to purchase 'certain lands and tenements, rents and services', to the value of 40 marks a year. The reply was favourable, although nothing happened until 1440 when letters patent allowed them to acquire real estate to a value of £40 a year in order to help with the payment of the fee farm.[11] Soon afterwards the Winchester estate of Mark Le Fayre was purchased. He had been mayor in 1398-9, 1402-3, 1408-9, 1411-12 and 1413-14, and had bequeathed all his property in Winchester to his daughter and heiress, Katherine, and her husband, Henry Somer. The Somers rentals, from 1425 to 1438, show much empty property, rents falling, and a drop in the annual amount received as rent. By far the most valuable of the buildings thus acquired was *The George Inn* on the eastern corner of the junction of the High Street and Jewry Street.[12]

In 1442, another charter described the decay of the city and attempted to provide further remedies. Eleven streets, 17 parishes and 987 messuages were said to be in ruins 'chiefly because of pestilence and the withdrawal of those who dwell there for trade'. The fee farm was alleged to be the chief financial cause. The mayor and citizens were allowed, therefore, to keep the chattels of felons, fugitives and outlaws taken with stolen goods within the city; the grant also permitted the election of four aldermen as justices of the peace. The city quarter sessions began, a source of justice and profit.[13]

In 1449, further financial help was given by the royal licence to hold a market each Saturday and a yearly fair lasting 10 days, beginning on 14 July, the Vigil of St Swithun.[14] No better measure of the decline of St Giles' Fair could perhaps be found, though it still continued and was a source of occasional annoyance to the citizens. In 1451, the mayor and commonalty undertook not to disturb the Bishop's Fair in future and, after this agreement with Bishop Wayneflete, relations between the city and successive bishops improved.[15] A few months later there was positive help in the form of an annual grant of 40 marks from the ulnage and subsidy of cloth sold in the county of Southampton, including the

31.   The cathedral nave.

city of Winchester. It was made in the first instance for 50 years but renewed on various occasions.[16] This charter of 1451 appears to have been the result of a petition to Parliament that described the financial difficulties of the city. These included the fee farm of 112 marks, the 60s. paid each year to the hospital of St Mary Magdalene, the heavy burden of £51 10s. 4d. to which Winchester was liable whenever it was assessed for a fifteenth, and the expenses of burgesses 'coming to Parliament at 4 shillings the day'.[17] It goes on to describe the withdrawal of notable persons, the void houses, the inofficiate churches, and begs for a release of 40 marks from the ulnage, and subsidy of woollen cloth. The streets which were said to have fallen down were Jewry Street, Fleshmonger Street, Parchment Street, Colebrook Street, Calpe Street, Gold Street, Burden Street, Shulworth Street, Bukkestrete, Minster Street and Gar Street. A total of over 1,000 houses there were described as 'decayed households', and 17 parish churches were in ruins.[18] There were frequent difficulties in collecting the fee farm, even after this help, and complaints:

> Wynchester the viii day of May by the Bailiffs of Wynchester.
>   Howr mayre takyt no hede of us ... therefor we pray you send a wrytt down to the mayre and to ws for to brynge howr ferme ... wretyn at Wynchester the viii day of May by the Bailiffs of Wynchester.[19]

Bishop Edington's work at the cathedral had not been completed when he died in 1366. His reconstruction may have been interrupted by the Black Death but, judging by the architectural evidence, this is not likely. The great visual monument of his episcopate must be regarded as part of his plan for reviving the city and the priory of St Swithun's after the pestilence; it is notable for the very high standard of building construction, and the soundness of the craftsmanship. The front is not the cathedral's best feature, but it was greatly altered by Edington's successor, William of Wykeham, who filled in his predecessor's balustrading and raised the levels of the aisle roofs, leaving Edington's windows as isolated examples of how he had intended to complete the reconstruction of the Norman nave. This lengthy work was not finished when Henry IV married Joanna of Navarre in 1403. The overall effect is splendid, of great height and dignity. It should be judged with the knowledge that the windows used to be filled with coloured glass, and that originally there were no seats in the nave.

Another problem which Wykeham inherited was the scandalous state of St Cross Hospital. In 1383, he appointed John de Campeden as master. The brethren lived in buildings which included a cloister south of the church, while the master's house was on the northern side. It was there that the Earl of Kent stayed during the Winchester Parliament of 1393. Campeden spent much money on the fabric, and his main work was the improvement of the chapel, where he raised the height of the tower, roofed the building and set up, in 1385,

32. Winchester College gateway.

33, 34 & 35.   Winchester College.

a splendid new high altar of alabaster. In *c.*1407-10 the nave was revaulted, and the great church begun by de Blois effectively completed.[20] A little later Cardinal Beaufort founded a second order of almsmen who were to be members of his 'Noble Order of Poverty', men who had formerly been of some substance in the world but had fallen on difficult times – 'noble men or members of our family', in the words of the founder. In 1486, Bishop Waynflete changed Beaufort's arrangements and reduced his order to one chaplain and two brothers. The cardinal's endowment had included St James' church in the Romsey road; its ancient cemetery was eventually made available as a burial place for Catholics through the generosity of a 17th-century master of the hospital.

Wykeham's other work, the foundation of Winchester College, proved to be not only a notable addition to the topography of the city but a major contribution to the life of the nation. The first schoolmaster was probably appointed in 1373, but the royal licence permitting the foundation was only issued some nine years later by Richard II, followed in a few days by Wykeham's own charter of foundation (20 October 1382).[21] The buildings which he had begun to erect have retained their attractiveness and over the centuries a whole area of Winchester has been gradually added to the complex which makes up 'Winchester School', as distinct from the nucleus, 'Winchester College'. The original college buildings date from the years 1387-1400, and were erected under the supervision of William Wynford. The result, and in particular the chapel, main entrance and brewery building in College Street, previously the lane to Floodstock, forms a notable architectural addition to the city. A new element was created within the community, for many boys became scholars or joined the school as commoners. Amongst the first 70 scholars chosen, eight were from Winchester. It is clear that commercial and personal ties were soon developed.

Wykeham's contribution to his diocese and to his cathedral city makes him undoubtedly the greatest of the later medieval bishops. In the 80 years after his death in 1404, however, the decline of Winchester continued. Though it escaped the troubles of the Wars of the Roses, the signs of decline are only too apparent. An abundance of petty local officials, a multitude of charges on the fee farm made through central government, and the physical decay of the area were only some of the signs which marked the end of medieval Winchester.

Chapter Eight

The Reformation

Winchester was important to the first Tudor king. Henry VII wished to associate his family in the eyes of the civilised world with the rulers of ancient Britain. His eldest son, Arthur, born in Winchester, was christened in the cathedral, this proving to be the first of a series of visits by Tudor monarchs. Though the young prince did not live to become king of England, his brother and successor, Henry VIII, felt the same need to stress the ancient lineage of his ancestors and, in 1522, was proud to show Arthur's round table to a visiting Hapsburg, Charles V. Henry stayed at the castle, the table was specially painted for the occasion, and Winchester was once again a royal city.[1] These years of royal interest, years of comparative peace before the outbreak of the Reformation storms, were at first marred by petty internal disputes within the corporation. Some of the trouble arose from conflicts of personality; there were disagreements about administration, and about the method of electing the mayor.

During the first mayoralty of Thomas Baker, in 1515, all the most important early ordinances likely to be useful precedents or embodying major policy decisions were extracted from the court rolls and, with some later regulations, written down in a volume known since 1546 as the *Black Book*.[2] The latest entry is one of 1551, and from that date onwards decisions were kept in a magnificent series of 17 large volumes, the *Books of Ordinance*. These run from 1551 to 1835, although the second volume disappeared many years ago. Two additional folios of 'Proceedings of the Corporation' add some information for the reign of Elizabeth I, but the *Black Book* remains the main source of what was happening in civic circles on the eve of the Reformation, including the disagreements about the mayoralty in which Bishop Fox was asked to intercede.

Fox, who was already a beloved and respected figure in Winchester, was known to be anxious that the local monasteries should continue as active centres of the true faith. He had also set in hand a reform which led to the closing of a number of redundant and dilapidated churches by the familiar modern method of uniting benefices, preceding each union by calling a meeting of parishioners, and acting with the knowledge of, and in some cases at the request of, the city authorities.[3]

The appeal to Bishop Fox in 1520 to mediate 'for Reformation and peasying of the said variances' about the mayoralty did not go unanswered. A general assembly of citizens was called to meet at St John's and, as a result of the bishop's intervention, all previous enactments regarding the election of the mayor were repealed.[4] No future mayor was to hold office for more than three years, and the procedure for elections was agreed. two names were to be put forward by the citizens of the Twenty-four, and the then mayor 'at his pleasure, put out one of them'. In 1523, provision was made for the immediate ex-mayor to take up his duty again if the mayor died during his term of office. Fox also helped to obtain the royal charter of 1516, which permitted the mayor to take his oath of allegiance in Winchester; the expensive London journey was no longer necessary.[5] The mayor was still a paid official, and he usually received an annual fee of 20 marks at the end of his mayoralty. The *status quo* of the corporation was preserved, and the charters confirmed, in 1489 and 1514.

Two new fairs were allowed by a grant of 1518, each for a duration of two days. These local gatherings were attempts to improve the economy.[6] There is evidence in the *Black Book* which suggests that they were held in the vicinity of St Maurice's church. If further proof be needed of the happy relationship between Fox and the city fathers it can be found in the last year of his episcopate. When the old bishop became blind and had to have the help of a suffragen, William Hogieson, Bishop of Darien *in partibus*, the corporation leased St John's House to Bishop Hogieson as his Winchester mansion.

On the eve of the Reformation, Winchester was thus already partly 'reformed' and Church and State were on good terms, though the changes encouraged by Bishop Fox were slight in comparison with those which were to follow. Yet far too much of the Tudor corporation's time was spent on petty matters. In October 1573, for example, the then mayor, Stephen Ashton, was an innkeeper. This was not considered to be a suitable occupation for a mayor, and Ashton had to move into the east part of his house, which he was forbidden to use as an inn. For the mayor to ride alone, without a servant, was always a civic misdemeanour of great magnitude. William Godwin, mayor in 1558-9, had been wont to ride to Southampton without a man servant; it tended to the 'disworship of the city' and had to be stopped. Slandering or blasphemously speaking against the mayor and the aldermen made a man subject to imprisonment in the Westgate, though quite a number of Wintonians were prepared to take the risk. Punishments made to fit the crime included that arranged in April 1559 for William Brexton, who had 'revealed the secrets of the council house to strangers': he had to give 10s. to provide a new cupboard for the city records. The corporation was frequently required, and in fact obliged under penalties, to attend the cathedral with the mayor, not once or twice a year as now, but every Sunday and on all other principal feasts.

Tudor Wintonians were aware not only of the great religious changes of their time but also of the dangers and difficulties produced by international politics, for it was part of the ordinary man's duty to bear arms in time of crisis. A list of

'Able men with arms and weapons made in the city of Winchester 20 September, 1559' shows most Wintonians prepared to defend themselves with bills, and some with swords, daggers, pole-axes, and bows and arrows. Only one man had a firearm – Richard Bethell, the linen draper of Hyde. Some city 'harness' of the period may still be seen in the Westgate.

Important news, whether social, political or pseudo-political, was conveyed by proclamation. Wintonians who spoke against the marriage of Philip and Mary were proclaimed against in their turn; the royal proclamation on the execution of Mary Queen of Scots was read at the High Cross by the mayor on 13 December 1586.

There were often other serious matters, social rather than political or religious, which were the subject of proclamation and action by the city council. These included the intermittent outbursts of 'plague' which had always threatened town life. Local interest in medicine must have been encouraged by the appointment of Dr. John Warner as dean of the cathedral in 1559. Warner had previously been the first regius professor of medicine at Oxford, and two of his medical books, the *De Materia Medica* of Dioxorides and *De Natura Stripium* of Ruellius are in the cathedral library. Another doctor, Simon Tripp, was appointed physician to the dean and chapter at the end of the century. He was a man of great learning, a product of the Renaissance like Warner, having studied at Cambridge, Oxford and Padua. He lived in a house in Colebrook Street which he rebuilt after obtaining a building lease from the corporation, bringing the 'frame' out over the street *c*.1588 and leaving, in a first-floor room, the opening for the 'stillatory' mentioned in the inventory taken after his death in 1596.[7] An earlier doctor, Thomas Bassett, a Wykehamist and recusant who lived in the parish of St Peter Chesil, leased the charnal chapel which had belonged to St Mary's Abbey. This may have enabled him to use the bones there for medical teaching.[8] Throughout the whole of the Tudor period, Winchester College educated a number of boys who later became distinguished men of medicine, including several physicians and surgeons in the royal household.

The dissolution of the monasteries produced changes in the lives of the citizens, and in the topography of the town. Not only were there three large monastic houses occupying a substantial area of the city, but also smaller establishments that were shut down. Eventually most of the property owned by ecclesiastical landlords changed hands.

In 1536, when the first group of Henry VIII's commissioners arrived to see St Mary's Abbey, their report was excellent. It was a considerable establishment of 102 persons, of whom 26 were nuns, 26 were children taught in the nunnery school, and the rest were servants and lay officers, including the porter of Eastgate. Care was taken to consult members of the corporation and other persons of status in Winchester, but there was no one who was willing or able to complain about the good sisters, who were reported to 'have been and are, of very clean, virtuous, honest and charitable conversation'. The buildings, too, were regarded by the commissioners as being of importance in the life of the city: 'of a great and large compass, environed around with many poor households which have their only living of the said monastery'. Not the least of the abbey's advantages was the abbess, Elizabeth Shelley, a lady of much determination and ability, whose girls' school was patronised by many leading families, including the Tichbournes, the Philpotts, the Poles and, especially, those Lisles who were Plantagenets.[9] The abbess and her nuns escaped the first dissolution; they paid out over £300 and gave up their Wiltshire manors to members of the Seymour family. It was a vain sacrifice. In September 1538 the three Winchester houses were again visited, and within a few months the two houses for monks were sur-

36.   The Round Table.

rendered. Abbot Salcot signed away Hyde in April 1538, Kingsmill at St Swithun's gave in later, but Elizabeth Shelley held out until 15 November 1539. Huge and significant areas of Winchester became desolate as a result of these changes.[10]

The priory of St Swithun, however, was a cathedral church where the monks had the right of electing the diocesan bishop. The cathedral and the close survived, for the king turned the prior and convent into the dean and chapter in 1541, and the last prior, William Kingsmill, became the first dean. He belonged to a well-known Hampshire family and succeeded in keeping his church virtually intact, although he took no action when, at 3 o'clock in the morning of 21 September 1538, Thomas Wriothesley and two other royal commissioners, Richard Pollard and John Williams, set about breaking up the shrine of St Swithun and taking down the high altar. Wriothesley eventually left with many of the cathedral's treasures, including a great cross studded with emeralds and the 'cross called Jerusalem'; he was disappointed in the actual shrine for its jewelled decoration was counterfeit. The commissioners left the main store of cathedral plate untouched. They were in a hurry, and were doing their work at night in order not to attract too much attention. Significantly the mayor 'with eight or nine of his brethren' was present, and helped in the destruction.[11]

Kingsmill remained in what soon had to be called the Deanery rather than the Prior's Lodging. Many of his new canons were men who had been monks, and in the first list of peticanons one name, that of Thomas Daccombe, is singled out with the special description 'secular priest'. His name is to be honoured, for it was Daccombe who seems to have saved many of the cathedral manuscripts from destruction. He had become rector of St Peter Colebrook in 1519, moving later to another Hampshire living, but returning to St Peter's in 1541. He ended his life as a rector in Dorset, dying in 1567, but not before he had collected at least 12 magnificent medieval manuscripts, including the Ramsey Benedictional, the psalter associated with King Athelstan, and two Winchester cartularies, all now in the British Museum.[12]

The new chapter was not as rich as the monks had been, although it was still a very wealthy community. It was soon deprived, in 1545, of the duty of supporting Winchester scholars at Oxford and Cambridge, surrendering to the king the estates which were to maintain these scholars. But within the community there was a high regard for learning, and the old way of life continued in a quasi-monastic form. Of the first seven deans, only one was a married man, and he, Sir John Mason, was an exceptional appointment of Edward VI, for he was a layman and member of parliament for Southampton.[13] The first post-Dissolution documents which have survived amongst the cathedral archives show the community carrying on its old life, eating together in the common hall, as it was now called, rather than the refectory, and maintaining a small staff who kept the rood loft, oiled the bells, and wound the cathedral clock. The number of altars in the church had already been reduced to two: 'Jesus' Masse Auter' and 'the second Masse Auter'. The 'holy hole' behind the feretory, through which relics had been displayed or passed, was stopped up. In 1552, the cathedral was deprived of all its 'plate, jewells, ornaments, vestments, copes and bells', and further change came at the end of the century. There was already a significant element within the city and the corporation prepared to profit from reform, and this was shown in the way in which the areas of Hyde and St Mary's were redeveloped.

The commissioners surveying St Mary's compiled a fairly detailed description of the precinct, of much topographical value. In the hospital to the north of the nunnery buildings proper were 12 poor sisters, each receiving a yearly pension of 6s. 8d. They were allowed to remain and, on the southern side of the little pathway which separated it from the nunnery, the abbess' dwelling was to stay. The gate-house, barn, baking and brewing houses, garner, stable, and mill were all to be kept and committed to the charge of William Lambert, for the use of the king's majesty. 'Deemed to be superfluous' were the church, chapterhouse, dormitory, frater, infirmary, convent kitchen, two garners on the south side of the court, the lodging called Mistress Lane's lodging, the precentor's lodging, and the plumber's house. The church still had its famous steeple, with five bells, but it was soon a complete ruin along with the other 'superfluous' buildings. Provision was made for the abbess and one of her brothers, Robert Shelley, to retain all money due to the convent and pay its debts, but the real man in charge was Lambert, who was also given custody of the muniments locked in the abbey stronghouse. The king's receiver was given the key, and the documents were dispersed at some later date. Little indeed now remains of the archives and library of this once famous abbey.[14]

The buildings which were demolished became a stone quarry informally used by the citizens and sometimes made good use of by corporate bodies. Stone walls in the precincts of Winchester College were repaired with cartloads of stone dug from St Mary's in 1566, and years after the Dissolution lead from coffins found in Colebrook Street proved a useful parish asset. Until the early 19th century a stonemason's yard was one of the features of the former precinct.

Elizabeth Shelley and at least seven of her nuns continued to live in the area: they may even have stayed on in the abbess' lodging. She had been granted a pension from the king of £26 13s. 4d. a year, but as a member of a well-to-do family could certainly not have been left by her brother, Sir William Shelley, in any real need. When the former abbess made her will in March 1547 she left specific bequests to three nuns, former members of the house, and to the poor sisters of the Systern hospital. Wills left by other former nuns confirm that at least some members of the community were still neighbours, if not living in the same house, and probably sharing some sort of communal existence. The last nun whose will has been found was Agnes Badgecroft, the sub-prioress. She was alive in 1557, when the old form of religion had been restored. The abbess had died nine years previously, and it is some indication of her fame and learning that she was buried within the chapel of Winchester College.

The future of large areas of the abbey precinct, the Winchester property of the nunnery, and the problem of who was to be responsible for the maintenance of Newbridge and Eastgate were matters which were only resolved over a long period. Newbridge, at the west end of Colebrook Street, had been 'new' for hundreds of years since its construction over the stream in the High Street. It was henceforth maintained by the corporation, who stopped demanding tolls and pensioned off the last porter of Eastgate, John Torte, in 1551. The gate then began to fall into disrepair and was eventually demolished.

Within the precinct of the abbey, an important survival was the block of buildings to the north of the church within the nuns' cemetery, 'in St Mary's Litton'. In 1554, all the Winchester property of the nunnery passed to the corporation as a result of the charter negotiated by William Laurens, which compensated for the city's expenditure at the marriage of Philip and Mary. The most important sections of the northern group of buildings were the charnel chapel of Holy Trinity with its bone store and the hospital for poor sisters.

The sisters' hospital was a problem, becoming a refuge for the unemployed and social outcasts: the misfits of later Tudor society. At one point it was divided into 13 small lodgings; rents were allowed to accumulate, arrears forgiven. It was the official city bridewell from the reign of Elizabeth I, and its inhabitants were supposed to be put to work by a Winchester clothier, but the situation was never satisfactory. The place continued to be overcrowded, dirty, a public nuisance and a 'very great charge to the city and especially to the parish of Colesbrook', whose churchwardens were nominally responsible. It was also the haunt of 'young, lazy, and idle persons'. Nevertheless, it continued as a bridewell until the whole block of buildings was pulled down at the end of the 18th century. The other small properties in this central block were also let by the corporation to various tenants. Despite the proximity of the bridewell they seem to have been respectable people; indeed, on either side of the High Street two substantial houses developed out of the remnants of the religious houses. To the south, the house now called Abbey House had emerged as a privately-owned freehold by 1699. The corporation had previously let parts of the site to lawyers, Thorpes and Clarkes. Robert Pescod, who settled the property on his wife in 1699, was also a lawyer.[15] With the main house, these various owners retained a nucleus of property 'in the Abbey'; the inn called *The King's Head* in Little Minster Street (its site is now a car-park) followed the same descent.

The sites of the four friaries, all dissolved, eventually passed to Winchester College as the result of an exchange with Henry VIII in 1543. The whole precinct of the Black Friars was still being leased as a unit by the college as late as 1847. After 1538 St Katherine's church was demolished and the prior's house turned into, or rebuilt as, a private house. Further south, the church of St Frances, belonging to the Franciscans, was pulled down, but no one hesitated to live in the remnants of the dissolved friary. The inventory of an alderman who died in 1545 shows him in Greyfriars with vestments and altar cloths in his parlour and 31 tombstones in the back yard.[16] When the college took over this site there was still a 'Mension' on it called the Prior's Lodging, and the local 17th-century historian, Trussell, appears to have seen parts of the precinct wall. Most of the area remained an open garden space.

Amongst the devout officials noted as living near St Mary's in 1536 was Thomas Legh, receiver of the abbey, whose daughter Jane married the William Lambert who took a leading part in the dissolution of St Mary's, lived in Hyde Street and was churchwarden of St Bartholomew's. The Lamberts were the parents of another Jane, who achieved local notoriety. Married to Sir Gerald Fleetwood when he was only eight years old, this second Jane became the mistress of Sir William Paulet, third Marquess of Winchester, by whom she had four sons and a daughter. The Paulets eventually had a great house in Hyde Street.[17]

Lambert's fellow churchwarden, Richard Bethall, was another Winchester man who profited from the Reformation. He had been a tenant of Hyde Abbey before the Dissolution, as lessee of the manor of Woodmancote, where he is said to have spent much of his later life. He was a cloth merchant whose customers included Winchester College, and in 1546 he gained the lease of Hyde Abbey for the sum of £110. He obtained not only the main site, but some monastic property in the parish. What Bethell seems to have gained at Hyde was the Abbot's Lodging, with a barn and stalls, two granaries, a dovecot, a mill, the Prior's Lodging and the burial ground, with various pieces of meadowland and mead, and also the site of St Stephen's chapel. The great mass of the convent buildings remained in royal ownership, for the cloister, chapel house, dormitory, frater, convent hall, gate-house and lodging adjoining it were to be demolished, and the materials used for the king's benefit, as was the lead on the other buildings, the Abbot's Hall, the chapel, the treasury, the 'new' chamber and other houses.[18] Some of the Bethell property eventually passed to the Paulets and the Clarkes, and both of these families made considerable alterations in Hyde.

On the southern side of Winchester the hospital and its chapel in what is now College Street, which had been maintained by St Swithun's Priory, remained in the ownership of the new dean and chapter, and were leased to various tenants, chiefly individuals connected with Winchester College.[19] The Carmelite Friary off Kingsgate Street, acquired by the school in 1543, was too near the main college buildings not to be eventually used for school purposes. A major alteration was the demolition of St Elizabeth's College, the site of which the warden and fellows bought from Wriothesley in April 1544 for £350. The warden and

37. Moberley's in Kingsgate Street.

fellows may have intended to use St Elizabeth's as a boarding-house for commoners, the use to which they eventually put the sisters' building in College Street.

Winchester College survived the religious troubles of the early Tudor period: it was neither dissolved nor subject to major reformation, although there were divisions amongst the warden and fellows, and opinions varied amongst Wykehamists. When reform seemed imminent, the headmaster, John White, was a staunch Catholic, while his *hostiarius*, William Ford, was a reformer. The story of Ford's decision to pull down the images in the chapel, an act carried out by him in person, and the subsequent attack on him at night in a dark corner near Kingsgate, has often been told, but the details have been disputed. For the next few years the fate of the establishment was uncertain, but the school managed to escape the changes of dissolution and reform which so affected its church neighbours. Care had to be taken in 1536 when the school was 'visited' on behalf of Cranmer, and by Thomas Cromwell on behalf of the king. In June 1536 Cromwell appears to have been given a piece of plate 'for having his favour in the College cause', and when the king himself was at Wolvesey on 21 September 1536, oxen, sheep and capons were sent for the royal table with the same precisely stated object in mind. The act of 1536 exempted the universities and the colleges of Winchester and Eton from paying tenths to the Crown. The grouping of the two schools with the two universities was undoubtedly one of the reasons why none was 'dissolved'.[20] The old high grammar school was not so fortunate: it disappeared quietly and the building in Symonds' Street was let to Dean Kingsmill's mother. Some town boys must now have been taught in the college, according to an argument put forward by that school in the early 17th century.

Religious changes were bound to affect the life of the school and the careers of the boys who were educated there. The standard of teaching remained high, and there were plenty of young Wykehamists able to write congratulatory poems in Greek and Latin on the occasions of royal visits. Edward VI's reforms, as a result of a visitation in 1547, required that Bible readings and prayers in the hall should be in English, and that prayers or anthems directed to the Blessed Virgin should not be used. In Mary's reign there was one famous Wykehamist martyr, John Philpot, Archdeacon of Winchester, who refused to sign a declaration affirming the real presence at the Eucharist. As archdeacon he had excommunicated John White, then warden of the college. In 1555 White, the last of the Catholic wardens of Wykeham's foundation, became bishop, and he achieved some notoriety on the accession of Elizabeth I, when he preached her sister's funeral sermon, with an extraordinary mixture of imprudence and lack of tact: 'Better a living dog than a dead lion ... Mary hath chosen the better part'. He was deprived of his bishopric in 1559, but was eventually allowed his personal freedom.

* * * * * * * *

Outside the corporate bodies and the religious institutions, there were many ordinary Wintonians who found religious change perplexing and dangerous. It cannot be said that the religious and social changes of the Tudor period left Winchester a prosperous or united city. The extreme Protestant policies of Edward VI's government were not popular, though once again the city's privileges were confirmed, in an *inspeximus* charter of 1550. Wintonians were soon to see what the young king looked like in person, though his visit was made at an unfortunate time when both the Bishop of Winchester and the warden of the college were imprisoned in the Tower of London. He was loyally received at the Westgate, although there was some degree of public disorder, associated in the government's mind with disgruntled members of Bishop Gardiner's household, and one John Garnham was said to have made speeches openly inviting his hearers to rebellion.

One major cause for concern on the part of the corporation was the fact that institutions with which they were particularly concerned and which served useful local purposes, the hospitals of St John and St Mary Magdalene and the charnel chapel of St Mary's Abbey, were threatened with closure as suspected chantries. St Cross Hospital survived, but action had to be taken to try to preserve and maintain the other ancient foundations. A petition was sent to the king by Edmund Foster (mayor 1549-50) and the two bailiffs in the hope that the priest serving St John's Hospital chapel would not be regarded as a chantry priest: 'he is paid five marks a year', the petitioners said, and 'sumtyme more and sumtyme lesse as the mayor and Bailiffes could agree with him ... [this stipend had been paid] tyme out of mynde to one chantry priest within the said hospital ... whereas in truth there was no such priest there'.[21]

The real object of the petition was finance rather than devotion; there were the familiar complaints – Winchester was falling into great ruin and decay and scarcely able to pay the king the fee farm of the city. The king was asked to decide that the corporation should not pay any rent for St John's, and that the chapel was not a chantry. The affair was mixed up with other questions about Inkepen's charnel chapel, for his majesty's 'pour oratours' had always had certain rents from Roger Inkepen's foundation; these had been stopped, though the corporation offered to prove its case by the production of 'olde Anneyent Rentalls and other wryting redy to be shewyd'.[22] They were clearly not able to explain properly their relationship to certain Winchester institutions, and this misunderstanding of history was repeated again in the 17th and early 19th centuries. The corporation managed to keep St John's and its endowments in its own hands, however, the relationship being eventually confirmed by charter in 1587. The charnel endowments were passed to the corporation in 1554 as a result of the marriage of Philip and Mary. The chaplaincy in St John's disappeared, despite the careful sworn evidence produced by a number of Winchester citizens, and thus the mayors of Winchester lost their chaplains.

Another grievance was the action of central government in sending to Winchester for 'church goods'. It was now that the ancient parish churches and the cathedral lost their plate and vestments – their church treasures.[23] Many Winchester men now found that reformation had gone far enough, and were

38. A Spanish dance before Philip of Spain during the pageant (*c.*1908) associated with the 1905-12 works on the cathedral.

prepared to echo the scribbled words of the young cathedral priest written in the margin of a Sarum missal in December 1546: 'I praye God I lyve to see the masse to be said again, for that to see hit wolde glade my harte so much as any things in this worlde'.

The accession of Queen Mary and the reaction to the old faith which followed were without doubt welcome events to many Winchester citizens. Almost the first action of the new sovereign had been to visit Bishop Gardiner in the Tower and order his release, and she soon appointed Edmund Steward, one of his protégés, as Dean of Winchester. When it was learnt that the queen intended to marry Philip of Spain not all citizens were enthusiastic. Nevertheless, feverish preparations had to be made in the cathedral and in the city when it was known that the marriage was to be solemnised in Winchester. Decorating and cleaning of the streets were carried out, and visible signs of the Reformation disguised.

It would be interesting to know more about the *tabula picta* constructed for the occasion, with an iron frame and decoration by William Mosse. The possibility that it was yet another repainting of the round table cannot wholly be ignored. Mosse also painted the arms of the Lord Chancellor at Westgate in July 1554. The roads were made up, and 'le rubbishe' dispersed. The High Cross was hastily repaired: it had obviously suffered in the recent religious changes. Some scarlet gowns had to be bought, and preparations were so hurried and exhausting that one hopes the corporation had some personal share of the enormous amount of wine that was laid in before the coming of the queen.[24]

Within the cathedral there was renovation and preparation for the huge congregation. Unfortunately, the documents which once described these changes were lost when the archives were ransacked in 1643, but a number of contemporary accounts describe what was a magnificent occasion. On the Friday after the wedding, Mass was celebrated in the cathedral by a Spanish priest: 'Some were glad ... and others were sorry'. There were so many people in Winchester that when at last the king and queen departed, the court had to leave in separate groups in order not to overcrowd the accommodation available on the roads to London.

The Spanish match enabled the astute lawyer who was mayor in 1554 to make some useful financial arrangements for the city. William Laurens was not a native of Winchester, but he was one of the Twenty-four in 1540, and mayor in 1548, 1553 and 1554.[25] He could upset people, and his great rival, Stephen Bedam, a goldsmith and himself an ex-mayor, was committed to the Westgate for slandering Laurens 'with unfitting words in the presence of the auditors of the city in the said council house'. Laurens used the occasion of the royal marriage to plead Winchester's economic ills, and on 5 September 1554 the city was granted the farm of the ulnage. Letters Patent of 8 September 1554 gave the city 10 marks a year from the fee farm for 10 years, and 50 marks yearly for 50 years. Finally, on 17 September, a third grant was made, the only one to survive as an original in the Winchester archives.[26] It made over to the corporation the rents derived from properties formerly in the possession of St Mary's Abbey, South-wick Priory, Wherwell Abbey and the college of St Mary Kalendar. Amongst the buildings of special interest were the mill of the Abbess of Wherwell, Colebrook House (which had belonged to Southwick Priory) and the house known as Hell at the western end of the Pentice (40-41 High Street), which had been part of the endowment of the charnel chapel attached to St Mary's Abbey. The charter itself is full of repetitive legal jargon, but it shows how Mary Tudor's changes were undermined by the creation of new landlords, and her failure to restore monasticism.[27]

Laurens was also responsible for the successful conclusion of negotiations with the queen which resulted in the city being given the custody of the castle in March 1559, and for all those acts he was handsomely rewarded by a grateful corporation. Amongst his friends and clients was Ralph Lamb, whose portrait was painted by a Spanish artist in 1554. When Lamb made his will in 1558 he left £400 for the purchase of property for the benefit of the almsfolk in St John's Hospital. The endowment thus obtained included *The Dolphin*, where the present building bears the lamb and flag of the hospital, and six new almshouses were built behind St John's House.[28]

39. Ralph Lamb, benefactor of St John's Hospital, painted at the time of the marriage of Philip and Mary.

It can be said of Winchester in the late 16th century, as it has been said of Southampton, that although some inhabitants were wealthy, the city itself was poor. An influential and energetic group of wealthy city councillors were concerned with the reform of local government; perhaps they envisaged administrative change as an economic panacea.

In 1560, Laurens took the general charter of the city to London to be renewed, and the new queen's Letters Patent of 18 June 1561 confirmed Winchester's previous liberties.[29] This charter was overshadowed by that of 1588, which has been described as 'the grant of a new Corporation'.[30] In fact, it legalised the *status quo* of the constitution as it had developed during the Middle Ages, establishing the exact legal status and title of the corporation, its right to hold courts and to retain the hospital of St John. The title was henceforth defined as the mayor, bailiffs, and commonalty of the city of Winchester, property-holders, with a common seal. The officials, headed by the mayor, consisted of the recorder, six aldermen, one deputy-recorder or town clerk, two bailiffs, two coroners and two constables. The existence of the Twenty-four was also legalised. The mayor, recorder and aldermen were to sit as justices of the peace within the city, and the county justices were forbidden to 'intermeddle'. No previous charter had ever before outlined the duties of the chief officials in this way, nor even named them, and the grant also specified the functions of the ordinary city court of record, of borough-moot, and of pie powder. The weekly markets were confirmed (Wednesday and Saturday), as were three fairs. Earlier charters restricting the power of the sheriff in Winchester were confirmed *de facto* though not by strict *inspeximus*.

Thus the mayor and commonalty were given the right of making returns to all writs, discharged from suit at county and kindred courts, and freed from a variety of petty tolls and customs. The corporation's right to hold and to be given property of all kinds without any special licence was also confirmed; altogether a most satisfactory stage in the city's constitutional history. The city also received a new set of weights and measures, a new seal was made in 1589, and the great chest for keeping money and documents, now housed in the Westgate, probably belongs to this period.

As the charter itself states, a leading part in the negotiations which preceded it was taken by Sir Francis Walsingham. At an assembly held in St John's House on 21 May 1582, Walsingham, the queen's secretary of state and a privy councillor, had been appointed the first high steward of the city for life. He received an annuity of £6 13s. 4d., paid in advance, and it must be assumed that the appointment confirmed Winchester's connections with the pro-Walsingham party at court and in the House of Commons. The court connection was maintained in other ways. Sir John Wolley, who represented the city in parliaments of 1584, 1585 and 1586, always with Thomas Flemyng, was the son-in-law of Sir William More of Loseley, and thus to some extent a member of the anti-Howard faction and a supporter of Walsingham. In the parliament of 1593 Flemyng sat with Sir Edward Stafford as his fellow member. Stafford should indeed have brought glimpses of the outer Renaissance world to his constituents. He was an experienced diplomat whose mother was mistress of the robes to the queen, while his second wife was a Howard, and his personal chaplain was Richard Hakluyt. Yet the continuity at Westminster was maintained by local members, and Winchester's most distinguished M.P. was probably the recorder, Thomas Flemyng, who sat in the parliaments of 1584, 1586, 1588 and 1592, had a house in the city, and was paid as M.P. at the rate of 52s. for 21 days' service. He was once one of

England's most important lawyers, became Lord Chief Justice and sat at the trial of Guy Fawkes.[31] Born at Newport in the Isle of Wight, he was buried at North Stoneham.

The chief officials named in the charter of 1588 were the mayor, Edward Cole, and Flemyng. Cole was the tenant of much city property, including the site of the mill outside Eastgate, where a condition of his lease was an obligation to rebuild. He was mayor again from 1598-9 and 1612-13, and for much of this time was also bishop's register, being a lawyer by profession. There is a memorial to him in the north aisle of the cathedral dating from 1617, and his portrait hangs in the Guildhall next to that of his son-in-law, Lancelot Thorpe. As a practising lawyer, Cole was of great use to the city in negotiating the details of the charter, and he was the founder of an early 17th-century dynasty of much importance in local government.

Administrative reform and the existence of a few wealthy citizens in new large houses, those belonging to Sir Walter Sandys (commander of the garrison) in Lower Brook Street and Dr. Tripp in Colebrook Street for example, could not disguise the fact that the city was in a state of economic decline. There was a reduction in the number of citizens who could be taxed as well as a fall in population.[32] The drift to the centre, the High Street, meant empty property in the side streets and made it possible for 'interlopers' to set up as temporary tradesmen. There were endless complaints about these non-freemen, and the craft guilds were frustrated by what they regarded as unnecessary interference by the civic authority.

A notable attempt to deal with the city's social problems was made by one Wintonian – Peter Symonds, stepson of Richard Bethell and a member of the Mercers' Company in London, where he spent most of his life. In his will of 20 April 1586, Symonds left a considerable endowment from property in Essex for the founding of a new almshouse in Winchester. The occupants were to be six poor, old and unmarried men, and four poor young children. In addition, two scholars were to be maintained, one at each of the ancient universities. The bequest was to be administered by a governing body (gubernatores) headed by a warden (conservator), who was to be the warden of Winchester College *ex-officio*. On St Peter's Day every year the entire foundation was to attend a commemorative service in the cathedral. The mayor and corporation were required to be present, and the founder's portrait was put on view, bunches of flowers being laid before each of the almsmen, who were to wear chains of silver round their necks 'as the musicians of London usually have on High Festival Days'. Symonds' family was not pleased with the will and disputed it, so it was some years before the bequest could be carried out. The charity was incorporated by Letters Patent of James I in 1606, and the hospital building erected on the corner of what soon became known as Symonds' Street. It was constructed with stones from Hyde Abbey by a local builder, Thomas Paice the elder.[33]

40 & 41. Peter Symonds' almshouses and (*below*) detail of the wall plaque.

SYMONDS
PETER FOVNDER
16 07

The social problems of Tudor times were too great, however, for private solutions. Early attempts by the state to intervene had put the onus for poor relief on the parish: poor rates had to be levied, collected and distributed on a parochial basis by the overseer of the poor or the churchwardens. It was an insufficient remedy, and for those whose poverty was held to be a result of their social irresponsibility the solution was a bridewell or house of correction.

An impressive house of correction was set up in Winchester by the county justices in about 1578, just two years after the act which required them to provide a place where the poor could be set to work. The Winchester house was in part of the castle precincts, and it provided an opportunity for men to learn many skilled trades and occupations, including weaving, wool-combing, cloth-drying, corn-grinding and hat-making. Women were also instructed in a variety of employments, including the knitting of stockings. The full 'course' lasted five years, three spent in learning and two in working within the building to repay in labour the cost of the first three years. It was an advanced institution, though genuine unemployed folk were not the only inhabitants, for the Justices used the place as a correction and detention centre for men and women who had committed minor misdemeanours.[34]

This was primarily a county institution, and it is not certain that it took in Wintonians to any large number.[35] The onus of poor relief in the city remained with the parishes, which had to maintain their local poor by rates collected in each area. For the historian, one of the most useful results of Henry VIII's religious changes was the requirement of 1535 that parish priests should keep a register of births, deaths and marriages. Along with churchwardens' accounts, these registers provide a vast mass of information about Winchester families and parochial history. It is the parish records which tell much of the events and effects of the Reformation at a very local level. Many of the early Winchester registers have disappeared, but Tudor survivals are to be found in the outlying parishes of St Bartholomew (from 1563), St John in the soke (from 1578), and St Peter Chesil (from 1597). The only central parish to have retained its records is St Maurice, where the records begin in 1538 and there is an occasional early entry in Latin, for example in 1538 when a Kingsmill marriage was recorded. In the 1580s the registers were kept by the clergyman Henry Lurkyn, a writer of dreadful verses:

> Hit is verye necesarye
> This book True to kep
> for some shalt have occasion
> The ayges her to seek.

It ought also to be recorded that a parishioner of this church called his son Hamlet long before the rest of England had heard about that Danish prince. There are more sinister undertones in the burial entries for 1543 and 1544, years of plague in the city when deaths are recorded as 28 and 17 respectively, compared with four in both 1541 and 1542.

Religious changes are also reflected in the churchwardens' accounts. In 1548-9 the churchwardens at St John's sold the silver gilt chalice, and in 1550 followed this up by selling off one-and-a-half hundredweight of parchment books, brass from the church, a piece of alabaster and a gilded image. Between 1551 and 1554 they sold another chalice and a cross, for the large sum of £22 17s. 10d. The churchwardens who held office at the end of Mary's reign, and for the first year of Elizabeth I's, had to pay various charges, and their account included sums for setting up the holy water stoup and buying a holy bread box, but finished with the ominous entry 'for pulling down the altar two shillings and four pence'. In the neighbouring parish of St Peter Chesil, the first churchwardens' book was a gift to the church presented by a devout parishioner two months after the royal wedding in the cathedral, and it begins with the full statement of the royal titles, though the accounts only run from 1566. Here, too, a chalice was sold off and in 1560 the churchwardens, loyal subjects, bought what they called a 'Nomelly Buke of Rebellion'. Even in that late year they retained in use a number of objects clearly displeasing to the diocesan bishop, Robert Horne, for St Peter's still owned surplices, a font cloth and a silk cloth to hang over the altar which had not yet been replaced by a communion table. This is part of the evidence which suggests that the old faith and its practice still had followers.

In the very month that the Act of Uniformity was supposed to be enforced it was noted that the new service books were not acceptable in the Winchester neighbourhood, and that men wanted to continue to hear the mass. A few months later the newly- appointed bishop, Robert Horne, a notorious reformer who had the cathedral glass broken and statues taken down, found cause for concern in the citizens' stubbornness. Catholic priests were known to be in the city, and the civic authorities showed no willingness to apprehend them. In 1564, the then mayor, Robert Hodson, and other members of the corporation were taken to London and thrown into prison because of their failure to act against papists. Hodson himself was a papist, and Bishop Horne's list of suspects included Hodson, Richard Bethell and his son, William Laurens and Roger Corham. Corham was a noted recusant from Hyde. The situation became even more difficult after 1570 when the pope excommunicated Elizabeth, as there were soon more repressive laws against Catholics. In about eight months of 1570, 38 Winchester papists were cited for non-attendance at church; even the dean and chapter were regarded with suspicion by Horne. Dean Steward had already been replaced.

Winchester was described in 1576 by the future Cardinal Allen as one of the most Catholic towns in England. Their numbers increased, rather than diminished, and the execution of two priests, convicted of treason, did not discourage

> CHRIST'S HOSPITAL
> Which was founded
> In the Year of our Lord 1607
> By PETER SYMONDS
> a Native of Winchester
> and afterwards a Mercer
> in the City of London.
> The Endowments of this House
> are applied to the maintenance
> of Six Old Men, One Matron, and Four Boys;
> and also to the assistance
> of one Scholar
> in each of the Two English Universities.
> The name of such a Benefactor
> Is rememberd with gratitude by Posterity.

42. Notice from Christ's Hospital.

the faithful. John Slade was executed at Winchester and John Body, who had been a scholar in the college, at Andover. These martyrs have recently been commemorated by a window in the Catholic church. When a return of papists was made in 1583, there were 51 names for the Winchester area alone, out of a total of some 300 for the diocese generally.

All kinds of Winchester people were recusants. David Ringstead, underkeeper of the gaol, admitted quite freely that he was a papist; he could and did help many Catholic prisoners. James Bird, executed in 1593, was a young man who attended mass in 'My Lady West's house' in St Peter Street. Lady West, the wife of Sir Owen West, had been under suspicion since at least 1578; no really punitive action was ever taken against her. Other suspected ladies included Elizabeth Norton and Averia Heath, fined in 1592. Bird was the son of the mayor, Anthony Bird, who searched Lady West's house in 1583 and found much evidence of covert Catholic worship, including missals, vestments and an altar. From this time onwards St Peter Street became particularly associated with the old faith, as it still is today; so too were certain households in the soke and at Hyde.[36]

The queen, like her predecessors, visited Winchester on several occasions, which encouraged the citizens to believe that it was still a royal city. Elizabeth I probably visited for the first time in August 1560, and perhaps again in September 1569 on a journey between Southampton and the Vyne, Basingstoke; on this later occasion 'Lady Masson's house' was prepared for her reception. Early in September 1574 she was addressed by the scholars of Winchester College with verses in Greek and Latin expressing their loyal affection. The scholars were active young men: Camden records that they went down to Dartford and adorned *The Golden Hind* with appropriate verses after Drake's great voyage. The queen was in Winchester again in September 1586 and May 1591, when the corporation presented her with a handsome silver gilt cup, tipped the minor officers of her retinue, and had the town pump mended in an effort to improve the water supplies. The chamberlains overspent and had to borrow £10 out of the coffer to cover their expenses. The churchwarden of St John in the soke noted the 3s. spent on 'Drink, ringing for the Queen'. When the queen died in 1603 it was indeed the end of an era, and the beginning in Winchester of further years of trouble and unrest.

Chapter Nine

Winchester under the Stuarts

Early Stuart Winchester was a city of division and decline, and the chamberlain's accounts record a continuing period of physical change.[1] There were ruined churches; others were used for secular purposes. Small lanes continued to be enclosed or built over by influential citizens such as the Coles and Hobsons. Eastgate and Newbridge had to be repaired at public expense. In 1613 there were only five guildsmen: one, Thomas Godson, was a future mayor; another, John Lampeir or Lampard, a future prisoner in the Westgate; and a third, William Fletcher, was the dean and chapter's clerk of works. The mayor, Richard Adderley, was still getting the usual fee, in two instalments of £5 each; the recorder, John Moore, received the traditional £4 a year; and minstrels were engaged 'when the Mayor went to sup with the Recorder'.

In contrast to the wealth of a few citizens, amongst them the Clarkes of Hyde Street, there were about five hundred people out of work. The area of Abbot's Barton had become notorious as a place of refuge for beggars, and the county magistrates even contemplated using a building off the High Street as a house of correction.[2]

Not surprisingly, the corporation's main concern was the city's economy, and once again they were able to use a royal visit and the expenses arising from it as an economic lever with the Crown. James I arrived in Winchester in November 1603 on the occasion of the trials of Brooke, Cobham, Young and Raleigh for their alleged conspiracy in the 'Bye' and 'Main' plots. The trials had been moved to Winchester because the plague was once again raging in London. On 3 November 1603 the king had written from Wilton requiring the warden and fellows to remove themselves and the scholars, and 'give their houses and lodging to the king's Judges whilst the Courts are kept at the Bishop's Palace at Wolvesey'. As a result of this order, the scholars were sent off to Silkstead, but the courts opened on 12 November in the great hall of the castle, not at Wolvesey.

James' charter to the city, dated 15 December 1604, was specifically given 'because of the decay of the city' and the great outlay and expense incurred by the inhabitants during 'the arraignment of sundry persons', and during the period when the king and queen, and their son Henry Prince of Wales, had been staying in Winchester. This long and involved charter confirmed Philip and Mary's grant of the farm and subsidy of the ulnage for a further 60 years, together with a remission of part of the fee farm and the right granted by Philip and Mary of exporting cloth at half the regular rate of custom of tonnage and poundage. A large section of the charter is taken up with a recital of the Act of Parliament of Edward IV by which dimensions of manufactured cloth were defined. The charter was followed by further negotiations about the ulnage, negotiations left almost entirely to Sir Thomas Flemyng and the recorder. As a result, the city was able to let the farm of the ulnage to the Duke of Lennox in 1613 for a payment of £400; he promptly sublet it. Lennox's grant forms the last real appearance of the ulnage in Winchester's history, and Flemyng was given a piece of plate by the grateful corporation 'for the kindness he had shown the city'.[3]

There were other ways in which the corporation hoped to improve the prosperity of Winchester. In August 1617 the city paid the expenses of a certain Captain Sason, 'staying in this city four days in travelling to Southampton to view the river and make it navigable from Winchester to Southampton'. The corporation had sent a delegation to London, headed by the mayor Richard Adderley, with Edward White and Lancelot Thorpe, the town clerk, to interview the Bishop of Winchester about his ancient rights on the river. To further their interests they presented both the bishop and the Archbishop of Canterbury with sugar loaves and started a lottery to raise money.[4] Nothing happened, and the plan was shelved until after the Civil War. Winchester was still an important market centre, and the rebuilding of the Market House in the Square was another project designed to encourage economic recovery. It proved to be a rather delicate matter, since part of the building had to be erected on land belonging to the dean and chapter. Two wooden arches from the fabric can be seen in the museum, bearing the initials of Lancelot Thorpe and Edward White and the date 1615.[5] The Square became an increasingly important centre of city life.

The activities of the corporation were of considerable interest to the dean and chapter, but the diocesan bishops were rarely in Winchester. In 1625 part of Wolvesey was being used by the Marquess of Winchester as a munition store, full of powder, shot, match and muskets, dangerous items which were later moved to Netley.[6] The first three bishops of the 17th-century diocese were all men who supported the Laudian revival in the Anglican Church. Bishop Lancelot Andrewes (1619-26) was buried in the church which is now Southwark Cathedral, but one of the mourning rings distributed after his death can be seen in Winchester's Fiforium Gallery. His successor Richard Neale (1626-31) soon became Archbishop of York, and the diocesan who proved to be the mainstay of the revival of Winchester was Walter Curle.

Contemporary with these three bishops was Dean John Young, and it is the historian's good fortune that this particular dean kept a diary.[7] Young was a shrewd Scot and a devoted royalist. His diary contains a mass of information about local affairs and local people, and it is an essential source book for the troubled years before the outbreak of the Civil War. In the cathedral the services under his direction were conducted in the spirit of the Laudian revival, and in 1616 the dean 'moved the sermon' to the body of the church, restoring the choir to something of its erstwhile seclusion. There was trouble in 1629 about Dr. Moore, a Wykehamist canon, as the rest of the chapter did not approve of his views. The dean asked him to submit copies of his sermons in advance, and Moore refused. He was too much of a puritan for the cathedral and resigned in 1631 after a final sermon on the text 'I dwelt among my own people' which he preached, to the annoyance of his colleagues, in a gown and without a surplice.

When the cathedral was officially visited by Sir Nathaniel Brent in June 1635 as vicar-general, the dean tactfully asked Peter Heylin, rector of Alresford and Laud's future biographer, to be the preacher. In January 1636 another sermon produced a major crisis, when a kinsman of John Harris, warden of Winchester College, concluded his efforts with the words 'pray God to have mercy upon England for the sin of Idolatory and breaking of the Sabbath'. It was agreed that Hill could preach in future, but on the understanding that 'the Warden should answer for it'. These were public sermons and, of course, their content fell on some sympathetic ears. There were many changes in the cathedral fabric, too. A new Inigo Jones screen containing brass statues by Le Sueur of James I and Charles I separated choir from nave; the central tower crossing was ceiled in and decorated in an appropriate manner; 'Laudian' altar rails, now in the lady chapel, were placed in front of the high altar; and the great west window was reglazed. It was almost inevitable that some Wintonians would not approve of these changes, and the crisis over ship money in 1637 worsened relations between the dean and chapter and the corporation.

It began as a parish pump quarrel and degenerated into a serious dispute. Ship money had to be paid to the high sheriff and in 1636 this duty of collection fell on John Button of Lymington. Button had assessed the close separately and the dean and chapter paid up promptly. To their indignant horror, they were then faced with a second demand, from the corporation, who seemed to have been prepared to ignore the fact that the chapter treasurer, Doctor Alexander, already had a receipt for the money. The chapter would not pay again, and the corporation then arrested first one and then a second member of the lay staff of the cathedral, both residents of the close, and consigned them to the Westgate. There was a clerical uproar, and some members of the chapter advocated the pulling down of the corporation's new Market House. Dean Young counselled moderation and appealed to the king. The situation worsened when the corporation used this opportunity to raise the whole issue of their rights within the close, and whether or not they could carry the maces there. Another point of difficulty was the vexed question of where the mayor was to sit in the cathedral. In the years which passed while these disputes dragged on there were difficult mayors; one came to church late, one wore his hat and left early before the sermon, while another fell over the legs of the Archdeacon of Winchester 'kneeling at the Commandments'.[8]

This pantomime of civic affront had an ominous undertone. Both the corporation and the dean and chapter were anxious to get their privileges confirmed, but only the efforts of the cathedral body were successful; the Caroline Statutes of 1637 were agreed by Laud and by the king, and the influence of the dean and chapter was so strong that the corporation never succeeded in getting the city's charter renewed. Moreover, both parties had had the honour of meeting the king, for Charles had wished to listen to certain aspects of the dispute. He had vacillated, and the impression which he had made on the corporation's chief adviser, their recorder, was not favourable. This was unfortunate, for the corporation's recorder was John Lisle.

It took time, however, for the divided loyalties of the country to appear within the city, but in April 1640, when the Short Parliament assembled, the two members returned for Winchester were John Lisle, a future supporter of Cromwell, and William Ogle, commander of the Winchester garrison, a loyalist but not yet a royalist. The two men were returned again in the autumn of 1640 for the beginning of the Long Parliament, which eventually ended its own existence only after it had been purged by Colonel Pride, agreed to the execution of the king, and declared England to be a Commonwealth.

When the king raised his standard at Nottingham in August 1642, Winchester had a royal garrison under Lord Grandison in the castle on the western hill. In the autumn, the castle surrendered to forces led by Sir William Waller. Though there was not much fighting, it was unfortunate that Waller's troops were, as usual, unpaid, and they took the opportunity of looting the town, particularly the cathedral and the close. *A true and exact relation of the great overthrow given to the Cavaliers in Winchester*, published in 1642, described the parliamentarian victory, and was quickly followed by another piece of propaganda from the royalist press, *The King's Majesties Message to the inhabitants of the city of Winchester*. This was a royal reproach because the city had surrendered: 'So will wee throw by all respects or remembrances that you were our subjects'. Waller was a freeman of the city, and he was disturbed by his troops' behaviour. Early in the New Year (March 1643) he came back, intending to apologise, but his troops were still unpaid, there was further looting, and in one nasty incident a young royalist was tortured in *The George Inn*.

By this time support for the parliamentary cause was not as great as it had been, and when Ogle, disabled by the Commons, declared for the king he was able to re-establish a royal garrison in the castle. The frequent absences of John Lisle, who was increasingly busy in the Commons and unpopular in Winchester when he was there, encouraged royalist revival. The garrison, under Ogle, maintained its control of the castle until September 1645; then Cromwell himself arrived and after a short sharp attack accepted its surrender. The war in Winchester was over but its effect, with that of the policies of the Rump Parliament, was tremendous. All the old institutions were threatened in one way or another - by physical assault, reform, extermination, and by the imprisonment and persecution of individual members of the community; but there were still royalists amongst the corporation.

In December 1648 Charles I arrived at the Westgate on his last journey to London, and a royalist mayor presented the keys to the king in the traditional way, only to be set upon by the guard. The king's execution, in January 1649, was the end of an era in the life of the nation. On a local scale, it marked the temporary end of much of Winchester. In February, the royalists in the corporation were turned out by the Commons and a new corporation set up by parliament's ordinance.[9] The only local institutions to survive were Winchester College, St John's Hospital, St Cross, and Symonds Hospital.

It was fortunate for the school that one of the most powerful men in parliament was Nicolas Love, Ogle's successor as member of parliament for Winchester from 1643 and a Wykehamist, whose father had been headmaster. Dean and chapter was abolished, as were bishops, but Winchester College went on. When it was visited by parliamentary commissioners in 1649, Warden John Harris proved himself a diplomat. He was accused of bowing at the name of Jesus, preaching in support of bishops, praying for the king's army, and supporting Sir William Ogle, governor of Winchester castle. His careful answers included one to the effect that though he had prayed for the king he had not prayed for the confusion of parliament. He was undoubtedly helped by the fact that some extremely influential parliamentarians were Wykehamists; as well as Love, Nathaniel Fiennes had stayed in the school in December 1642, the very day before Waller took possession of the castle. Fiennes' visit appears to be the origin of the confused story of the survival of Wykeham's chantry chapel, which he is said to have protected from the violence of his fellow parliamentarian soldiers. Whatever the truth of this particular legend, assigned to various dates and occasions, neither college nor chantry was harmed in the war.[10] Love was responsible, in fact, for a significant gain, though part of it was temporary. In 1652 he persuaded the Commons to send an important group of manuscripts to the school, books which had survived from the cathedral library. In the following year a list of the school establishment for 1653, the so-called long roll, was compiled. It appears to be the oldest list of its kind for any school in England, and shows how well the foundation had managed to survive the Civil War. In 1657-8, Warden Harris built the attractive small building called Sick House off Kingsgate Street on the site of the Carmelite Friary. He died in 1658 and was succeeded by William Burt, who had been the schoolmaster and was not unsympathetic to some measure of 'puritanical' practice. He managed to survive the Restoration, remaining as warden until his death in 1679. Burt deserves to be remembered for what might be called his repair work on St Swithun's Street, an area which had suffered as a result of the Civil War, though not a street with much building in it before 1642. He was given preferential treatment by the corporation, who granted him building leases on favourable terms, and thus made it possible for some of the destruction wrought by the war to be repaired quickly and economically.[11]

There were other major changes in the Winchester scene. A stream of orders arrived from London demanding the demolition of the castle on the western hill, already damaged in the siege of 1645 when the western part of the town had also suffered. St Clement's church, on the northern corner of St Clement's and Southgate Street, was occupied by troops and could never again be used for church purposes. It is hardly surprising that Wintonians hesitated to rebuild in the immediate vicinity of the castle, and the redevelopment of the upper part of the High Street began only in the 19th century. Effective demolition of the castle began in late 1650 and continued into 1651 under the supervision of Richard Major of Hursley, a county justice and the father-in-law of Richard Cromwell. He had to report that it was a difficult building to destroy; the walls were thick and the foundations of strong flintwork: 'it be a works of a long time, and of a vast charge, if not impossible'. Nevertheless it was work which went on and only fragments of this once famous castle survived when the monarchy was restored in 1660. The south-east tower keep was leased by the corporation in 1664 to an ejected cleric, Henry Complin of Avington. Certain lengths of wall and some massive foundations including the so-called 'secret passages' also survived the destruction, but the most significant survival was the great hall, which passed with the rest of the fragments to Sir William Waller in 1656, by gift of parliament. Waller sold it off to trustees for £100 for use as a county hall. The remaining fragments of the castle he gave to the corporation, who were thus able to return it to Charles II as the site for a new palace.

On the other side of Winchester, Wolvesey Castle was also virtually demolished, becoming, as St Mary's Abbey and Hyde had been 100 years before, a mere stone quarry. The cathedral close was much affected. After Dean and Chapter were abolished, and the prayer book replaced by the directory of worship, its clerical inhabitants left Winchester. Their houses were parcelled out amongst supporters of the Commonwealth, headed by Nicholas Love (given the Deanery), while John Lisle had a smaller house to the east of the dean's mansion. He was still the recorder and, as a commissioner of the great seal, perhaps the most influential of the politicians concerned with the city.

Lisle's neighbours in the close included Humphrey Ellis and Leonard Cooke,[12] who were the two ministers charged with the responsibility of directing the religious life of the city; a third preacher, John Brayne, appointed for the soke, was dead before 1652 when his widow, Dorcas, was pensioned by the government. Ellis, who was given or assumed a lead in local affairs, was not an altogether attractive character. He acted as chaplain to the corporation, and preached at least one election sermon in St John's House at mayor-making, for which he was paid 10s. He was not the only Winchester man to quarrel with John Woodman, the solicitor dealing with the sequestrations of royalist property, and also resident in the close. In one unfortunate incident Ellis was attacked by a crowd led by Woodman in St Maurice's church, his Bible was taken out of his hands, and he was forced to leave the building. Ellis also fell out with Cornelius Hooker, Lisle's eventual successor as recorder, who alleged that he (Ellis) had spoken against Cromwell.[13] It was an unfounded libel, and Ellis remained on good terms with the rest of the corporation. He was allowed to leave the close and settled in Tripp's old house in Colebrook Street.

Only cautious but energetic action by local men saved the cathedral from demolition, for the Commons naturally discussed the fate of the greater churches. A Winchester alderman, Christopher Hussey, was fortunately present at the committee meeting which might well have taken an irrevocable decision; he had the item deferred, and the recorder, Cornelius Hooker, an objectionable man in many ways, drafted a petition opposing the demolition. The petitioners claimed that the building was 'an ancient and most beautiful structure, the most convenient and spacious place for the hearing of God's word'. It was saved, but the fabric was in poor condition: the choir stalls had been damaged, their pinnacles broken off, and the series of biblical scenes which adorned them smashed; the great glass window at the west end, reglazed by Dean Young, had been broken; the brass statues of James I and Charles I had been the 'object of attack by the soldiers'. These latter were now taken down and, apparently at the mayor's suggestion, sold. The money was used to repair the churches of St Thomas and St Maurice. A small amount of money, under £40, was collected, and urgent repairs to the building carried out in the midsummer of 1654 with the hope that 'dayly decay through want of reparation' might be halted. No details have survived of what was actually done, and the degeneration of the fabric certainly continued. Its physical decline, and that of the close houses, was almost inevitable.

The hospital of St Cross was more fortunate. The mastership was bestowed on John Lisle, and vacancies in the almshouse used for the pensioning of parliamentarian ex-soldiers.[14] It is not clear how much Lisle received from this additional office, perhaps less than £200 a year; he soon gave it up, and was succeeded by another extremist lawyer, John Cooke, who was solicitor general and the chief prosecutor at the trial of Charles I. At least these arrangements had the advantage of preserving the fabric, and some attempt was made to increase the stipends of the almsfolk.

The hospital of St Mary Magdalene on the eastern hill did not fare so well. Its continued existence had always been rather uncertain, simply because it had little endowment. By 1545 the number of inmates had been reduced to nine.

Occasional donations helped to keep the place going, as in 1611 when the then master, Dr. John Ebden, left an annual sum of £10 to be divided amongst the almsfolk and also provided for a gown to be given to them each Christmas Day. The hospital had suffered in the Civil War through the activities of royalist troops. In 1643, a petition was sent to Lord Hopton describing how the hospital's flock of sheep had been killed and eaten by the soldiers, who had stalled their horses in the sanctuary. Every possible piece of wood that could be found had been burnt as fuel, including the main altar of the chapel, and the master and brethren had been turned out.[15]

The parish churches also suffered though it was argued in 1660, not unfairly, that many of them had been in poor condition before the Anglican services and the prayer book were abolished, and before the 'reformed' corporation decided to let most of the churches for secular purposes. As far as the old parish life of Winchester was concerned, the rule of the Rump was the final disastrous blow in the slow process of decline which had begun with the Black Death. In evidence offered to the House of Lords in 1660, the surviving members of the royalist party in Winchester listed a long series of crimes against the city's parish churches. The corporation were alleged to have demolished the belfry tower of St Clement's church, taken down the bells, and let both church and parsonage house to a tenant who used the font for washing clothes, cut a door through the east end behind the altar, and erected a furnace and oven inside the chancel. In defence, it was argued that St Clement's was 'a very little church, incapable of holding any considerable congregation ... in time of war ... utterly ransacked and torn to pieces ... and most part of the parish burnt down in the war'. St Peter *in Macellis* was admitted to have been in poor repair before 1642, the stone belfry having been taken down and the material used to pave the streets. It was suggested that no harm had been done by this, since the church had been a notorious ruin for years, 'known to be a loathsome, noisome nuisance to the parts of the city adjoining it'. In the High Street, St Mary Kalander had been leased to a layman who 'dug for a well amongst the dead bodies' and altered the High Street frontage into a butcher's shop and smithy. In defence of this action it was argued that this church had not been used for divine service within the memory of man, that there was no sign of its belfry, and its roof had gone, leaving 'only a ghastly sight of two ruinous walls lying open for butchers ... to empty the bellies of their killed beasts'. In Colebrook Street, St Peter's church had been leased to a layman, a tanner by trade, who made a hay-loft at one end and moved tan pits into the nave of the church. It was argued in this case that for at least 14 years this 'inconsiderable little place ... extremely untiled ... had had nothing in it but grass weeds and nettles'. St Swithun-upon-Kingsgate was another sufferer, let to a tenant who had kept pigs in one end and lived in the other; it was argued in justification that the place was ruinous already, and quite unfit for a congregation. The church registers in fact refer to the church as being 'down' in 1632. The fate of St Lawrence was happier, though it lost what medieval fittings had survived since the great repair of 1475. The font was taken away, as were most of the pews, the stones used for paving the streets and the building turned into a school.

Only two parish churches, St Thomas and St Maurice, were put to ecclesiastical use by the reformers. St Thomas was said to have been retiled, reseated, reroofed and made into a 'decent near handsome church ... the like never seen in the city'. St Maurice, too, was repaired and was also described by the parliamentary party as 'a most handsome church'.[16] Away from the city's centre, at Hyde and Abbot's Barton, the inhabitants suffered from the marauding armies of both parties. Cathedral property fell into disrepair. John Lisle's brother-in-law, Thomas Chandler, the owner of Abbot's Barton, was swept up into the royalist army, fined heavily and died a ruined and bankrupt man.[17]

The accounts kept by John Woodman as 'Receiver in the Civil Wars' speak for themselves. He paid out alms to 310 'poor people' of the soke and city, and found it impossible to collect all the rents which had been part of the cathedral's income: 'Several leasehold tenements ... many of them pulled down and burnt in the late War by the forces in the Castle of Winchester'. There were even some houses 'where poore people dwell in that have not anything to distreine' in lieu of rent.[18]

When Charles II was welcomed back, the 'return of the church' was to a city in some fair measure of decline and decay.[19] Soon after 29 May (the exact day is not certain) the king was proclaimed at the High Cross, and the 'restored' corporation went to the cathedral in the old way. There they heard a 'very loyal and eloquent sermon' from the rector of Avington. At the Cross a special dais had been erected from which to read the proclamation, and a cathedral choir of sorts had been collected, including the survivors of the pre-1649 singing men, led by 'Mr. Burt', aged eighty. Their singing of a suitably amended version of Byrd's famous anthem composed for Elizabeth I, beginning with the words 'O Lord make thy servant Charles our gracious King to rejoice in Thy strength', marked the beginning of a new period in Winchester's history.

Almost immediately an attempt was made to revive the Winchester-Southampton canal project. On 14 November 1660 the new corporation petitioned the Marquess of Winchester, the new bishop (Brian Duppa), the restored dean and chapter, the warden and fellows 'and all other pious and charitable hearts in the county' in the hope that all these distinguished people might support the making of a canal.[20] Winchester, wrote the petitioners, was greatly impoverished after the Civil War, there were 200 poor families, and 'trading altogether decayed'. A group of public-spirited individuals, led by Sir Humphrey Bennett, were authorised by act of parliament to make the Itchen navigable from Alresford via Winchester to the sea at Southampton, and construct any necessary new channels, locks or weirs. They were required to complete the work by

1 November 1671 and not to charge for carriage more than half the price required for land carriage, a requirement which ensured that there could never be enough return on money invested. Another reason for the project's failure was the resistance of Southampton, for although much of the work seems to have been completed, the transporters found themselves restricted by Southampton action to the carrying only of 'coals and the Norway trade'. Apparently the rival corporation had indicated that it was the intention of the Winchester group to carry on a clandestine trade in dutiable goods 'to the prejudice of His Majesty's revenue'. The rector of Weeke, William Emes, recorded in his diary that the first unladen trial boat came up from South-ampton in 1697 and the first load of coal on 18 April 1698. Defoe's verdict *c*.1724 was probably correct: the navigation 'never answered the expenses so as to give encouragement to the undertakers'.

The return of the plague in 1665 and 1666 was another factor hindering economic revival. In September 1665 the mayor's annual feast had to be can-celled, Winchester College was shut and the boys were sent to Crawley. The school was closed again in 1667 from August until the end of December, and the wardens of New College and Winchester met at Hursley rather than in the city. 'Election' was held at Newbury.

These outbreaks, particularly that of 1666, were severe. 'Plague' accounts have survived for two of the most severely affected parishes, St John in the soke and St Peter Chesil. The pest-house, thatched with sedge, was in constant use. Many families were shut up in their own houses and relieved only by the church-wardens, who also had to apprentice the many orphans and distribute relief money. This flowed from the Isle of Wight, Southampton, Romsey, and from a few villages near Winchester whose inhabitants hoped to prevent the spread of pestilence.[21] According to local tradition, the dead were buried in communal graves between Twyford Down and St Catherine's Hill in Plague Pits Valley. One of the saddest records is of the death, in St Maurice's parish, of the entire family of John Jerome, the cathedral painter and craftsman whose work had included the painting of the pinnacles of the choir stalls which had partially replaced the woodwork broken by Waller's troops. Jerome, his wife and their children died as a family. The situation was disastrous for those children who were left as orphans and it was to help them that the Charitable Society of Natives and Citizens came into being; the first annual feast was held on 29 August 1669 and the proceedings were henceforth in the charge of two annually elected stewards. There was junketing, but the purpose was the serious one of appren-ticing and educating the orphan children of Winchester citizens. A Society of Aliens followed in July 1720, and an obelisk, erected in 1758 outside Westgate, records the origin of the two organisations.

The restoration of the monarchy had created almost as many local political problems as it had solved, and the policies of Charles II and his successor

43. The obelisk and (*right*) a detail of the inscription on the base.

perpetuated the divisions of the city. Strenuous efforts were made by central government to control local government, for if a majority of Winchester freemen were king's men, Winchester's two members of parliament would *ipso facto* be of that persuasion. Even in 1665 Clarendon was writing to local justices of the peace asking for their help 'in discovering the machinations of those men you know to be ill-affected to the government'. The relations between corporation and central government continued to be reasonably friendly throughout the next few years; early in 1674 Charles gave the city the customary form of financial relief by reducing the fee farm to half the nominal amount of 100 marks.[22] In September 1682 the king and his brother, the Duke of York, were both made freemen of the city. A court party had clearly established itself within the corporation under the leadership of the mayor, Thomas Coward, who agreed on 28 September to admit Edward Harfell as a member of the corporation at the direct personal request of the king. Harfell was a lawyer who practised in the Cheyney court and was the son of a former chapter clerk.[23] All of the senior aldermen immediately opposed Harfell's election. The opposition was led by Anthony Yalden and Thomas Wavell, the latter a linen draper and member of a famous family whose connections with the city and with Winchester College went back to the 15th century. They fully appreciated that Charles II had begun his attack on the city's independence.

On 29 September the mayor declared that 'Because his gracious Majesty was pleased to honour the city with his presence for that and for other reasons I think fit to deliver up our charter, not doubting that his Majesty will please to grant it again'. He went on to allege that he had asked all the aldermen to meet him on that particular day, but that only two had appeared.[24]

The charter which the king was demanding was that of Elizabeth I. Its surrender was bitterly opposed, especially by Thomas Wavell and a few other men who may be called Whigs, who found themselves in an increasingly difficult situation, opposed by members of the corporation whose commercial interests and political loyalties lay with the Crown. For in 1683 Charles had decided to build a new palace in Winchester; Christopher Wren was employed, and the foundation stone laid in the same year, after the corporation had handed over the site of the castle for the proposed new building.[25] Within a year the Court party had gained a stranglehold on the corporation, and at a meeting on 28 June 1684, when 46 members were present, it was unanimously decided to surrender the charter, and on 12 July it was agreed that the common seal of the corporation be put to the deed of surrender. The mayor hired a special coach to take the charter to the king in person; Charles was at the Winchester races. In early September a petition asking for the return of the charter was sent to London, again to the king in person. Charles passed it on to the attorney general. Nothing was done, and soon afterwards the dukes of Richmond and St Albans were made freemen of the city. Ominously, the corporation did not meet again until 8 February 1685 when James II was proclaimed.

No formal enrolment of the surrender was made in the city minute books, but a copy was made in the city lease-book, in an almost furtive manner, and the deed of surrender preserved amongst the papers of the Duke of Norfolk, presumably because Bernard Howard was active for the king in Winchester and was eventually nominated as recorder by James II.[26] At the meeting of the corporation on 16 March, two Tory candidates had been chosen as members of parliament: one of them was Roger L'Estrange, the king's pamphleteer and propagandist. Royal control over Winchester was complete, and the execution of Alice Lisle on 2 September 1685 must be considered in local terms as a further attempt to strike terror into Winchester hearts.

In reality, its effect was to strengthen the opponents of James II, and by the time a writ of *quo warranto* arrived in late October 1687 opposition to the king had hardened and was still led by Thomas Wavell. In 1688 the corporation had to agree to accept a new charter, dated 15 September, which effectively ended local liberties. The corporation were all named and officials were chosen by central government, while machinery was provided by which they could be removed at the king's wish. The man appointed as mayor was Thomas Pescell, the town clerk was Arnold Capdeville, and the only members who had previously been freemen were Roger L'Estrange and Bernard Howard. All the members were Roman Catholics or had Catholic connections. Removal of members was by simple notification via the privy council, and the charter also embodied exceptions from the Test Act, the Corporation Act and the oath of allegiance as laid down in the Act of Supremacy of Elizabeth I.

James' end was drawing near. The new charter only lasted a few weeks, and the old privileges were hastily given back by Letters Patent of 2 November 1688. The old corporation was restored: Thomas Wavell became mayor, Richard Harris of Silkstead was appointed recorder and, though there were new members who might be classified as Tories (Godson Penton and Ellis Mews, for example), the Whigs' triumph in Winchester reflected the national success of William of Orange.

In 1683, in the halcyon days before his attack on the charter, Charles II presented the city with his portrait, a painting by Lely in a fine Clarendon frame. It is still on display in the present Guildhall, but the royal palace, designed by Sir Christopher Wren for the site of the old castle on the western hill, survives only as a series of fragments, a few drawings, and a glorious memory of what might have been. The overall plan as conceived by Wren did have an important effect on the topography of the city, even though the building was never completed. The foundation stone was laid by the mayor, Anthony Yalden, on 23 March 1683, though the king himself was at the races as usual. The city's bells were rung and bonfires lit on the tower of the castle and on St Catherine's Hill. According to the historian Wavell, who described the unfinished building from personal observation, it was to have contained 150 rooms and was to have been 328 ft. long on its west-facing front; the building was to be dominated by a large cupola, and there were to be a magnificent external colonnade and a splendid staircase supported by marble pillars given to the king by the Grand Duke of Tuscany. The exact centre of the east-facing front was to be on a line with the centre of the west end of the cathedral, whence it was to be connected by a great avenue 200 feet wide and 'lined with the houses of nobility'.[27] Landowners whose ground lay around the area were not to be permitted to renew or re-lease that ground. Wren envisaged a large park with a circumference of 10 miles, stretching towards St Cross and including both the cathedral manor of Thurmond's and the land leased to Robert Badger.

This plan made the city most attractive to courtiers. In St Swithun's Street a large E-shaped house with wings topped by twin cupolas is traditionally described as having been the Winchester house of the Duke of York; it has been altered, but remains essentially a late 17th-century building, with a grand approach from St Thomas Street. At the west end of Canon Street, Queen's Lodge, an L-shaped building on the corner site, is associated with Catherine of

44.   17th-century homes in Canon Street.

Braganza, and a notable house in St Peter Street (No. 4) is supposed to have been built for the Duchess of Portsmouth: it is now the probate registry and has lost one wing, its railings and a bust of the Duchess which it displayed in the 19th century. The initials E.G. on one of the lead cistern heads have persuaded some observers to associate the house with Nell Gwynne, but in fact they commemorate a later owner, Edward Grace, a wealthy benefactor of St Thomas' church. At the eastern end of the town, a courtier, Sir Robert Mason, built his family home (Eastgate House) from the remnants of the Black Friars' buildings, a house depicted as a marginal illustration in Godson's later map of Winchester but demolished in 1844. Amongst the important new inhabitants of the city was Sir John Clobery, who had a large mansion in Parchment Street. He had taken a leading part in the political and military arrangements which made the return of the king possible. The Duke of Buckingham, another courtier, was said to have lived in Kingsgate Street.[28]

Although the corporation had no real cause to be grateful to Charles II or his successor, the city owes much of its best-surviving domestic architecture to the restoration of the monarchy and Church, and there are some splendid examples in the close and in the soke.

Dean Young had died in exile at Exton in 1654, and six other members of his Chapter died during the Interregnum. The new dean appointed in 1660 was Alexander Hyde, a cousin of the all-powerful Earl of Clarendon, Charles II's chancellor. By March 1661 financial prospects seemed good, rents were coming in, as well as the large income derived from fines set on new tenants taking leases or copyhold of Chapter property. It was agreed that the 'Cathedral and the Close houses shall be re-edified at the common cost'. The Deanery was a particular problem, since much of it was derelict, but in December 1661 the Chapter engaged Richard Frampton, a Kingsgate Street architect, to repair it. It was he who built the new long gallery, now such a striking feature of the close, and repaired the Great Hall.[29] The building of four new houses in Dome Alley was carried out under the direction of the cathedral's clerk of works, William Fletcher. These were houses built as quickly and economically as possible, with the cheap material of the age – brick. The bricks were burnt in the close, although the moulded bricks for the cornice had to be bought elsewhere, and the buildings were also decorated with functional lead work, water pipes and cistern heads from earlier Tudor buildings. At the north-east corner of Dome Alley a fifth 'new' house was built, or reconstructed, all of stone. This is the gabled building now known as Church House, and its traditional form is in marked contrast to the Dome Alley houses.[30] When Archbishop Juxon held a visitation of the cathedral in 1662, the chapter was able to give a good report of the cathedral fabric and to say that the work of restoring their houses was well in hand.

By far the most notorious of the new chapter was Dr. Gumble, who had been

45. Dome Alley, built after 1660 by William Fletcher, clerk of the works to the Dean and Chapter.

46. Zincograph by J. B. Dixon, based on a sketch of October 1841, showing Dr. Gumble's house in the close (*left*) which was demolished in the middle of the 19th century.

chaplain to General Monck. Dr. Gumble was too often away from Winchester and would not undertake a fair share of the repairs needed by his house, a building which became a local *cause célèbre*. In the autumn of 1673 he pulled most of it down, and built a three-storey addition in another style, at a cost of £200. It was hardly surprising that the chapter refused to allow this sum in their accounts, held back Gumble's 'dividend' of £170, and appealed to the bishop to declare his prebend vacant. Dr. Gumble's eventual successor in this house was Thomas Ken, who had become a canon of Winchester in 1669, but the house was demolished in the mid-19th century.[31] Ken's contemporaries included a number of very able men: William Hawkins, son-in-law of Isaac Walton, living at

47.   The surviving wing of Wolvesey Palace, begun by Bishop Morley in 1684.

7 The Close; John Nicolas (at 3 Pilgrims' School), who was also warden of Winchester College where he was a wealthy contributor to the building known as School ; and above all George Morley, Bishop of Winchester from 1662-84.

It is difficult to escape from Morley in Winchester. A visitor to the Guildhall will find his astute piercing gaze looking down from a Lely-like portrait in the Banqueting Hall. A short distance to the west of the Guildhall, in the outer close, is Morley's College, a 19th-century rebuilding of the group of almshouses endowed by the bishop in 1673, and constructed in part of the cathedral church-yard. This 'College for Matrons' was to be a home for the widows of clergy from the dioceses of Winchester and Worcester, and the manor of Taunton Dean, Somerset. There were usually eight matrons and also three junior out-pensioners. In an age when the status of the wives of parish clergy was still not established, and there were no clergy pensions, Morley's endowment was generous and far-sighted. His less famous projects include the rebuilding of Black Bridge and the reform of Cheyney Court. His major addition was the rebuilding of Wolvesey, not as a fortification, but as a large domestic palace.[32] It is said to have been begun in 1684, the year of his death. In his will Morley made a further important contribution to Winchester – his library, which he left to the dean and chapter and which now forms the Morley Library in the cathedral, a splendid and valu-able collection indicative of his care for the learning of the dean and chapter.

The liking which Charles II had for the city, and perhaps even the outbreaks of plague and smallpox, were factors which continued to encourage well-known doctors to settle in late 17th-century Winchester.[33] The fashionable general practitioner of the period was Dr. Nicolas Stanley, '*nulli secundum*' according to his gravestone. He was really a London doctor, but was presumably buried in the cathedral (in 1687) because he was the son of the headmaster of Winchester College. Dr. Arthur Taylor was also a successful doctor, whose official appoint-ments included that of physician to St Cross Hospital in 1663, a more or less honorary job which did not prevent him from having a successful private prac-tice. He had a large house (probably in the close), kept a coach and three horses and died worth over £1,600. William Coker, who died in 1704, was also buried in the cathedral and had practised in Winchester for 26 years. Dr. William Over was able to leave a large sum of money to found a free school for boys. It is hardly surprising that the movement to found the first county hospital outside the London area should have originated in Winchester. Clerics and lawyers also flourished, as did innkeepers and carriers. Amongst the latter, the Waldrons proved to be most successful, founding a firm which continued into the late 19th century.

Yet late 17th-century Winchester had become a city with large houses, growing social distinctions and not much civic pride, though the corporation registered the city arms with Garter's Deputy in 1686, and there was a short-lived plan in 1693 to convert the Market House into a new town hall, the Parchment

48.   Decoration from the entrance to the Pawletts' great house of Hyde,
now resited in Victoria Road.

Street elms being cut down for that purpose.[34] Too great a proportion of local
prosperity had come to depend, as it had in other parts of England, on patronage and politics. The hearth tax returns of *c*.1669 show substantial numbers of
families on the poverty line 'discharged' because their homes contained only one
hearth.[35] Local great men included Sir Robert Mason, living in the house which
his father had built out of Black Friars, later known as Penton or Mildmay
House, and Essex Pawlett of Hyde House who left a will ordering his mansion to
be sold after his death.[36] Nonconformity perhaps offered some hope for a demo-
cratic future, but chapel-going grew only slowly in a city where the established
Church was strong and where there were many influential and tolerated Papists.

Chapter Ten

From Queen Anne to Queen Victoria

Town life in 18th-century England has often been described in terms of poverty and corruption, elements which can certainly be found in Winchester in the century before the great era of early 19th-century reforms. Yet local circumstances often produced individuals or groups prepared to devote themselves to the cause of social improvement. There was political corruption, but there eventually emerged amongst the inhabitants a strong feeling of local pride and patriotism, and an interest, tinged with regret, in the city's ancient past. Significantly the title page of the first Winchester guide-book (*c*.1780) bore the words *Winchester ... its foundation, splendour, and decline.*

Much of Winchester's 18th-century façade can still be seen today, and the fine *East Prospect of Winchester* drawn by Nathaniel and Samuel Buck gives an excellent impression of the city *c*.1736. The *East Prospect* shows all the great buildings, the parish churches, and Southgate, Eastgate and Northgate. Notable houses individually visible include Abbey House before the alterations of *c*.1751 by Pescod; Hyde House, the home of the Benedictines, a fine building with a walled garden and gazebo; Eastgate House; and the so-called Duke of York's house at the west end of St Swithun's Street, its wings each topped by a cupola. Two bowling greens can be seen, one below the ditch of the castle near Southgate, and the other in what is now North Walls; Winchester College and St John's House are also visible, as are the High Street, the river navigable to Southampton and Blackbridge, and the Castle Hall.

Some 14 years after the *East Prospect*, the corporation took the important decision of employing William Godson of Basing to make a detailed survey of the entire city. His map of 1750-1 is of the greatest value and shows the old layout still extant, with narrow streets leading to the walls. Northgate was standing, but the North Walls area was undeveloped except for the part of the ditch which was used as a rope walk. St Swithun's Street had little building and Southgate Street had become a road of large mansions; College Street, in contrast, had both its frontages. At the Morn Hill end of St John's Street stood Cheyney Court prison and the stocks, and the Quakers' burial place was situated on the side of the hill. The smaller and more detailed maps which Godson drew of Hyde Abbey farm and the manors of Barton and Thurmonds at St Cross have a particular value.[1]

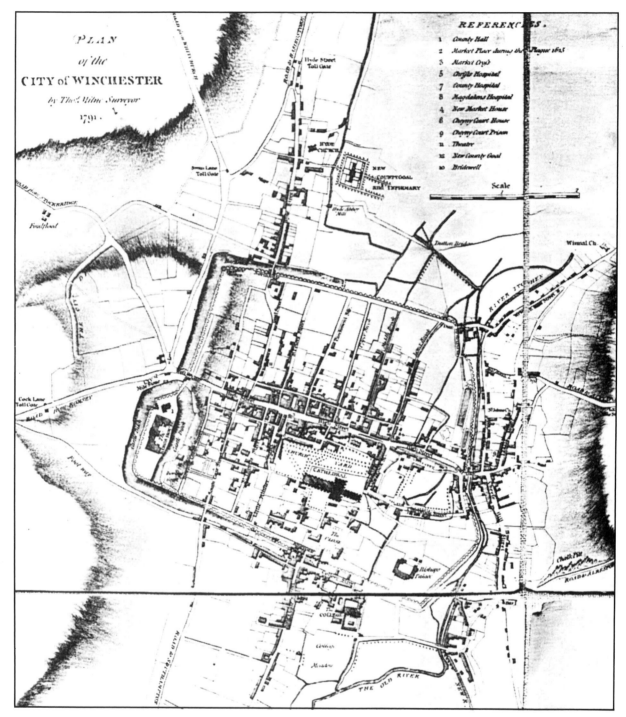

49. Plan of the City of Winchester by Thos. Milne, Surveyor, 1791.

Another surveyor, Thomas Milne, mapped Winchester in 1791 with little detail. In 1784 the first Winchester *Directory* had been published by John Sadler, and 'Godson' and 'Sadler' provide a clear picture of the city and the community as they were in the second half of the 18th century. From 1771 there exist the records of the paving commission, providing detailed evidence of many changes during the next 100 years.[2]

It could be said that what was left of medieval Winchester survived despite the 18th-century inhabitants. Northgate had collapsed on a christening party in 1755, and was pulled down soon after, like Eastgate, and Southgate was demolished by the paving commission. Kingsgate remained, as did Westgate, simply because a large room on its first floor had been let by the corporation, and there was no wish to turn out their tenant, John Gauntlett, who was an influential wine merchant. It had been used as a prison as late as 1742.[3] The city walls were slowly eroded, and the great hall of the castle was subdivided by a rough partition put up in 1764.[4] The ruins of Wolvesey Castle continued to be used as a quarry, and about two-thirds of the new palace was pulled down in 1781.[5] The crypt of the cathedral was used as a wine vault, and the north aisle as a works yard. Architectural advice was sought (but not accepted) by the dean and chapter from James Wyatt in 1794, and the remnants of the cloister and refectory were pulled down *c.*1797. The chapel of St John's Hospital was turned into a free school soon after 1701 and, on the outskirts of the town, the entire medieval hospital and chapel of St Mary Magdalene was demolished. The parish church of St Bartholomew at Hyde was in decay, and the ruins and foundations of Hyde Abbey became the site of a new county bridewell (1787).[6] Only in 1770 did the citizens as a whole take some apparent active interest in any part of their medieval inheritance: in that year the corporation proposed to sell the City Cross to a neighbouring landowner, Mr. Dummer of Cranbury Park. In the Gothic taste of the time, he wanted to adorn his garden with suitable relics, and when the inhabitants woke to find the Cross in scaffolding there was an angry demonstration, with the result that it remained.[7]

If the medieval past was neglected, much of the new building was in excellent taste and a delightful addition to the present-day appearance of the town. By the time of Godson's map there were many private houses which were either entirely new or faced in the new classical style. Horace Walpole, however, writing in 1755, thought the city 'a paltrey town and small', while Wren's palace was 'The worst thing I ever saw'. One wonders what he would have thought of the public buildings of the last half of the century: the bridewell at Hyde (1787), the new prison in Jewry Street (1788), the magnificent hospital in Parchment Street (1759), and the theatre in Jewry Street (1785). He would have approved of the new Catholic chapel of 1792 in St Peter Street. which was superbly decorated by William Cave and designed in the Gothic style for Bishop Milner by John Carter.[8]

The 18th century opened auspiciously enough. Queen Anne paid the town a visit in August 1705 when David Wavell was mayor. She brought with her the prince consort, George of Denmark; bells were rung, streets and lanes decorated, lights hung before every door, and the royal couple were presented with a loyal address and a purse containing 100 guineas.[9] It was the queen's intention to finish the building of the great Wren palace and bestow it upon Prince George in case she died before her husband. There was a feeling that Winchester might again be a royal city and a special committee, set up in 1711 to improve the Guildhall, met under the chairmanship of Thomas Godwin, an apothecary. Work on the Guildhall was finished when at long last there dawned what the corporation called, in their address of congratulation to the monarch, 'a glorious peace after a long and expensive war'. The generosity of Winchester's two members of parliament allowed the addition of a statue of Queen Anne and a town clock to the 'new' civic building. The Latin inscription which also adorns it, *Anna Regina Anno Pacifico 1713*, was a message of hope at the beginning of what seemed to be a new era of peace and prosperity.[10] There are still many 18th-century house façades left, some in mutilated form, for many shops have lost their original ground floors. The *Hampshire Chronicle* office is a notable exception, and there are other bow windows in Kingsgate Street. 105 High Street has an outstanding 'Adams' front, and was built for an apothecary, George Earle, in 1772. Perhaps the best private house is that of William Sheldon in Southgate Street, finished *c.*1748 and now known as Serle's House.

Unfortunately Anne's successor was not interested in Winchester, whose last royal resident was Lady Derwentwater, Charles' bastard daughter.[11] George I began to dismantle the palace. In 1756 about five thousand Frenchmen were imprisoned there. It was used again as a prison during the War of American Independence, and in the later wars with France and Spain. After the French Revolution the building provided a home for hundreds of refugee priests who had been forced to leave their native land, and the stone just within the northern door of St Peter's Catholic church commemorates their stay in Winchester.

From 1796 onwards the 'King's House' was used as a barracks, and was profitable to some tradesmen. The remnant presence of a gaunt and semi-derelict building meant that Winchester shopkeepers no longer served courtiers, but had to rely on customers not always expecting London standards or London prices.

There were other factors which made Winchester less prosperous than it could have been for much of the 18th century. The sad state of Winchester College had an effect: the number of commoners declined rapidly from 93 in 1737 to eight in 1751, as the school had a not undeserved reputation as a breeder of Jacobites. Recovery began in the 1750s with the appointment of Dr. Wharton as second master, but even his subsequent years as headmaster were marked by outbursts of violence, particularly the rebellions of 1770, 1774, 1778

50. Avebury House,
St Peter's Street.

51. The old Guildhall.

52. 18th-century bow
windows in Kingsgate
Street; the first-floor window
is modern.

53. The attractive offices of the
Hampshire Chronicle.

and 1793, in which there was sometimes an element of town versus gown. The school was something of a mixed blessing as far as the townsfolk were concerned, and in non-academic circles the prevalent impression was that it bred reactionaries and high Tories, and that it was a rough and tough school. The rebellion of 1770 began when the landlord of *The White Hart* asked boys from the school to leave his inn, and there are graphic accounts of street-fighting between Wykehamists and town boys in 1770 and 1774.

Perhaps the chief reason why the town's prosperity was limited was its lack of industry, though this did mean Winchester escaped the worst consequences of the Industrial Revolution. Celia Fiennes had touched on this lack of industry *c.*1696, when she described Winchester as a mere market town; the Magdalen Hill Fair was its most exciting commercial event, 'the goods sold chiefly hops and cheese'. The town already had a traffic problem because of the large numbers of wagons coming in, particularly from the West Country. Daniel Defoe, writing *c.*1724, was more explicit: 'Winchester is a place of no trade ... no manufacture ... no navigation', and 10 years later it was noted that the city was 'in a county that is thin of people and has no settled manufacture'. The main employments of Winchester men and women remained the retail shop trade, private domestic service, and clerical work connected with the Church, the Law or in the departments of quasi-local government administration. The latter was still limited to the offices of the clerk of the peace, the deputy sheriff, the county treasurer and the paving commissions. Where there was industry, most was dependent on Winchester's chief surviving economic asset, her water supply: brewing, milling of grain, and the thrusting of silk employed a small proportion of the population. Towards the end of the century a silk mill in St Peter Street employed about three hundred people, including women and young children. It was an expanding business which the owner, William Shenton, moved in 1793 to enlarged premises in the Abbey Mill, Colebrook Street, but it is almost the only example of a major industrial development in Winchester before the coming of the railway. By Shenton's time there were other hopeful signs of revival.[12]

The picture which emerges of Winchester as a whole in the last quarter of the 18th century is of a community where life could be pleasant and prosperous. In a city of shopkeepers and small retail businesses, families mixed easily with their professional neighbours - the doctors, lawyers and clerics whose presence helped to make Winchester what it was then and what it is today. Since there were no town planning laws, what industry there was could be found wherever it had grown into existence, though it is interesting to note that the dean and chapter paid a local whitesmith, Malkin, 20 guineas in 1784 to move his premises away from the Widows' College.[13]

Sadler's *Directory* of 1784 gives a reasonably accurate impression of the inhabitants in the last quarter of the century. One paid, however, to have an entry

54.   105 High Street, built in 1772 by George Earle, a Winchester apothecary.

included, and there are other omissions in what in any case was primarily a list
of traders. Winchester in 1784 had at least eight bakers (of whom four were in
the High Street), nine butchers, 12 grocers (seven in the High Street), four
gentlemen's hatters (three in the High Street), seven breeches makers, four
booksellers (three in the High Street and not including the offices of the local
newspaper), eight women milliners, 14 shoemakers (half of them in the High
Street) and a large number of innkeepers. In the High Street there were at least
12 inns, and parts of the frontages of *The White Hart, The Chequers* and *The White
Horse* remain. *The Chequers* in 1784 had a landlady, Mary Pinnock, as did *The
Marquess of Granby* on the western junction of Middle Brook Street.

There were a great many 'monopolists' – shops or small industries offering a
specialised service. There was one coffee house, in the Square, under the direction of John Savage, who was also a brewer. Charles and Joanna Green offered
another new service; they were fruiterers in a High Street shop which was also
the post office. Letters for London were accepted each day until 9 p.m., and a

cross-post went out daily across the country, though these letters had to be posted before 5 p.m. Communications were good: carriers left each day for London, Portsmouth, Chichester, the Isle of Wight and Southampton. There were also regular coach services, including a thrice-weekly service to Salisbury and Reading. All these services were associated with specific inns: the Winchester-London carriers had their main headquarters in *The Queen's Head* in Upper Brook Street, and there were general carriers in Colebrook Street. The Portsmouth coach started from *The Coach and Horses* between Silver Hill and the High Street; wealthier travellers could change horses at *The George*, post-chaises could be hired from Laurence Darkin at *The White Hart* and from *The King's Head* in St Thomas Street.

Other monopolists included a fishmonger, a watch- and clock-maker, and a whip-maker called Inigo Jones, whose name is perhaps the cause of the tradition that the offices of the *Hampshire Chronicle* were once owned by the sons of the great architect. There was a 'china and glass man', a 'japaneur' and a 'man's mercer' in the Square; inevitably there were a great many tailors, two stay-makers (both men), makers of perukes, a perfumer and a hairdresser.

The century saw an increase in the number of practising lawyers, including a dynasty of town clerks with a private practice in Parchment Street; George Hollis, the proprietor of the navigation, in Gaol Street (Jewry Street); and John Ridding, clerk to the dean and chapter, in Southgate Street. There were at least a dozen other lawyers, the most distinguished legal figure being Serjeant Kirby, who acted for the dean and chapter on an embarrassing occasion in 1792 when the cathedral was burgled and the ancient plate irrecoverably lost.[14]

Second in number amongst the professional men were the doctors who, like the lawyers, tended to found dynasties. Dr. John Littlehales had a fine house in Southgate Street; he died in 1810 and is commemorated by a memorial in the cathedral. An equally well-known doctor, Matthew Combe (d. 1748), who practised in Winchester for over 54 years and lived in what is now Chernocke House in St Thomas Street, is also commemorated in the cathedral, as is Dr. Andrew Crawford (d. 1824), the father of a famous and beloved physician of Victorian Winchester. Perhaps the best-known medical dynasty was that of the Lyford family. Charles Lyford lived in St Peter Street and held appointments at the hospital and the prisons. Henry Lyford (1769-1819) was Jane Austen's adviser.

As well as doctors, surgeons and lawyers, two other groups of professional men left their mark on the 18th-century city – schoolmasters and clerics. The splendid house in Hyde Street, until recently *The Hyde Abbey Hotel*, was for many years the home of a famous private school for boys. The headmaster, the Revd. Charles Richards, was a well-known classical scholar and disciplinarian, whose pupils included Canning, the future prime minister, Dean Garnier, and J. M. Colson, the architect. He had succeeded to the headmastership after the death in 1779 of his father-in-law, the Revd. Reynell Cotton, who had founded the

school in 1760. Richards was the patron of Sir John Soane, whose schoolroom of
1795 remains (in rather a mutilated form) in Hyde Close and was opened in
1796 with 'several performances in elocution before a numerous genteel and
learned audience', but he allowed much of his own church (St Bartholomew's)
to become a ruin, took his boys to St Laurence, and became a canon of the
cathedral in 1820.[15]

Almost every visitor to the cathedral in the 18th century made the same
general comment – congregations were very small and the clergy lived comfortable and wealthy lives. Some of the canons were hard-working and conscientious,
though their cathedral duties were not always their only tasks within the

55.   Minster House, originally built as a private bank by the Waller family.

established Church. Zachary Pearce (dean from 1739-48) became a well-known bishop. Dean Thomas Cheyney (1748-59) was renowned for different reasons, as a Wykehamist and as an astute financier. In 1760, by investment and careful lending, his fortune had increased to £28,000, and he was long remembered for the party he gave at the Deanery in 1756, an entertainment for the Hessian troops then encamped on the edge of the city, and for his funeral, a magnificent occasion.[16] Cheyney's successor, Jonathan Shipley (1760-9), was a friend of Benjamin Franklin and became a great supporter of a free United States of America: 'I look upon North America', he said, 'as the only great nursery of freemen left on the face of the earth'. In fact, many 18th-century canons of Winchester were interesting and well-read men of character. John Mulso, appointed canon in 1770, the uncle of Hester Chapone, was a great friend of the naturalist Gilbert White of Selborne, and left behind a massive correspondence with that friend, which reveals him as a realist and a man of humour and affection.[17] An earlier member of the chapter, Robert Lowth, Archdeacon of Winchester, was the author of a famous life of William of Wykeham and was also a well-known Hebrew scholar and a poet of distinction.

Successive deans and their chapters were often criticised for non-residence, and it must be said that deans did not always provide the best examples, though their excuses were varied. At the November chapter in 1783 a brave vice-dean, Canon Lowth, brought up the fact that Dean Ogle had only been in residence for a total of 60 days in the last year. At the December meeting, the dean was present to explain that he had, in fact, done more than the 90 days required of him, but had been confined to the house with gout for five weeks.[18] The chapter met in the chapter-house in the south transept; the room was repaired and 'beautified' in 1743, although little was done to the main fabric of the cathedral, except to add an ever-increasing number of memorials, many of them attractive, but few in keeping with the architecture of a great medieval church.

The accounts kept by successive treasurers make it quite clear that the chapter took seriously its responsibilities towards the poor. The prisoners at the county gaol were invariably provided with a Christmas dinner at the dean's personal expense; there was concern, too, lest the upkeep of the roads round the close wall should fall too heavily on the inhabitants of the neighbouring small parish of St Swithun, and careful arrangements were made with the paving commissioners so that the general public should have the benefit of improvements in the outer close paid for by the dean and chapter. The declivity at the west end of the cathedral was 'made more easy' and the area gravelled to make a parade ground. In the same year (1770) 20 lamps were provided to light the great churchyard. The gravel walk in the churchyard was regularly repaired, and the walk from the parade to St Maurice's church paved, though in 1800 iron rails were placed along the west part of the cathedral, for the citizens had not always treated the outside of the building with due respect.

Individual members of the cathedral chapter were conscious of the dangers and misfortunes which could be the lot of humbler members of society. One of the most important contributions made by the cathedral clergy was the foundation of the county hospital by Alured Clarke (1696-1792) who lived in the close because influential relations had obtained for him the wealthy dean and chapter living of Chilbolton as well as a canonry of the cathedral. Subjected to long bouts of painful illness, he devoted his available energy and most of his income to the relief of suffering. Clarke preached in Winchester Cathedral on St Luke's Day (18 October) 1737, at a service which marked the opening of his Winchester Hospital. It was a foundation based on that of St George's, Hyde Park. He seems to have put the idea forward for the first time in May 1736 and within a year had secured 'by a common engagement by several persons of the most consequence ... and every denomination or party, an influential list of sub-scribers and an income of about six hundred pounds a year'. To administer this large sum he obtained the help of Robert Waldron, a man of known integrity, the owner of a fine house in Kingsgate Street and mayor in 1728.

A detailed set of rules was drawn up, covering patients, doctors, surgeons, nurses, and every member of the hospital establishment. All accounts were to be examined every week, bills paid promptly, and no one was ever to accept or offer any kind of 'fee, reward or gratification' for any service done on account of the hospital. A regular panel of visitors, chosen from the contributors, was to tour the hospital every day to prevent abuses and to examine (by conversation) the patients, in the absence of the medical staff; prayers were to be read every day by a rota of Winchester clergy. There was a comparatively large staff: two physicians attended, in turn, every Wednesday morning, and there were two surgeons who dressed their patients' injuries and finished their rounds before 11 o'clock each day. The house apothecary was a full-time officer who could not be absent from the hospital for more than two hours at a time without special leave and was not to 'presume to attend any other business than that of the Hospital'. His arduous duties included the fixing of the patients' diet sheets to their beds.

The matron was responsible for all the nursing staff and the general servants; she kept the keys, the inventories of goods and furniture, and was to report to the committee if the house visitors or the visiting clergy failed in their duty. The first matron appointed was a Mrs. Aston. Nurses were to dine together at a stated time, and were allowed a pound of meat and three ounces of butter and cheese each day. In summer they were to clean their wards before seven in the morning, in winter before eight, and they were to 'serve up *all* the breakfasts within an hour after the Wards are cleaned'. There were severe restrictions on the types of illness dealt with: it was not a lying-in hospital and pregnant women were not admitted, being turned out if discovered. Nor were patients with infec-tious or terminal diseases allowed in. Life was not easy for the in-patients. They were expressly forbidden to play any games, or smoke, and anyone who could work had to join in the general duties of the ward, such as nursing the other patients, washing, ironing, or anything that the matron required. Out-patients were required to attend regularly, not to be disorderly, and not to approach or leave the hospital via the great gravel walk in the cathedral churchyard 'in order to avoid offence'.[19]

Clarke had had the great fortune to find a suitable building within easy reach of his own house in the close, and the new hospital was accommodated in an L-shaped building, once the home of the Pescod family, on the south-west corner of Colebrook Street. Here there was space for men's and women's wards, a matron's room, dormitories for nurses and a 'herb-garrett'. Appropriate texts were painted on the walls. The demolition of this

56. Statue of John Clobury in Winchester Cathedral.

building in 1959, the first county hospital outside London, must be counted as a severe loss in the history of Winchester.

The successful foundation of the hospital was followed, in 1758, by its transference to a much less restricted site in Parchment Street, where the house which had once belonged to Sir John Clobury was pulled down and a plain functional building designed by John Wood, of Bath, remained for the next 100 years as a permanent reminder of the 18th century's concern for its less fortunate members.

Life in the close could be lively and amusing. Chancellor Hoadley and Archdeacon Eden founded an amateur orchestra of local clerics but close parties were select. Outside the wall there was a willing, but not always well-behaved, audience waiting to fill the theatre in Jewry Street. The decision to build a new theatre had been taken in 1785, by a Mr. Collins of the Collins-Davis Company. It was a further sign of the revival of the town at the end of the century, and proved a great success.[20] It was due to open on a Monday but was not quite finished. The workmen and decorators, who were partly unpaid and very disgruntled, put on their own particular performance – a strike. There was some hasty paying of bills, and the theatre opened the next day. Its outwardly plain façade, of which one wing remains, belied its highly elaborate internal décor, painted by William Cave. The building was constructed to Collins' directions by a local firm of builders, Kernot and Dowling. According to the *Hampshire Chronicle* the interior was resplendent, with a gilded proscenium arch.

> In the centre is a bust of Shakespeare, over which is the following motto – '*Omni Tulit punctum qui miscuit utile dulce*' – and on either sides are the arms of the city and county. The pillars that support the green boxes are superbly painted after the manner of those at the Parthenon: the ceiling is painted in imitation of a blue sky, with some well painted clouds ... at the four corners Thalia and Melpomene, as the Comic and Tragic Muses, Apollo as an emblem of the Opera, or music, and Pero as the representative of pantomine: the pannell next the ceiling is decorated with festoons of flowers, and the whole house is finished in a style of elegance which does great credit to the taste and judgement of Mr. Cave, by whom the whole of the ornaments are designed and executed.[21]

The whole theatre was lit by candles, presenting a brilliant spectacle, and a dreadful fire risk. Collins' death in 1807 marked the end of a theatrical era, and though his Jewry Street theatre lingered on, it never maintained the somewhat tawdry brilliance of its opening years. Charles Ball, writing in 1818, described it as possessing all the requisite qualifications for a place of amusement but two, namely cleanliness and convenience, though it was not closed until 1863.

Another popular amusement was racing, under civic patronage since at least 1634. Charles II was a frequent visitor to Winchester races, which were held at Stockbridge and Worthy Down. James II thought Winchester better than Newmarket, and Queen Anne's visit in 1705 also included some time at the races. By far the most famous 18th-century horse was 'Beware Chalk-Pit', an animal belonging to Paulet St John, which had once fallen into a chalk pit some 25 ft. deep, jumped out, and the next year (1734) had won the Hunter's Plate at Worthy Down. Stockbridge Down was the place for flat-racing; steeplechasing was enjoyed, at a rather later date, at Worthy Down and at Abbotstone.

Racing attracted a varied clientele and was popular with the young gentlemen of the college, as was cock-fighting, which was held on a number of local farms in the surrounding villages. One of its 18th-century Winchester headquarters was at *The Fighting Cocks*, an inn next to the Westgate. After David Wemyss, a wealthy young commoner, joined the school in 1734 he spent most of his spare time as a 'constant spectator at cock fights' or fisticuff encounters 'between Rustics for a purse presented by the Lord of the village'. There were also some well-known Winchester semi-professional pugilists, one of whom attained a kind of local notoriety by resigning from *The George* whist club after he discovered that an unpopular town clerk, Harry Green, had been made a member.[22]

The many Winchester inns, each serving its particular clientele, all played their part in the city's social life. The whist club run by James Dibsdale at *The Chequers* moved with that landlord to *The George*, the leading Winchester hostelry after Dibsdale's rebuilding of 1769; it was a large coaching inn with a driveway from the High Street into an inner courtyard. Dibsdale came from Avington, and his association with the Chandos-Brydges families gave his inn prestige and political importance.

With the community of clerics, gentry, professional men and tradespeople, there lived the men, women and children who were prisoners in the county gaol or in the two bridewells. What to do with these unfortunates was a serious problem for the authorities. A suggestion made in the Commons in 1785 that instead of transporting felons to Africa, the king's palace at Winchester should be converted into a place of confinement, found an immediate opponent in the then speaker, a Winchester man, Wolfran Cornwall. The city, he said, 'was the residence of a Bishop, the seat of a great public school, filled with inhabitants of opulence and gentility', and no more was heard of this particular project. Instead, a new county gaol, entirely for felons, was constructed in 1788 on the west side of Jewry Street, with the approval of the great prison reformer, John Howard. Condemned prisoners were dragged off to the gibbet nearly a mile away amidst the jeers of crowds who loved a good hanging and also came in their thousands to watch female prisoners burnt to death, still the punishment for murdering a husband. The burning of Mary Bayley in 1784, and the last execution of this kind in Winchester, that of Mrs. Huntingford in 1819, were watched by so many people that the magistrates decided that all executions in future should take place within the precincts of the county gaol instead of at Gallows Hill, about a mile out of Winchester on the Newbury-Andover Road. The accommodation for prisoners in the county gaol was improved in 1805 by the construction of a new prison for debtors along the street frontage, to the design of a well-known architect, George Moneypenney. Its handsome appearance was criticised by a committee of inquiry in 1817, however, for the object of a gaol was to inspire terror not architectural admiration.[23]

The system of regular inspection by visiting magistrates, begun after 1817, put an end to some of the major social problems within the prison. Attempts were made to find employment for the prisoners and to regulate the charitable gifts supplied from the ancient foundation of St Cross (a penny loaf for each prisoner six times a year) and from Winchester College, which had provided four sheeps' hinges every Wednesday, a bullock's head every Saturday, oatmeal, salt and bread each Thursday, and a daily supply of broken biscuits. Parts of the façade of this Jewry Street prison with its rusticated stonework can be seen today.

The county bridewell which replaced a building in the castle was erected in

1787 on part of the site of Hyde Abbey, and its construction was a major antiquarian scandal. It, too, had a resident keeper, a small chapel and a detached
infirmary. Its unemployed inhabitants were 'slight' offenders, with 'only half
corrupted minds', were illiterate, clothed in filthy rags, and had little or no
proper bedding. It is unlikely that conditions were much better at the small
bridewell maintained by the corporation in the centre of what is now the Broadway, a survival of the hospital for poor folk maintained by the nuns of St Mary's.
After Thomas Weld bought Abbey House from the Pescod estate c.1798, the
whole of the centre block was pulled down, and this part of the High Street
became known as the Broadway. A new bridewell was erected on the west side of
Abbey Passage and remained for many years as the headquarters of the Winchester City police force.

The corporation was corrupt and inward-looking. It was the paving commission, formed in 1771, that concerned itself with the improvement of the roads,
lit the streets, regulated sedan and hackney carriage traffic, made pavements,
and granted permission to build bow windows. These were considered to be,
even at first-floor level, a form of encroachment on the highway. Almost the first
act of the commission was to number the houses in the High Street and then to
gravel the surface there.

When the commissioners had collected the paving rates they were able to
finance other improvements. In 1778-9 the road from the Square to the turn-
stile at the corner of the close by Minster Street was paved, the road at Bubb's
Cross was repaired, and lamps were placed in parts of the city. In 1791 the commissioners opened a subscription list, so that they could create a footway
through the Westgate at a cost not exceeding £50. Another improvement nearby
was the 'stopping up' of the south end of Gar Street at the request of the barracks commissioners, agreed to because the paving commissioners thought that
it would 'keep the City much more private from the Barracks'.

The corporation was occupied with its own affairs and above all the fact that
it was still only members of that corporate body, the freemen, who had the right
to vote in both local and national elections. To have a vote was to possess a tan-
gible asset. Winchester was not a pocket borough, always supporting the same
party, but many of its electors were corrupt, supporting, as the occasion arose,
the two rival families of Paulet (Dukes of Bolton) from Abbotstone and Hack-
wood, and Brydges and Chandos from Avington. The Paulet interests were
maintained by George Durnford, a lawyer who lived in a fine house in Jewry
Street, and Avington supporters were organised by the city's recorders, including Thomas Coward, a man who held both the mayoralty and the recordship,
and William Pescod.[24] The city returned two members of parliament so there
was ample opportunity for manoeuvring by two parties. It had been a Winchester M.P. from Avington, George Brydges, who gave the statue of Queen
Anne in 1713 when a Paulet gave the town clock, and in 1749 another Brydges

left a considerable sum for the improvement of St John's House. After his death, Avington passed to his cousin, the first Duke of Chandos. The second duke, Henry, was high steward in 1754, and it was his influence which helped to secure the charter of 1761. His successor, James, the third duke (1731-89), was also a high steward and mayor in 1773-4, for a part of 1775 after the death in office of Thomas Waldron, and again in 1784-5.

It is obvious from the Chandos correspondence that freemen were added to the corporation in order that they should vote in a particular manner.[25] A classic study of the House of Commons has made it clear that in elections for parliament between 1761 and 1774 the Duke of Bolton's influence was paramount.[26] Voting in the parliamentary election of October 1774 was preceded by a year in which Chandos had been mayor, and was succeeded by his alliance with the powerful Winchester family of Penton, who, father and son, held one of the two Commons seats from 1749-96. That family had emerged as a political force in the late 17th century, and the large house at the east end of the High Street soon became known as Penton (or Eastgate) House; it was here that George III and his queen stayed in 1778 when on a visit to Winchester. Henry Penton senior (1705-62) represented Winchester from 1747-61 and was a government supporter, holding the sinecure of king's letter carrier. He resigned both his office and his membership of the Commons in favour of his son, Henry Penton II, recorder of Winchester and a Wykehamist (1736-1812). The younger Penton was able and became a political force of importance in Hampshire, supporting Lord North and occasionally advising him. The Avington influence continued when the third duke's daughter, Anne, married Richard Grenville, Marquess of Buckingham (1776-1839), Earl Temple, who succeeded to his father-in-law's title and occasionally lived at Avington when he was not at Canons or Stowe.[27]

The papers of the two rival ducal families reveal the pressures and the corruption within the corporation, but its official ordinances are dull and always discreet, concerned with the leasing of city property, including that of St John's Hospital, and the occasional appointment of officers. There were still two assemblies of freemen each year, and elections took place at that in September. There was a great deal of private 'arranging' within civic circles. The mayoralty was restricted to a few families: three Wavells and three Waldrons averaged three mayoralties each, George Durnford was mayor five times and died in his sixth term of office. He was a lawyer, but the great majority of Winchester mayors in the 18th century were prosperous local tradesmen elected by the freemen in St John's House at their autumn meeting. The corporation had its critics, and it was sometimes an object of ridicule rather than of local pride. In the family tradition, David Wavell became mayor in 1704-5 and held the office again in 1710-11. Another member of the family, Gilbert (d. 1742), was mayor from 1716-17 and 1737-8, and was the corporation's tenant at *The George*. Later,

the Wavells left local government, and the three most prominent members of
the family in Winchester were two clerics, Daniel Wavell (d. 1738), rector of St
Maurice's church, and Richard (d. 1779), master of St Mary Magdalene Hospital, a noted local historian, the third being Loving Wavell, surgeon at the county
hospital.

The Wavells, like the Waldrons and a number of other Winchester families,
were not only many in number but also to be found in varied strata of local society, for men still progressed easily and comfortably from trade to profession
and vice versa. The Waldrons supported Avington; Robert (d. 1741) lived in
Kingsgate Street and was mayor in 1728 and 1732; earlier members of the family
had included a Winchester scholar (David, in 1668), and carriers and maltsters
in the city. Some Waldrons were cousins of Dean Young, and one member of the
family, William (d. 1717), lived in the outer close and had a notable library of
books in Latin and English on history and the law. Two later Waldron mayors
were carriers, working from Upper Brook Street – William, mayor in 1731, 1732,
1742, 1747 and 1754, and his son Thomas, mayor in 1741, 1744, 1753 and 1775,
when he died in office; his obituary in the *Hampshire Chronicle* appears to be the
first published obituary of any mayor of Winchester.[28]

The Cave family was another, later, civic dynasty; they were painters, decorators, artists and craftsmen. William Cave senior (1737-1813) became a freeman
in 1797, and was bailiff of the Twenty-four; his son and namesake became mayor
in 1813, and another son, James, illustrated Milner's *History of Winchester* in
1798. They were devout Catholics but were prepared to accept occasional con-
formity. Thus they were able to undertake civic office.

All these 18th-century mayors were served by a more or less perpetual dynasty
of town clerks, appropriately called Clarke. The mayor in 1712-13 was Robert
Clarke; his brother, Henry, had become town clerk in 1705, and the office was
next held by Robert, town clerk from 1729-58, reappointed with his brother
William, 1758-79, and then succeeded by William's son, yet another Robert
(dead by 1790), who was appointed joint town clerk with his father after his
uncle's resignation.[29]

The Catholic community in Winchester had long had its centre in St Peter
Street, as well as in the neighbouring suburb of Hyde. The large house near *The
Royal Hotel*, which had been 'my Lady West's', was sold *c.*1674 by Roger Corham
to the recusant Smiths. A Smith daughter, Anastasia, became the second wife of
William Sheldon from Warwickshire, the son of General Ralph Sheldon who
had served James II in exile. The Sheldons left St Peter Street, and built the
splendid mansion now called Serle's House in Southgate Street, though the
heart of the Catholic community remained in St Peter Street. After Roger
Corham had sold his old house to the Smiths, he built a new one on the opposite side of the road as a home for the priests who served the Winchester community. Mass was celebrated in the first-floor room at its north end. A small

chapel in the garden was rebuilt completely in 1792 in the style of the Gothic Revival. It was designed by John Carter, a London architect working under the direction of Dr. John Milner, of whom more later.

This church, now Milner Hall, used to be one of Winchester's most important buildings. Though it was small, it contained almost every feature of the revived Gothic architectural style, an elaborate fan-vaulted roof and painted bosses. Its painted decoration and its altarpiece were the work of William Cave. Its architect, John Carter (d. 1817), and his patron, Milner, played an important part in the Gothic Revival movement; they were careful, too, to incorporate in the new chapel the old main porch from St Mary Magdalene Hospital on the eastern hill, the sole remaining fragment of an important local building. The act of 1792, which permitted the licensing of Catholic chapels, had made Milner's church possible and secured its continued use for the Catholic community.[30]

This community became more important now for various reasons. Tolerance, on both national and local levels, was only one factor. In Winchester the community increased dramatically with the advent of large numbers of refugees from Europe. Milner's own strong-minded leadership was another reason for the strength of Catholicism within a predominantly Anglican cathedral city. In

St Peter Street the old house on the eastern side was handed over in 1795 to a refugee order of nuns from Brussels, following the Benedictine rule, who remained housed there until 1857. A similar arrangement had been made for Abbey House, where Thomas Weld gave a home to Franciscan nuns, who altered the house and set up a school in Colebrook Street which they maintained until their departure for Taunton in 1808.[31] Both orders owed much to the help and encouragement of John Milner (1752-1826) who became pastor of the Catholic community at Winchester in 1779.

Milner was a tailor's son who had been trained for the priesthood at Douai; he was an orthodox Catholic of the old kind, a great believer in papal infallibility

57. Miniature of Bishop John Milner by George Anthony Keman, painted at Bristol in 1805 when Milner was 55 years old.

and, though he wanted Catholics in England to be tolerated and free to follow their faith, he was completely against any suggestion that emancipation could be advanced by the work of laymen. It was natural that he should have a great personal interest in the history of the Catholic Church in England and in the revival of the architectural styles of the medieval Church. A short time after his arrival in Winchester he became absorbed in its local history, and published in 1798 *The History, Civil and Ecclesiastical, and Survey of Antiquities of Winchester*. The book's reception was mixed: the Society of Antiquaries of London made him a Fellow, but his attack on Anglican acts and clerics could not pass unnoticed. In consequence some of the reviews were very critical. The Revd. J. Sturgis called him a popish wolf in the clothing of an antiquarian sheep. Nevertheless, his *Winchester* went into several editions, and its numerous and delightful illustrations by James Cave helped to make it a bestseller; it remains the standard history of the town, despite its inevitable and multitudinous mistakes.[32]

'Milner' remains a useful book, but is only part of the legacy of 18th-century Winchester. It was a century which left behind excellent buildings, a famous hospital, and an increasing number of citizens used to the democracy of dissent. For there was soon a steadily increasing number of chapels and other meeting houses near all the parish churches. 'The preaching house in the lane from High Street to Lower Brooks' (1773) and the building in Silver Hill 'newly converted into a Chapel' (1786) had been preceded by humbler meeting places, such as the house of Thomas Vinn, a shoemaker (1737).[33] These were missionary chapels, preaching the word all over Hampshire and forming powerful and persuasive communities in the next century, communities to whom the need for political and social reform was obvious.

Chapter Eleven

Reformers

Perhaps the most influential advocates of reform within the early 19th-century corporation were John Ventham, Samuel Deverell and John Earle. Ventham (1784-1856), 'a sound liberal', already had behind him a long career of public service when he joined the corporation in 1824. He was an actuary who had become clerk to the united Winchester parishes in 1806, then resident manager of the Trustee Savings Bank, founded in 1816, and was mayor in 1854. John Earle (1775-1845), an apothecary, was the nephew and successor of that old Winchester Whig, George Earle, and a friend of Samuel Deverell (1763-1849), a lawyer from a county family who lived near St John's Hospital in Simon Tripp's old house in Colebrook Street.

If political reform was to mean anything, a start had to be made at St John's. The few Whigs, not radicals, who had penetrated the corporation, were dismayed to find that no-one knew how or when that body had acquired the bulk of its real estate. City rents and St John's Hospital rents were only nominally separate, and the leasing of hospital property was often a matter of obliging friends. No attention had been given to the almshouses since Tylny's rebuilding of 1699: 18th-century beneficence had been concentrated on St John's House, which had become the great social centre of Winchester, while the chapel was used as the free school. Pressure mounted for an inquiry into the affairs of the hospital, and into the nature of corporation and hospital property.

On 21 March 1811, after certain information had been obtained from the churchwardens and overseers of the ancient central parishes, the attorney-general began a general action in chancery against the mayor and corporation with the object of finding out the extent and nature of the charitable funds administered by them. On the same day, a second suit was begun on behalf of the poor folk residing in St John's, asking for a proper account of the hospital's funds and for the appointment of trustees in lieu of the mayor, bailiffs and community in whom the hospital had been vested since the charter of 1588. Orders were made in January 1818 that appropriate inquiries should be made in both cases, but chancery moved slowly and the inquiries were not completed until 1827, when the corporation lodged an appeal. It was already apparent that, if the management of the hospital was to be handed over to the trustees, an Act of Parliament would be necessary to enable the corporation to give up the duties

58. St John's Street.

which it was supposed to carry out under the charter.

An Act of 1829 made this possible and 13 men were named as the first trustees, headed by the Bishop of Winchester and including Henry Giles Lyford, Richard Hopkins, and Samuel Deverell.[1] In fact, little could be done. In 1833 Richard Hopkins, a member of the corporation and a trustee, resigned in disgust from that first body; he felt he could do more as a trustee, and a notable improvement in the conditions of the almsfolk within the hospital soon became apparent when a new almshouse was built. This was St John's South, completed by 1834.

Hopkins' resignation had the effect of hardening opposition to reform within the corporation. About one hundred and seventy new freemen were admitted, hastily, during the very meeting at which his letter of resignation was read. They included Charles Bailey and Charles Woolridge, both lawyers; Richard Baigent, the first drawing master at Winchester College; and the Duke of Wellington. It must be fairly stated that, although most of these new freemen were Tories, not all were Tory die-hards. Most were men of integrity, and in November 1833 an investigation of all the corporation's property was ordered. As an indication of how confused the administration had become, it was even necessary to set up a special committee to examine the title of the corporation to the Guildhall: no one knew who owned it.[2] Eventually the properties were divided between the two bodies, the hospital's finances properly settled, and new almshouses on the north side built. The mayor who instigated this inquiry was a young man, Charles Witman Benny (1794-1870), a grocer from Portsmouth only recently arrived in Winchester, who became a great capitalist in the later Victorian city. In 1820 he had bought a grocer's shop in the High Street from Mrs. Lloyd, and he became mayor in 1834. Benny retired from civil life in 1853.

Important as the reform of St John's was considered to be by the Wintonian reformers, it was a small matter when compared with the Whig government's proposals to reform Parliament and to extend the franchise, in corporate boroughs, to the male occupiers of property rated at £10 a year or more.[3] It was not difficult to gather local support for Lord Gray's bill, introduced into the Commons on 1 March 1831. The two sitting Winchester members were Paulet St John Mildmay (from Mildmay House) and Sir Edward Hyde East, from Worcestershire. In the two general elections (May 1831 and December 1832) brought about by opposition to reform, Mildmay topped the poll as the reform candidate. An important public meeting on 14 May 1832 under the chairmanship of the then mayor, John Earle, gave him its full support. In the December election of that year Bingham Baring, the second candidate and a member of the great banking family, was supported by some of the local dissenters who were urged to vote for him as 'the Champion of Civil and Religious Liberty'. The third candidate, James Buller East (1789-1878), Sir Edward's son, was known to have the support of the Duke of Buckingham and his son, the Marquess of Chandos. He was also supported by the college, especially the warden, Robert Barter, and headmaster, Dr. William Gabell. Despite this support there were plenty of virulent attacks on him, for example:

> Then up with Baring, down with East
> No Tory nominee,
> Though crawling slaves may lick the dust,
> No crawling slaves are we.

The real contest was between Baring and East; Mildmay was a diplomat, whom the cynical local politicians distrusted:

> I am Mildmay, gentle Paulet
> I can charm with honied word
> From these lips a speech to gall yet
> Whig or Tory ne'er has heard.

His unkind nicknames included 'Mr. Soft Speech' and 'St John in the Wilderness' after his defeat on 10 June 1835. His letter of thanks to his supporters was a model for all defeated candidates: 'I should still be your representative but for a misunderstanding that worked to my prejudice'. He was 'in' again for Winchester in July 1837 until 1841, when East topped the poll. James Buller East continued to represent the city until 1864, when he retired. 'By Church, out of College ... he won the St Stephen's Stakes seven times', but from 1847 onwards was in second place to a Liberal, John Bonham Carter.[4]

Reform, in fact, did not mean the end of the influence of Avington House. In vain did the Winchester radicals ask such questions as 'Why does such apathy prevail in Winchester', or make libellous comments on the corporation's morals and their political sympathies. Open voting was still the real difficulty. In a list of 1841, published in mockery of the real lists of voters, the names of some highly respectable voters occur side by side with the reasons alleged for their support for East, the Tory candidate. Amongst them are:

Benjamin Bishop	– Hatter to the College
James Batchelor	– College Washing
James Burnard	– Golden reasons
W. Gover	– Carpenter to the Church
A. Holloway	– sells Tory beer
Charles Hurst	– Ratted for sterling reasons

Parliamentary representation was only one aspect of the problem. It was widely accepted that the reform of Parliament could be only the prelude to other reforms. On 24 May 1832 a general public meeting was held at the Guildhall to form a Winchester police force, the first in Hampshire. A committee was set up, and an inspector appointed at a salary of £1 per week, with seven constables under him.[5] Suitable recruits proved difficult to come by; the pay was small, and the duties onerous. The force tended to attract men who had failed elsewhere, were drunkards, or pseudo-pensioners – a gardener from Avington, for example. The first inspector, Robert Buchanan, resigned in less than a year; more than half of his force had been dismissed as unsuitable or had left of their own accord.

In 1834, the Poor Law Act dealt with one great problem of local administration, the relief of the poor. The old parish system of poor relief came to an end in Winchester and in 1836 'The Union' was built on Oram's Arbour on the western hill, a utilitarian building in a severe classical style designed by the man who was to become Winchester's borough surveyor, William Coles.[6]

In the meantime, a Royal Commission of Inquiry into Local Government was uncovering a mass of general corruption and inefficiency all over England. Elections were still a farce and the decisions of local authorities were arrived at in complete secrecy; there were all sorts of political evils, and anyone who

59. Chesil Street.

wished to inquire into the affairs of a corporation could only do so by obtaining
a writ of *mandamus* or *quo warranto*. There was financial corruption and mis-
management of estates. Too much power was concentrated in too few hands;
the same men were both magistrates and members of corporations. Town clerks
held too many local legal offices, and in their own financial interests had sometimes advised corporations badly, even corruptly. The Municipal Corporations
Act of 1835 put an end to much of this; the council in a municipal borough was
to be elected by ratepayers who had resided in the town for three years and were
on the 'list of those able to vote'. It had been agreed in the course of the bill's
passage through Parliament that it would be inadvisable for local government to
be entirely at the mercy of the ratepayers, and it had been suggested that aldermen should hold office for life. This was not accepted, and in the end aldermen
had to be re-elected every six years by the council. Justice was to be separated
from municipal administration, and at first it seemed likely that Winchester
would lose her separate commission of the peace.

The last Book of Ordinance gives only a poor impression of the interest
aroused in the city by 'Reform'; a more detailed account is to be found in the
minutes of the council's *de facto* (though not *de jure*) executive committee which

60.   Portrait of John William Chard (1765-
1849), mayor of Winchester 1832-3 and organist
of Winchester Cathedral from 1802 until his
death, from a pastel portrait taken at Bath in
1791.

met regularly before council meetings to decide agenda. The discussions of this important junta are recorded in the series known as Proposal Books.[7] The mayor, on the eve of the reform, was John Young: his proposal committee consisted of John Mant, William Barnes, Richard Littlehales and Giles King Lyford. They first met on 21 October 1834 and discussed only leases of city property, notably those which it was intended to grant to Lady Mildmay, the M.P.'s mother. They did not meet again until 23 February 1835, when they chose several people to receive certain local charities and discuss the proposed new corn exchange. They met briefly on 7 March to discuss the corn exchange again, and on 18 March agreed on the sale of land to Lady Mildmay. Further meetings were held dur-ing the following months, but subjects of local interest, not matters of reform, were apparently the only things discussed.

After the Municipal Reform Act had been passed on 26 December 1835, the retiring mayor, John Young, took the chair at a meeting of burgesses which resulted in the election of the new council, six members for each of the three wards of St Maurice, St Thomas and St John. Five days later the new councillors nominated six aldermen, and on 1 January 1836 John Young, proposed by Mr. Deverell and seconded by Mr. Bird, was unanimously elected as a fit person to fill the office of mayor. At the same meeting, three nominations for the town clerkship were received and, after a vote, Charles Bailey was elected. The city treasurership was entrusted to Robert Jessett, a banker.

Under reform the city lost its quarter sessions, and the new council consid-ered that one of its most urgent tasks was to obtain a re-grant of this right. On 11 January 1836 a watch committee was set up, and the council agreed that a petition should be sent to the king 'to continue the Quarter Sessions', and that the recorder, Philip Williams, should meanwhile be re-appointed at a salary of 40 guineas a year. At the next meeting of the proposal committee the design of the new city seal was approved, and an address of gratitude drafted for dispatch to the king: 'We feel thankful especially that your Majesty has been the willing instrument in the hand of Divine Providence for effectuating the great alterations in the state of your empire ... we cannot but particularise that great and salutary measure, the Municipal Reform'. At the same meeting the Marquis of Chandos was removed from the office of high steward and a county member of parliament, Charles Lefevre, appointed in his place.

In May 1836, however, the council received a rude shock; the petition for the continuance of the quarter sessions which had been sent to the privy council was refused. By 13 May a new petition was ready, and it was decided to send it to the Home Office via the new high steward. In less than a fortnight a favourable reply was received, and on 27 May the council unanimously resolved that 'Charles Edward Lefevre Esq. ... High Steward of this city and borough has by his assiduous attention to the rights and privileges of this city ... deserved the warmest thanks of this corporation and that the Mayor be requested to convey the same to him with expressions of the gratitude we owe and of the respect and esteem in which we hold him'.

The newly re-appointed recorder, Philip Williams, was deeply interested in the history of Winchester and it was to him that the city owed its first muniment room. The council unanimously accepted his suggestion (made through the mayor) that the room over Westgate 'be converted into a Muniment Room', and thanked him for his offer to sort the different documents into a chronological order. 'Ugly Phil', as he was called by his wide circle of family and friends, seems to have been a delightful man; he was the son of another Philip Williams, last of a long series of pluralist rectors of Compton, and his wife, Sarah Collins, was the daughter of the second master at Winchester College. Philip Williams' interest in local history was shared by the town clerk, Charles Bailey, who in 1856 published a series of extracts from the city documents under the title *Archives of Winchester.*

Perhaps the greatest innovation was the degree of control imposed on the corporation by central government through the treasury. It was a minor measure in some respects, but it was also an indication of the future. Treasury permission had to be obtained before the corporation could borrow money or sell property. Winchester was able to appoint a finance committee, raise local revenue through rates, and spend it, chiefly on the city police force, a permitted corporation activity. In the fairly general permission which allowed the corporation the right to make by-laws for the good of the town there was some wider scope for future activity, but the effect of the Act was to hand over local administration to a limited circle of shopkeepers and professional men, whose chief object was to keep down the rates. It was not always easy to find money for general improvements, and, moreover, the pavement commissioners retained their particular responsibilities: washing, paving and lighting the roads and maintain-

61. High Street and Westgate.

ing the footpaths were still nothing to do with the corporation. Nor was the corporation always willing to take up its options. Public health was an important issue in growing Victorian towns, but too much legislation envisaged only optional action by corporations. Councils were not forced to use the model clauses for health regulations in the Clauses Act of 1845; the Public Health Act of 1848 might be applied in matters of drainage, but the option rested with the authority. In these public health matters, Winchester soon gained an unfortunate reputation.

The newly-reformed council met once a quarter, in the first week of February, May, August and November. Council members were expected to attend regularly, and were fined if they could not produce a valid reason for absence – for example, a doctor's certificate. Only aldermen wore gowns; a motion that councillors should wear 'distinguishing vests' provided at their own cost was soon turned down. The mayor was elected at the November meeting; it was a real

annual general meeting, including a public reading of standing orders by the
town clerk. There was often more than one candidate for the mayoralty, as in
1864 when the shopkeepers on the council wanted William Budden and
secured him by a narrow majority. His opponent was Charles Warner, a lawyer,
whose chief sponsor had suggested that he would be better able to represent the
citizens as a whole, including gentry, professional men and clergy. The mayoralty was of real importance and the holder had to be, though it was not always
so, a good chairman. At the November meeting, tactful new mayors sometimes
invited their predecessor to continue in the chair for the business that followed
the election. The mayor was also the chief magistrate and presided over the
bench, however inexperienced and ill-suited he was for the task. Mayors, in fact,
had too much to do, and had to be energetic and in good physical health. The
Act of 1853, permitting for the first time the official appointment of a deputy
mayor, was an important innovation. Past mayors had occasionally appointed
deputies, with the consent of the council, but these individuals had little real
standing until 1853.

Mayor-making was always followed by a great dinner in honour of the retiring
mayor. This was held at St John's and catered for by one of the local hoteliers.
In November 1853 when the retiring mayor, William Forder, was entertained in
this way, there were 119 people present, including four choirmen from the
cathedral who sang during the evening and interposed all the toasts with the
appropriate 'renderings'. After the loyal toast, and one to the Prince and
Princess of Wales, there was a succession of speeches, in honour of the bishop,
the clergy of the diocese, the army, navy, militia, and the volunteers; the health
of the ex-mayor was proposed by the senior M.P., Sir James Buller East, and
Mr. Forder responded at length. This was not all. Other toasts and responses followed to the dean and chapter, the warden and fellows, city magistrates, the
agriculturalists, aldermen, council and town clerk, and the professions and
trades in Winchester. 'There were a few other toasts before the company
retired', including the press, responded to by Mr. J. Johnson, of the *Hampshire
Chronicle*, and finally the ladies. This toast was received with acclamation and
the singing of a glee, 'Sleep, gentle ladies'. There were no ladies present to
respond, but Mr. A. Smith, of Hyde House, answered for them.

The corporation carried out its work by means of committees, of which there
were at first only two standing bodies, the finance committee and the watch
committee. It was their duty to present reports every quarter and recommend
the making of an appropriate quarterly rate. The first printed treasurer's
accounts appear to be those of 1 September 1838 to 1 September 1839. Total
income was just over £2,000: the police cost £437, the town clerk £112 10s. 0d.
and the recorder £42. The 'General' rate was prepared by the finance committee; in May 1852 its recommendation was for a penny rate in the ensuing quarter, which produced £181 19s. 2d. In 1863, the same recommendation produced

62.   North view of the Benedictine convent, St Peter's Street, now *The Royal Hotel*.

£211 8s. 6d. and throughout the century the product of the general rate rose, as it was bound to do with the growth of the city.

Convenient headquarters for the police were fortunately available in the city bridewell on the western corner of Abbey Passage: the bridewell prisoners were henceforth left in the county gaol in Jewry Street, while the building itself was converted into a police station and fire engine house at a total cost of just over £100. The city police force continued to have its headquarters on this site for the rest of its existence, and the Winchester police superintendent and his staff became a familiar part of the city scene. Superintendents wore top hats, frock-coats and boots, and were indeed venerable figures. One of their duties was to raise the fire alarm and then call out the 24 volunteer firemen who manned the engine. The alarm was a bell kept at the Guildhall, where the curfew was still rung at 4 a.m. and 8 p.m. each day on the fine bell made by Clement Tosier in 1702.

Occasionally *ad hoc* committees were formed to deal with specific problems. A lodging house committee in 1853 reported the filthy and unsatisfactory conditions of most of the Winchester lodging houses: it was decided that none of them could possibly be registered as common lodging houses under the new Act of Parliament. In 1857 a market committee eventually produced the new market house on the corner of Market Street and the High Street. The perambulating committee travelled the town on foot to see what was happening in various parts of the town and whether there were encroachments on corporation property. It was this committee which arranged the original layout of the on St Giles' Hill, a difficult problem since five parishes, and thus much legal expense, were involved.

The decision to sell off the corporation's real estate, and invest the money obtained in government stock, was important. This enfranchisement went on over many years and was done simply to produce a better income, as it did, through investment in the 'Three Per Cents'. It was intended to prevent the corruption which had prevailed in the past, and in 1852 was appropriately proposed in council by E. C. Faithfull, a friend of Samuel Deverell and legal adviser to the Cobbett family. The tradition continued of keeping the corporation money in a private bank, whose manager or senior partner was the corporation's treasurer. The first London Joint Stock Bank appeared in Jewry Street in 1859, an ancestor of the National Westminster, but the most successful Winchester bank was that of Mr. William Wheatear Bulpett. This was largely a farmers' bank which moved from the eastern end of the High Street into 105 High Street in 1852, and became the ancestor of the National Provincial.[8]

Chapter Twelve

Progress and Change

One result of franchise reform was that local elections were fought increasingly on local issues. The great issue in mid-Victorian Winchester was that of public health, the question of whether or not the city should have a sewage scheme. 'Muckabites' and 'anti-Muckabites' fought for seats on the council, but nothing happened, and the inability or unwillingness of local government to deal with the problem discredited the corporation.

Winchester had always had an excellent reputation as a healthy town, with a good water supply, hospital and plenty of wise and experienced physicians. In 1844, however, a lecture at the Mechanics' Institute given by Mr. H. Newman, sanitary inspector to the corporation, was so disturbing that the matter was referred by the mayor to the pavement commission, the only authority appropriate to deal with drains, for drains disturbed road surfaces and footpaths. The commissioners agreed that something ought to be done, but took no action, despite ominous comments in *The Times* that linked effluvium with disease, persistent outbreaks of 'low fever' and sore throats in the town and college, and a general article in *The Builder* in 1854 concerning cholera.[1]

63. Alderman Charles William Benny, from the portrait in wax by Richard Cockle Lucas.

The situation deteriorated further as more households were connected to piped water supplies, for the prime cause of Winchester's health problems was the lack of drainage to dispose of used water, especially as there were no water-closets or plumbed-in kitchens. New houses at West End Terrace and Fairfield Villas had been supplied with piped water in 1856, and a huge cast-iron pipe supplied the Union in the same year. Amongst other early users of piped water supplied by C. W. Benny's Water Works Company were the brewery owned by William Buss in Little Minster Street, the corn exchange, St Michael's school in Canon Street, Joseph Moreton (a plumber) in St Swithun's Street, Thomas Goodrich's wine vault in St Peter Street, and a number of inns including *The White Hart* and *The Three Tuns*. The water company's biggest contract was with the Board of Ordinance for the supply of water to the barracks, and it also supplied water to the college, the new training college, and the corporation fire engine. Special arrangements were made for those inns served by James Simond's Hyde Street Brewery: *The Crown and Cushion, The Dolphin, The Compasses, Rodney's Head, The Cart and Horses, The Britannia* and *The Black Bear*. A large number of private households also were connected to the main.[2]

In 1857, Newman gave another lecture to the Mechanics' Institute, in which he was very specific, referring to the disgusting state of the High Street and the small packed houses in areas where 'the ground is little better than one mass of corruption'. He suggested a main sewer, starting in North Walls and ending with an outlet in what was then called Bull Drove. The effluent was to be deodorised, filtered and used as a fertiliser, which could be pumped up to Morstead and Chilcombe where there was ground which would benefit. It is largely the scheme which is in use today, but it met with much opposition. Amongst Newman's specific complaints were the siting of pigsties near the county hospital in Parchment Street and the ghastly overflow from the hospital cesspit which emptied into the Upper Brook, still an open stream.

Nine years went by without any real action from the commissioners or the corporation. The local Board of Health, in fact the corporation, was presented in August 1866 with a petition

64. W. Barrow Simonds, M.P. from 1865-80 and mayor in 1852.

signed by all the leading doctors and surgeons. Two days before this was printed another meeting had been held at the Mechanics' Institute. The Archdeacon of Winchester, in the chair, was urged on by the dean, and committees were formed to publish information about the drainage and sewage of Winchester. The first committee, which included C. W. Benny, W. W. Bulpett, the Woolridges and other city men, was stiffened by the inclusion of the headmaster of the college, the Revd. Dr. Moberly, George Ridding (second master of the college) and Canon Carus. The facts included some damning statistics: in well-drained towns the average expectation of life was 58 years; in Winchester as a whole it was 50; in the parish of St Peter Chesil it was under 42 years. The house visitation sub-committee reported in detail on the disposal of Winchester's sewage: much of it went direct into the Itchen, into cesspits or old wells, which contaminated other wells from which a considerable proportion of people still obtained their drinking water. Some particularly unpleasant examples were specified – of houses where the windows could never be opened because of the stench of privies outside, of privies opening directly into the Brooks, and of wells becoming filled with dirty water and sewage. The town pump well was contaminated and the hospital cesspit, even though it had been cemented over in 1861, remained a major cause for concern until the new building in Romsey Road was completed in 1862.

Not surprisingly it was the committee's 'earnest hope that the time is not far distant when Winchester shall cease to remain a city of cesspits'. Their economic conclusion, that the existing system cost £600 a year and that it would be cheaper to put in drains, made some converts. Yet many more years were to pass before the recommendations won the general approval of the city council and a proper drainage system was agreed. Even then, it was generally believed that nothing could have been done if George Ridding had not encouraged Frederick Morshead, one of his housemasters, to become a councillor in order to push the scheme through.[3] Morshead was mayor in 1872-3, and the Garnier Road pumping station was opened in 1875.

In other respects, the corporation was quick to take advantage of permissive legislation. The Museums Act of 1845 allowed local authorities to use the product of a halfpenny rate for the maintenance of a local museum, and a public meeting in Winchester held on 6 October 1846 unanimously passed a resolution to the effect that it was 'highly desirable a general public museum for the county should be established in the city of Winchester'. Donations and subscriptions were asked for, and on 15 July (St Swithun's Day) 1847 a Hampshire county museum was opened in Hyde Abbey School. The first archaeological specimen to be handed over from a Winchester excavation appears to have been a Roman urn found whilst digging for the foundations of a gas-holder in Water Lane. There was plenty of enthusiasm but not much money, and it was decided to apply for the protection and help of the city corporation. On

6 February 1851 the first museum committee was appointed; the Winchester bushel, of Henry VII's time, was filled with strong beer and passed round amongst members in proper celebration. Winchester's city museum had come into existence, and the city also took over the museum's books. Thus was the public library created.[4]

Neither museum nor library would have survived if it had not been for the energetic first curator, Henry Moody, a remarkable character. His museum was transferred in 1851 to a section of the old gaol in Jewry Street, where it remained until c.1871. In 1853 Moody produced the only complete catalogue that the museum has ever had, and gave countless lectures on all sorts of subjects. He also wrote numerous articles and books, invaluable for their references to Winchester as it was in his time, and for their record of memories of older men and women he had known. He eventually resigned the curatorship under a cloud in 1871, for he had sold off certain articles without permission. In 1883 Moody's daughter was acting as guide to the collections, then housed at the top of the new Guildhall. She told a casual visitor that her father had been an antiquary, who had 'half ruined himself by publishing archaeological works, but she was not sorry for it'.[5]

Winchester must surely be the only cathedral city to have a sewage pumping station named after a dean. Social reform in Victorian Winchester owed much to the great 19th-century deans: never, said one of them, would the dean and chapter forget their duty as citizens.[6] Thomas Rennell, dean from 1805 until his death in 1840 at the age of 87, was a liberal-minded churchman who, as a younger man, helped to support the French priests in exile and the Alton Quakers. He is remembered in Winchester for the 'restoration' of parts of the cathedral fabric between 1815 and 1820. This was largely the work of an enthusiastic member of the chapter, George Frederick Nott, and was only nominally under the control of the newly-appointed cathedral architect, William Garbett.

65. Silhouette of Dean Rennell in old age.

When the roof bosses in the cathedral presbytery were recently restored, a note dated 1817 was found behind one of them. It stated that Nott had done more to the cathedral fabric than any of his predecessors in two or three hundred years. Nott's 'crimes' con-

sisted of his destruction of Perpendicular work in the transepts, replacing it with
'Norman', and in his removal of medieval memorials from their original situa-
tions, replacing them in the retrochoir. These activities were cut short in 1817,
when poor Nott fell 20 ft. from a ladder, but, though he was no longer able to
supervise the restorations in person, his interest in the work continued. A serious problem had been brought to light in 1820 when Garbett reported on the
condition of the nave pillars near Edington's chantry. Rennell wished to employ
a consulting architect, while Nott supported Garbett's scheme for repair. In the
end the dean won the day, the Chapter appointed John Nash (not the dean's
original choice) and the pillars were repaired with a new material, cast iron,
which was cased in cement. They have recently been extensively strengthened
and rebuilt.

During the next few years, the dean and chapter obtained advice from different men for specific projects. The difficulties which had arisen over the restoration of the nave pillars disappeared with Garbett's death, but the chapter took
no action over his reports on the south transept. The wall plates were in a poor
condition, and the perilous state of much of the south side of the whole fabric,
particularly at the east end, must surely have been visible to the naked eye. An
architect was not needed to demonstrate that some of the cathedral walls were leaning out-
wards, and that much of the stonework was decayed.

For a brief period after Gar-
bett's death the chapter was advised by a Mr. Hodgson, but in 1857 he was replaced by John
Colson, who quickly advised that the stonework on the west front was in urgent need of repair.
Exactly a year after his appoint-ment, the chapter set aside the sum of £1,000 for this work, but
they were not prepared to entrust its supervision solely to their new and young adviser. In
1860 it was decided to seek an outside opinion from Euan Christian, who was a friend of
Canon Carus and was already known in Winchester for his new church, Christchurch, in Harold

66. Thomas Garnier.

Road. Christian's report, accepted and approved by Colson, concentrated the chapter's energies on the west front, where much stone was removed; in fairness to Colson, he was also concerned about the south wall of the presbytery and, in fact, the chapter did some repair work there in a small way in 1881.[7]

All the differing activities of Anglican church life, such as the building of churches, teaching in the new schools, the work of societies which called for support from devout laity, inevitably came into contact with Thomas Garnier, Dean of Winchester, a man of devotion and piety, of tact and determination, who could identify with the needs of the poor and the homeless. He also enjoyed preaching before Her Majesty and staying at Osborne. Garnier was a man of wealth and of great integrity. His family was of Huguenot origin, long settled in England, and the dean's father, George, had been high sheriff of Hampshire in 1766.[8]

Thomas, the second son, had been taught at Hyde Abbey School and Winchester College. As a young man he had managed to travel abroad in a brief interval of the war with France, and had been presented to Napoleon in 1802. In 1807, Garnier became rector of Bishopstoke, a living which he held until 1868. Already a member of the Linnaean Society, Garnier was a knowledgeable botanist and a lover of rare trees and shrubs: his rectory soon became famous for its garden. It is he who is said to have planted tulip trees in the close, and in 1867 at the age of 91 Garnier celebrated his birthday by planting an oak in the Deanery garden. He was a great believer in the education of working men, and was an active supporter of the Mechanics' Institute, serving on its committee for many years. He took an active interest in that new Winchester feature, the railway, and when John Dean, Supervisor of the Great Western Railway, retired in 1853, it was Garnier who presented him with the appropriate testimonial and inevitable silver salver. The Dean of Winchester could preside with sincerity and affection over a huge tea party for Winchester children and act as a generous host at the Deanery when he gave a musical evening for 'one hundred and fifty of the élite of the city and neighbourhood'. 'The best Dean we have ever had or ever will have', was the comment of an elderly verger in 1883, adding that despite his generosity Garnier had left more money than any previous dean.

Garnier was an admirer of Scott, and his memorial in the cathedral is Scott's wooden screen which separates choir from nave; there is also a fine medallion memorial of him in the south transept. But for countless men and women in Winchester he needed no memorial, being remembered as a man who had fought injustice, bad housing, unemployment and poverty. It would be unjust to Charles Sumner, however, to pass over that bishop as of little influence in the city, for, under his guidance, the parishes were reorganised.

The first church to be considered was that of St Maurice, in the centre of Winchester and a small building for a large central parish with an increasing population. The plan adopted was of complete demolition, except for the

67. The church of St Maurice and St Pantaleone, built in 1841 and demolished in the 1950s. It incorporated the Norman tower and arch from the original church which was taken down in 1840.

68. The Norman south arch of St Maurice's which can still be seen on the south side of the High Street.

Norman tower, but there were endless difficulties in bringing the work to completion. It is not absolutely certain that William Garbett was the architect appointed to design this new church, but Garbett's death in 1834 could certainly explain why his anonymous successor found it difficult to complete the work after the old church had been taken down in 1840. Garbett was fond of grey-headers, which he had used with admirable effect at St John's Hospital, and the new St Maurice's was built almost entirely of these bricks. Its foundation stone was laid in July 1841, and the work was finished within a year, the bishop presiding at a great ceremony of commemoration.

By 1838, the Revd. William Williams, Richards' successor at Hyde, had begun the renovation of St Bartholomew, and had partly rebuilt the ruined chancel. In 1834, before Garbett made his will, there were already plans not only to rebuild St Thomas' church but to move it to an entirely different site in Southgate Street. This was to prove a long and expensive business, and there were many Winchester people who, like the antiquarians and archaeologists who visited Winchester with the British Archaeological Association in 1845, deplored the proposed demolition. The decision to rebuild on a new site was taken, however, and the old church was pulled down, though the churchyard was allowed to remain. The main fabric of the building which replaced old St Thomas was finished in 1846, to the design of E. W. Elmslie, although the spire was not completed until 1856-7. Though that feature has sometimes given trouble, and the church, in fact, had to be repaired almost as soon as it was opened with the help of a local architect, J. Colson, the spire was a notable addition to the Winchester landscape.[9]

After work had begun on new St Thomas, yet another change occurred. A new parish was carved out of St Maurice's, and was centred on a new church, Holy Trinity, in North Walls. This church was designed by Henry Woodyer of Guildford in the French Gothic style – with a small flèche. It was completed in 1859.

Two other new parishes completed the mid-Victorian organisation of Anglican Winchester. One was Christchurch, which was the result of the energetic activities of William Carus. It is worth considering its creation in some detail for it was a real community effort, 'typical Victorian Winchester'.[10] Carus was one of the city's great personalities: born in Liverpool in 1802 he had studied at Cambridge and become a disciple of Charles Simeon, the great evangelical. His ability, confident manner and powers of persuasion soon brought him preferment. He became vicar of Romsey and canon of Winchester in 1851, and in 1854 rector of the new St Maurice. Carus was a close friend of another reformer, the Revd. L. M. Humbert, master of St Cross. It was not difficult to persuade Humbert that the time had come to make a new parish in what was really 'his' part of Winchester, and Bishop Sumner agreed to support the scheme. On 16 April 1858 it was announced that he had assigned a district to the new church 'the spiritual wants of a new neighbourhood will require the additional accommodation' – and had given £40 towards the fabric. Carus himself at once gave £2,000 and an additional £1,000 to the endowment. It was decided to call the church Christchurch.

The possible sites were fully discussed, but representatives of the Conservative Land Society, including a number of local tradesmen, offered a free site of four plots of the Society's land in the new Harold Road, an offer which was gratefully accepted. A subscription list was formally opened, headed by donations of 20 guineas from each of the two Winchester Members of Parliament. There was already 'a new built villa' next to the chosen site, and this became the vicarage. From the very beginning, a large and spacious church was thought necessary, and a comparatively large sum of money was required, in contrast to Winnall church which was rebuilt in 1858 for £412.

Carus laid the foundation stone 'as though he was quite au-fait in masonry' and got an excellent press from both the *Hampshire Chronicle* and the *Winchester Quarterly Record*. In a generous speech he omitted all references to his own gifts to the church, thanking instead his bishop, the dean and chapter, the Diocesan Church Building Society, and his committee.

The church took just over a year to complete, and Carus' own personal donation to the funds reached a total of £3,500. On the last day of 1860 the new church was consecrated, and Harold Road soon lost its name. It can hardly ever have been doubted who the first vicar would be. On 29 January 1861, Carus was instituted and in his new parish found a real outlet for his abundant energy. He stayed there for 10 rigorous years, and was greatly helped by his first curate, the Revd. W. C. De Boinville, whom he took with him from St Maurice. Carus retired to Bournemouth in 1870, retaining his interest in Winchester, and keeping his canonry till 1885. He died in 1891, indeed a great Victorian.

In 1873 yet another new Anglican church was added to the Winchester landscape, that of St Paul in Weeke parish. It was designed by John Colson senior, but suffered a number of delays, and was not finished until *c.*1910, when the aisles were completed by Colson's son and namesake.

From the renewed fabrics of the ancient parish churches, the new churches, and the vigorous parochial clergy, the citizens of Victorian Winchester were offered a wide variety of activities designed to make them active members of the church militant. All parishes had regular parochial dinners at local inns, as they had done in the 18th century, and these were hilarious occasions, unsuitable sometimes for ladies, who were not often present.

The corporation took, and was expected to take, a leading rôle in this sort of activity: in 1858 the mayor presided over a large public dinner in St John's House attended by all the local clergy and churchwardens; the object of the evening was to discuss 'the well being of the clergy'. The inaugural meeting of the Scripture Readers' Union in 1853 was presided over by the then mayor,

W. Barrow Simonds. Anglican ladies were encouraged to support the Winchester Refuge for Distressed Females, which opened *c*.1844 and within 10 years
had helped about one hundred and fifty girls. Good needlewomen could support the United Dorcas Society, which handed out clothes to the needy once or
twice a year at the Corn Exchange. There was a flourishing Church of England
Young Men's Society, which provided an adult evening school, originally meeting in Upper Brook Street, and becoming so large that it had to move to Holy
Trinity School. Victorians also had endless opportunities for participating in a
multiplicity of activities in support of foreign missionaries.[11]

One important feature of this Anglican activity was the creation of a system of
excellent local schools, each associated with a particular parish. A large central
school, St Mary's, was set up in Colebrook Street in 1812. It was followed by
schools associated with particular parish churches: St Peter Cheesehill (1840),
St Michael, St Thomas, Holy Trinity, St Bartholomew, and St John. Perhaps the
most famous of the early headmasters was G. W. Mason, the first headmaster of

69.   Colebrook Street, *c*.1830.

St Michael's Practising School, who gave a series of public lectures in order to raise funds to build a schoolmaster's house. One of the smaller topographical changes of recent years has been the disappearance of these early schools and their houses. The Diocesan Training College, now King Alfred's College which opened in a new building in 1862, was one of the great contributions made to Winchester and Hampshire society in the mid-19th century.

The training college produced qualified teachers. A start was made in 1838 when a group of five students met at 27/28 St Swithun's Street under the direction of the Principal and only member of the staff, the Revd. D. J. Waugh. The object was to produce teachers whose Christian vocation had been proved, and a master who was 'humble, industrious and instructive'. High standards were demanded, food and other creature comforts were only modest, but the demand for places increased. The students moved about from one home to another, spending 20 years at Wolvesey under the second Principal, the Revd. Mr. Smith. The college opened eventually in a splendid new building designed by John Colson on that part of the western down which had come to be known as Sleepers Hill. From that day onwards, the students have become a recognised and welcome section of Winchester society. The training college building could never have been completed, or indeed initiated, without the vigorous support given by the Anglican diocese, and in particular by the secretary of the Diocesan Board of Education, the Archdeacon of Winchester, Philip Jacob (Inst. 1834, d. 1885). He was the grandfather of Professor E. Jacob, the historian, and was an impressive figure in the group of clerics who served the cathedral in the 19th century. The Garnier tradition was carried on by the next dean, another liberal, John Bramson. The Cathedrals Act of 1840 had reduced the number of resident canons by seven and the intellectual standard of this smaller chapter was high.

A substantial minority of Winchester's inhabitants, however, kept to the old faith, and the Roman Catholic parish which had been built up by Milner grew rapidly after the Catholic Emancipation Act of 1829. Richard Baigent, Winchester's first registrar of births, marriages and deaths, was a Catholic, and the Baigents became a notable family, as did the Gudgeons, descendants of Robert Gudgeon, a well-known cabinet-maker and 'upholder' (auctioneer), whose firm eventually acquired the Gauntletts' house in Southgate Street.

The heart of the Catholic community remained in St Peter Street, where the priest lived near Milner's St Peter's chapel, and where the Benedictine nuns remained until their departure from Winchester in 1857. In 1826, Coram's gabled house was replaced by three new houses (7, 8 and 9) built with a sum left by a devout parishioner. This development took place when Father James Delaney was in charge and when Milner's church was still big enough for the parish. Father Ignatius Collingridge (1848-83) left the residue of his estate for the erection of a new church, but many years went by before a suitable site could be found, and the building was not completed until 1927.

For dissenting churchmen the 19th century was also a period of growth and challenge. The small Independent Congregational chapel in Parchment Street was rebuilt in 1807 when the congregation was under the care of Richard Adams, a minister described in his funeral sermon at Lymington in 1846 as 'somewhat peculiar but eminently good'. He can claim to have initiated the first 19th-century rebuilding of any Winchester church of any denomination. It was still too small, however, and it was left to William Thorn, a later minister who was reasonably wealthy, to plan a new chapel and to buy a manse for the minister. Two houses in Tower Street, 1 and 2 Portland Terrace, were purchased in 1850-1; the Thorns moved into one of them and found themselves neighbours of William Budden and his large family, then in Tower House. Other neighbours who became close friends were the Warrens, local printers and publishers in the High Street.[12] All three families, incidentally, supported the Liberal Party. In 1851 Thorn's building committee instructed Charles Benny to buy Lot 3 at the auction of the old county gaol in Jewry Street. Here, on the site of the northern debtors' ward, a large new church and school were built to the design of W. F. Poulton of Reading in the Early English style. The chapel has proved to be an increasingly admired part of the Jewry Street frontage, and can hold 1,000 people. The words 'British School' can be read over one of its entrances. Pupils paid 2d. a week, bought their own slates, and paid extra for books. Brave children ventured into the cellar below the main school room where the names of debtors could be read, scratched onto the wall. Children came from all over Winchester: one boy even walked from Sparsholt every day. Thorn's work was missionary work, and he preached and lectured over a wide area, also giving generous donations to the chapels at Cheriton and Bishop's Waltham. He also initiated the tremendous annual Whit Monday 'treat' for his school, when three or four hundred children ate a large tea and then walked to Oliver's Battery in procession, with flags and banners flying, to spend the rest of the evening playing games. The school was welcomed by people who did not wish their children to receive Anglican teaching (no denominational instruction was given) and its closure in 1892 for financial reasons was a severe blow.[13]

Wesleyans and Baptists also made their contributions to city life, the latter in the new church built in City Road and opened in 1862. The Salvation Army's first venture in Winchester was at Hamilton House, Canon Street. It was used as a home of rest for women and girls in moral danger, a project which had been started in 1884 by Josephine Butler, the famous social reformer, wife of one of the cathedral canons and grandmother of 'Rab' Butler. A Norwegian Salvationist living in Southampton began working in Winchester in 1886 with the idea of forming a corps and depot, and in the next year Mrs. Butler gave Hamilton House to the Salvation Army. Funds for a permanent citadel were raised by 'ham, jam, and glory teas' at the Corn Exchange, and the work of the Army soon spread to surrounding villages. The citadel in Parchment Street was opened as headquarters in 1889.[14]

Chapter Thirteen

The Expansion of Winchester

Only a small proportion of families continued to live in Winchester for generation after generation. The census of 1851 shows a considerable number of men, women and children who were not Winchester born, and a majority of the better-known personalities of the late Victorian city were 'aliens'. The two Thomas Stophers, both architects, father and son, came from Saxmundham in Suffolk; amongst the Liberals, William Budden was born in Chatham; the Drews were of Huguenot origin from Portsmouth, a town which also produced Charles Benny,

70. Thomas Brassey (1805-70).

the Conservative entrepreneur; Richard Moss, another Conservative, came from London; and the 'printing' Warrens came from Southampton. Edwin Hillier decided to buy a Winchester nursery merely on the toss of a coin. The Wells were, exceptionally, a Winchester family of several generations and, like the Hilliers, have already celebrated more than 100 years in the city. Edmond's the draper's, another firm with a long history, were not a native family, although connected on the female side with the Yaldens. Some premises have long been associated with a particular trade but under different families. Hunt's the chemist's, Kingdon's the ironmonger's, and the former ironmongers of the Baker family in the Pentice are cases in point, as are the numerous public houses and earlier inns. The *Hampshire Chronicle*,

71. Chesil Street railway station.

72. The London and South Western Railway station.

established in its present premises since 1820, has always been an independent family business.

The first railway company to run a line through Winchester was the London and Southampton, but its original proposal to bring the cutting through the centre of the city fortunately came to nothing.[1] The completed line opened on Monday 13 May 1840, and the excitements of opening day were concentrated at Micheldever station where there was room for the company to entertain the workers and their families, amongst them Thomas Brassey, the contractor, whose name has been preserved in Brassey Road.[2] The first down train left Nine Elms at 8 a.m. and was received with frenzied cheers and salvoes of artillery.

Winchester inns continued to offer a road service to travellers long after the railway came. In 1853 the proprietor of *The Crown* in Kingsgate Street was advertising not only well-aired beds but also post-horses, flies, phaetons, gigs and saddle horses for hire, and lock-up coach houses. For generations carriers had worked from the same premises in Upper Brook Street, and a new firm of railway carriers was set up in St Peter Street by Tom Mark Gillo. It was all part of an inevitable process, accelerated in the last quarter of the century with the opening of the Didcot-Newbury line, and the building of Chesil Station at the east end of the town just beyond the Soke Bridge. By this time the older company's title had been changed to that of the London and South Western Railway, and there was a new railway station at Shawford, just south of Winchester. This was opened in 1882 to serve the inhabitants of the substantial new houses there.

The turnpike roads radiating from the city still retained their importance, and this was enhanced when the first motor car (a Daimler) appeared in Winchester in 1897. The 1870s saw the freeing of these roads from tolls, and the sale of the toll houses – Magdalen Hill (1871), Weeke (1872), St Cross (1875), Bar End (1875), Cock Lane Gate (Hursley Road, 1876) and Twyford (1885).[3] Two of these little dwellings were still standing in 1932, one in Worthy Road at Abbot's Barton, the other in Andover Road near Old Gallows Hill.

The city now began to become more of a tourist centre, the railway making it possible for people to take holidays some distance from their own homes. Winchester began to experience a new phenomenon, the day tourist, who either made his own arrangements or visited on a special excursion. Inns and hostelries began to flourish again: in 1850 the proprietress of *The George* was able to advertise that 'an omnibus meets every train' and be quite certain that her establishment would benefit from increased custom. In addition, special trains from Winchester took families to Salisbury, Stonehenge, Southampton and, of course, London. A 'special' organised on 27 August 1852 took 200 people to Salisbury, and included transport to Wilton and Stonehenge. Not only did the hotels benefit. Since not everyone wished to stay overnight, establishments which only served meals began to flourish. A temperance hotel was opened in

Parchment Street, and Amey's coffee house in St Thomas Street offered moderately-priced meals for family parties. It is all the more surprising that one of Winchester's most famous inns, *The White Hart*, closed in 1857. Its severely classical front, 'put out' in 1806, remained, but the premises were divided into two shops, one becoming the headquarters of the lively Mr. Conduit, band-master of the Winchester Volunteers, the chief pro-vider of sheet music and musical instruments of all kinds, and the conductor of orchestras on many a social occasion. The landlord of *The White Hart* was a very successful man, and his skills were rather wasted in *The White Swan* to which he

73. *The Royal Hotel*, St Peter's Street, which opened in 1859.

moved briefly. In 1859, the enterprising C. W. Benny opened a new hotel, named *The Royal*, under the management of *The White Hart*'s ex-landlord. It was in the St Peter Street premises that the Benedictine nuns had vacated in 1857, and which the astute Mr. Benny had been able to buy. It was a most successful venture, and *The George* found itself increasingly threatened by the creation of new, private hotels, as distinct from the old coaching inns. *The Chequers* lost its licence in 1869 and was demolished in 1890.

Thousands of people came to Winchester as visitors, and some wanted a guide-book or souvenir to take away with them. A seemingly endless series of guide-books, histories, local views, and soon the inevitable postcards, had to be produced. It was for tourists as well as the inhabitants that William Tanner pro-duced his view of the new St Thomas' church, entitled *The Gem of the South*. The firm of Warren produced a whole series of *Guides*, ably written and well illus-trated. Canon Humbert followed the restoration of St Cross Hospital by writing its history. This was published in 1868 by William Savage, who illustrated it with the earliest landscape and architectural photographs of Winchester.

74. The Pagoda (now St George's Lodge), St James' Lane.

75. St James' Villas, built *c*.1840, provided quarters for the families of serving officers.

Savage was a most enterprising man; he was a descendant of the sporting artists, the Herrings, and started a small shop in The Square where he sold materials for the fancy needlework so beloved by the Victorians. This developed into a general trade in souvenirs, for the shop was well situated to catch visitors on their way to the cathedral. The proprietor, who later moved to the High Street, began to sell an assortment of 'Winchester' china decorated with local scenes put on by transfer. He developed this trade, and the great firm of Copeland-Spode 'published' a variety of china articles depicting Winchester buildings and Winchester objects. Delightful cups, saucers and plates of all sizes were decorated, in colour, with scenes of the college based on Ackerman's prints. There were views of the cathedral and St Cross, of the trusty servant, replicas of the cathedral font, and of the Winchester bushel, to mention only a few. Savage's own home, a delightful cottage *ornée* in St Michael's Road, is a perfect period piece. He was undoubtedly one of the first citizens to realise that much of Winchester's future would depend on its importance as a tourist centre.

The coming of the railway marked an important stage in the development of the downlands on the western side of the city. There had been little building outside the Westgate, and on the south-west side of Winchester the ancient areas of St James and Drayton were still rural, with only the occasional farm building. Fifty years later there was still only one house (The Old House), which was part of Drayton Farm, between the St Cross turnpike and the substantial farmhouse now called Freelands. Alderman Stopher, writing of Winchester as he remembered it in the early 19th century, recalled the sparseness of building in the western areas and the bareness of the open downland, a great contrast with the many trees which are there today.

The first building to be erected in Romsey Road in the 19th century was probably the small chapel at the Roman Catholic cemetery. In 1839 the Winchester Cemetery Company was formed, under the chairmanship of C. W. Benny, and began to construct a cemetery ground on the southern side of what had been Barnes Lane, but was now usually called St James' Lane. It was a successful commercial enterprise which helped Benny's career as a financier and which did not prevent the other side of the road from becoming a very fashionable part of the city. It was there that Richard Andrews, a wealthy Southampton businessman, decided to live. In 1848-9 he engaged a Southampton firm of architects, Hinves and Bedborough, whose quite astonishing design was in the Chinese style. Here, in the Pagoda, Andrews, five times mayor of Southampton, entertained a whole series of distinguished guests, including the European Liberal politicians Kossuth and Czartoriski, and gave generous parties on local occasions.[4] He died in 1859, but his Pagoda still stands, though it has lost a good deal of its pristine glory and is now disappointingly known as St George's Lodge. Other residents of the western hill included the Hampshire Constabulary, the building of whose headquarters was followed in 1847-9 by the construction of a new Winchester county gaol, which also had a frontage on the main Romsey-Winchester road. The façade of the new prison was severe but not unpleasing, and neither prison, police headquarters nor cemeteries seriously detracted from the amenities of the area as a whole; the presence of the army barracks produced problems of a different kind, but also increased the demand for houses. St James' Villas were built for the families of junior officers.

In 1850 Charles Benny made his second contribution to the area by getting together a small group of local men who formed the Winchester Water Works Company, mentioned in the previous chapter. A reservoir was built at the top of St James' Lane, and the engineer's private house (now Roadway House), facing Romsey Road, set a high architectural standard.[5]

Another Winchester group, headed by a solicitor, Isaac Warner, formed the Conservative Land Society, and in 1858 laid out in building plots and then resold a large area of land west of the St Cross Road. These developers were careful to give their new roads names likely to appeal to local patriotism. Harold Road, Edgar Road, and Beaufort Road came into existence as plots were rapidly sold off and the erection of houses and villas began. The demand for houses was stimulated by the decision to build the new hospital and the diocesan training college in western Winchester. The new parish had its own church, Christchurch.

76.   Residents of Peter Symonds' Hospital.

The governors of the county hospital decided to move from the city centre in 1862. The continuing deterioration of Wood's building, its cramped situation in central Winchester and the unwillingness of the corporation to provide mains drainage were among the factors which influenced the decision. It was also clear that with a rising population in the county the hospital would have an important future. Moreover, Miss Florence Nightingale was a Hampshire neighbour of the chairman of the building committee, Sir William Heathcote, and she was in favour of the new site in Romsey Road. At first the old hospital was to be kept for out-patients, but when this proved impractical, the Parchment Street site was sold and redeveloped, chiefly as small houses.

In October 1862 land on the south side of Romsey Road was bought from two owners for a mere £2,226. As the building was to be erected with money from public subscriptions there was inevitably some delay, though a gift of £200 from Queen Victoria, with the promise of an annual subscription of £100 as the hospital could serve the Isle of Wight, and therefore Osborne, encouraged other subscriptions. The committee engaged William Butterfield as the architect and his plans were agreed in November 1863. Tenders were asked for, but even the lowest was considered too high. In January 1865 a second list of tenders was considered and that of a Gosport firm, Rogers and Booth, was accepted. Needless to say, their price of £22,582 was considerably higher than the lowest tender previously rejected. In June 1868 the hospital chapel was opened; it had been erected in memory of a great Christian, Warden Robert Barter of Winchester College.[6] In the same year the hospital was generously permitted to add the adjective Royal to its ancient title. Appropriately, the new small road on the hospital's eastern boundary was called Queen's Road.

Further north of the main Romsey-Winchester road a large built-up area was already beginning to grow rapidly in the districts anciently known as Fulflood and Weeke, areas which had previously changed little. Weeke had been part of the great priory manor of Barton, and Fulflood a tithing within it. The ancient church of St Matthew at Weeke, which had survived that period of demolition and decay which resulted in the disappearance of other churches in the north-eastern area of Winchester, had been the parish church of the small group of farmers and shepherds who worked the land of the priory. Even as late as 1656 the sending of tithing men from Fulflood and Weeke to the court of the manor of Barton was the only form of local government for this great area of farmland. There were farmhouses at Weeke, Fulflood and Teg Down. Although Teg Down was free from the payment of tithes, it had to pay 'down silver', a peculiar tax of ancient origin. Winchester College was the only other main landowner; it had been endowed in the early 15th century with a small estate there, and by 1865 owned nearly 70 acres of farmland.

The development of Weeke was made possible by the major reform of cathedral finances in the mid-19th century. In 1857-8 the dean and chapter began the enfranchisement of their property, a process continued by the ecclesiastical commission in recent times. Some confusion arose because of the nature of the ecclesiastical parish: it was 'Weeke' as a whole, but there were parts which were really within the city, and a distinction arose between 'Weeke Without' and 'Weeke Within'.

In 1861 the population consisted of 392 people, exclusive of 137 in the newly-erected Poor Law Union on St Paul's Hill. There were 88 houses, but only 18 of them were technically within the city. Under the Local Government Act of 1894 Weeke was divided into two distinct civil parishes, Weeke Within (90 acres) and Weeke Without (over 1,000 acres). The diocesan authorities had already authorised the erection of a new parish church, St Paul's, on St Paul's Hill. An extension order of 1904 took in further parts of Weeke Without, which was reduced to a mere 755 acres. By 1911 there were barely 100 people resident in the civil parish of Weeke Without, while in the old ecclesiastical parish the population had risen to over four thousand. Winchester was growing rapidly and had long burst the bands of her medieval walls.

77. High Street, *c*.1900.

Perhaps the most striking change within the city centre was the decline of the large town house. After 1832 few men whom the 17th-century heralds would have classified as gentlemen lived in Winchester. The great Sheldon house was handed over by Peter Serle to the army. The fine building which had housed Hyde Abbey school was divided into seven tenements and shops. Hyde House was pulled down by a new owner, William Simonds, a brewer who eventually built himself a new house further north of Hyde and called it Abbot's Barton House. Only one wing of the 17th-century mansion survives, but some fragments were later incorporated into Hyde (School) House by Simonds, notably the stone pediment of the main gateway and a Jacobean plaster ceiling. The demolition of Hyde House made redevelopment at Hyde possible on a large scale, including the erection of great brewery buildings.

Within the walled town, the demolition of Eastgate House had important consequences for the future of the city. For many years it had been the home of the Dowager Lady St John Mildmay, William Pescod's granddaughter and the mother of Paulet St John Mildmay, the parliamentary candidate. This old lady, the daughter of Carew Mildmay of Shawford, had married Sir Henry Paulet St John in 1786, and he had later assumed his wife's surname. After her husband's death in 1808, the Dowager Lady Mildmay spent much of her time at Dogmersfield or in Eaton Square, but she still came occasionally to Winchester, where she dispensed generous and welcome charity to the poorer inhabitants of the city. By 1844 she was nearly 80, and the family decided to sell the house. It was put up for auction at *The George*, sold, and demolished. Some fragments of the fittings were incorporated into other Winchester houses: the staircase went into the new house Mr. Simonds was building at Abbot's Barton, the ironwork gates and railings were re-erected at Kingsland House in Chesil Street, and the panelling of one of the great reception rooms was reused in Kingsgate House. The gardens and grounds of the house were sold off in building lots.[7] 'Forty-six lots of freehold building land, the lawns' were sold in 1846 and the site was soon redeveloped, with a new road known first as High Street, Eastgate, with very attractive houses. By 1850 the shops east of St John's Hospital which marked the edge of the new development were finished, and it was probably at this time that Winchester gained its first plate-glass window, in 'premises suitable for a chemist' on 'the corner of a new street'. Tanner's *View of Winchester*, published in 1852, shows most of the redevelopment complete; 'in front, a new street recently built called High Street, Eastgate'. A local builder, Newlyn, was responsible for most of the redevelopment. He used chalk from the nearby St Giles' Hill for the new houses and, though they have not always proved easy to maintain, they make a notable contribution to the appearance of Winchester. The Dowager died at Eaton Square on 6 May 1857 and on the day of the funeral, a week later, the cathedral bells paid a muffled tribute to the last member of the great Pescod St John Mildmay clan.[8]

Abbey House, much smaller and less impressive to look at than Eastgate House opposite, survived the withdrawal of the Franciscan nuns to new premises and was not redeveloped. It passed instead to a series of local professional families, of whom the first was Robert Jessett, first treasurer of the reformed corporation and a private banker.

The demolition of Mildmay (Eastgate) House was accompanied by a considerable change in Jewry Street, when the county gaol was removed to a new site outside the Westgate, on the north side of the Romsey road. This meant that a large area of land on the west side of Jewry Street and in Staple Gardens was available for other use. The contemporary advertisement stated that it was ground which 'in the hands of the spirited capitalist is capable of advantageous conversion'. What was offered for sale was the residence of the governor of the gaol and about ten other lots as sites. The materials were also offered by auction; they included 2,000,000 bricks, and amongst the rubble was the only Roman inscribed altar ever to be found in Winchester. Despite constant advertisement, and much interest, an attempt to sell the whole site failed, and the gaol was withdrawn from auction. It was then put up in lots, and sold off for a mere £7,000 including the materials.

Though Winchester could not produce a 'spirited capitalist' with enough money to risk buying the entire block, the city did have an able and successful financier in the person of its greatly-loved grocer, Mr. Benny. He now acted as entrepreneur, and bought lots 3, 5 and 6, partly for the Congregational church. Part of the south end of the Jewry Street frontage was soon developed as the modest premises of the first London Joint Stock Bank to open in Winchester. On the other side of the road the closing of the old theatre in 1863 and the redevelopment of its centre and southern sections as shops completed, temporarily, the major alterations in the appearance of this street until c.1927.

Land outside the city wall, and lying east of the river, developed in a different way. The east soke, made up chiefly of Chesil Street, St John's Street, Water Lane and Wales Street, had had a long existence as a part of Winchester which was both within and yet separate from the city. Its growth was restricted by the limited number of river crossings, at Durngate, the Soke Bridge, Wharf Mill and Blackbridge. In 1813 the Soke Bridge was rebuilt by public subscription to the delightful design of George Forder, surveyor to the dean and chapter. During reconstruction, the foundation of the medieval structure came to light. The improvement was largely intended for the convenience of Winchester traffic leaving the city via Bar End for Portsmouth, and it was not followed by any immediate increase of building on the eastern hill. The main economic features of the east soke which had helped to build up its profits in the past were in fast decline. The mills at Durngate, Soke Bridge and the wharf were not prospering, and the old fairs of St Giles and Magdalen Hill were fading away.

In 1784 there were only two buildings on the eastern hill: the farmhouse still called Palm Hall, and the residence of Dr. John Smith, who won a certain amount of notoriety in Winchester because of his policy of inoculating patients against smallpox, as distinct from the later successful process of vaccination. The hill remained underdeveloped as a grazing area and occasional fairground. The creation of a new corn and cattle market in another part of the town doubtless had the effect of hastening the decline of the east soke, and the creation of the new market house in 1857 was a further detraction. By *c.*1850 the Sheep Fair on the eastern hill still took place on the first Monday in Lent and the Cheese Fair, held on the fairground in the lower eastern end of the High Street, also remained; it was held on 24 October in accordance with the charter of Elizabeth I. St Giles' Fair had degenerated and had acquired the name of Magdalen Hill Fair; in Milner's time it had still been important, but by *c.*1850, although still held on St Mary Magdalen's Day (2 August), it was just a temporary arrangement for getting rid of surplus country produce and yet more cheese.

St Giles' Hill still belonged to the bishop, but when the diocese lost its real estate in the financial reform of the mid-19th century, development of the hill became possible. Until 1851 it was not the policy of the ecclesiastical commissioners to sell off the bishopric's land. In 1878 the corporation bought a large area (the 'front' of the hill, facing the city) direct from the commissioners, for £1,250, and they soon made further acquisitions.[9] A small section was bought from the Didcot, Newbury and Southampton Railway; the appearance of this railway and the construction of what became known as the Chesil station had an important effect on the whole of Winchester. The purpose of these purchases by the corporation was to make what contemporary newspapers called a 'pleasure ground', and a further important part of the hill, the area sloping down to Morn Hill Road, was given to the city by Lord Northbrook in 1894. It was a generous present, made during the mayoralty of Thomas Stopher and reciprocated by an acknowledgement in the form of a vellum roll presented to the noble earl. The mayor's interest in the hill was that of a professional architect who had already designed many of the large private houses which Lord Northbrook had allowed to develop on the east of it.

The corporation borrowed £600 to lay out the pleasure ground area, and employed a well-known landscape gardener, called Milner, to advise them. The rateable value of the city was then £88,442, and a halfpenny rate produced £344 18s. The result of the corporation's enterprise on the eastern hill was the attractive wooded slope which looks down over the river and the city, and which closes the vista looking east along the High Street. It was a major change in the Winchester landscape, and one which brought protests from people who preferred the plain downland. There would certainly be protests now if the trees were felled. The rest of the hill was soon developed, using names derived from Winchester's historic past (Canute Road, St Catherine's View) or from the

78. Thomas Stopher.

Baring family (Northbrook Avenue, Baring Road, Stratton Road).

The 'East Hill' frontage had already begun to develop. By 1877 there were five houses and a new rectory for the parish of St Peter Chesil. A further major development took place with the erection of the last of Winchester's Victorian churches, All Saints'. This was finely designed by J. L. Pearson, the architect of Truro Cathedral, and built from the quarried chalk of the hill on which it stands, though the building is still incomplete. Many of the new houses which Thomas Stopher designed for the hill were for wealthy Winchester tradesmen who no longer wished to live over their shops. One incidental result proved to be the discovery of a number of Saxon relics. When 'the mansion next to Palm Hall' was built in 1894, two spears, a skeleton and a perfect iron sword were uncovered. Further discoveries were made in 1905 and, thanks to Alderman Stopher, almost all these relics were placed in the city museum.

The contrast between the development of the eastern down and that of the west was increased by the addition of new public buildings on the west side of the city.

A thorough repair of the castle hall was begun in 1871. The whole length of the building was now apparent for the first time for many years, and the Purbeck shafts of the main columns were visible as important features. Accommodation for legal business had to be provided, so a huge arch was opened through the east wall of the hall and an inner hall was built beyond, leading to new assize courts and offices on the site of the old castle ditch. The round table was taken down from the east end, repaired, and replaced at the west, after being carefully measured and studied. The windows were filled with new stained glass containing the arms of famous people connected with Hampshire, including many kings and bishops. In 1874 the west side was painted with a complete list of knights of the shire, those men who had represented Hampshire in Parliament, and, within the inner hall, the names and dates of the high sheriffs of Hampshire were similarly recorded. Every possible opportunity was taken to record the past history of the county.[10] The corridor which led from the crown court to the *nisi prius* court was decorated with the arms and escutcheons of the lords lieutenant of the county; a county magistrates' room was decorated with panels bearing the arms of the chairman of quarter sessions, culminating with those of Melville Portal himself, the man who had initiated the work of restoration and who became chairman in 1879. The restoration produced widespread interest and pride in county history, reflected within Winchester by a variety of local celebrations, and in academic circles by the formation of the Hampshire Field Club and Archaeological Society in 1888, and the creation of a Hampshire Record Society in 1889.

It was natural that the 'new' western hill should be the site of the headquarters of that new feature of local government, the county council. The Local Government Bill, which was eventually introduced into Parliament in 1888 and resulted in the setting up of county councils, was a radical measure of reform viewed with concern by many of the Hampshire magistrates, who had now to 'offer' themselves to the electorate if they wished to continue to serve as administrators. Accommodation was one of the first great problems and, in November 1890, plans were drawn up for a new set of offices and a proper council chamber. These were eventually erected in the centre of the great space to the north of the castle hall. The design, by Sir Arthur Bloomfield in association with the county surveyor, was carefully considered and the materials, flint and stone, chosen to blend with the environment. At the same time, the

79.   The bronze statue of Queen Victoria by A. Gilbert, which can be seen in its current position in plate 14.

opportunity was taken to make a new pedestrian way in the south side of the Westgate.

A short-lived addition to the area was the great bronze statue of Queen Victoria by A. Gilbert, the sculptor of Eros, which remained for some months under a hoarding until it was moved to Abbey Grounds, in the keeping of the mayor and corporation. It has since been replaced within the great castle hall, and its future situation is a current local problem. Bloomfield's new offices and their fittings cost a modest £22,000, and were generally thought to be a land-mark in more ways than one, for their building marked the beginning of a problem which is continually with the inhabitants of Winchester, the great growth of county administration and the effect of its needs on Winchester's amenities and appearance.

It was in the restored great hall that the diocesan bishops gave generous parties, and the new instrument of Anglican democracy, the diocesan confer-ence, met. On the eastern side of the city, however, the future of Wolvesey Castle and of the remnant of Morley's Palace remained uncertain: huge sections of the ruins collapsed; the bishops let their palace as a private house and as a museum for stuffed birds. Earlier in the 19th century it had become for a short time the diocesan training college, and later it was used as the diocesan church offices. Fragments of Morley's building were removed to adorn the front garden of Abbey House, and the Victorian bishops, still great powers in the land, pre-ferred to live in Farnham Castle. Not until 1938 did their successors return to Wolvesey.

Reform in local government did not stop with the creation of the county council. In 1894 the Act creating rural and urban district councils set up another authority, the Winchester Rural District Council, which had important powers in the whole of the area surrounding the city. In future, the expansion of Winchester could only take place at the expense of this authority, but by this time there had already been a considerable extension of the city boundaries, and land which had formed part of the rural approaches to Winchester for generations was being built over with alarming rapidity.

The late Victorian citizens whose needs and ambitions brought about those many changes were men who believed in progress and in party politics. Until 1880, when aldermen were no longer able to vote for themselves or for other aldermen in aldermanic elections, the Liberal party remained very influential, despite the national set-back of 1874. The parliamentary election of 1880 marked the beginning of a further decline in its fortune. A Liberal topped the poll then, but the party's great local leader, William Budden, was to some extent both helped and hindered by the active interventions of the Anglican Church and the college, organisations still viewed with some measure of traditional suspicion by humbler Wintonians, though many dissenters, urged on by the Warren-Thorn influence, always voted Liberal. Even the foundation of a Liberal

80. The idea of erecting a statue of King Alfred caught the imaginations of people not only in Britain but abroad in a way that was quite incredible, and on the day of the unveiling the streets were packed with enthusiastic crowds.

newspaper, the *Hampshire Observer*, eventually bought up by the Warren family, could not do much to hinder the great rise in popularity of Richard Moss, whose numerous local generosities were viewed by Liberals with much suspicion. He represented the city in the House of Commons and was high steward-elect when he died in 1901. It says much for Budden that his political rivals elected him again and again as mayor on the great occasions when the new Guildhall was opened and when the queen celebrated her Jubilee in 1887. His death in 1894 was followed by one of the last great funerals of Victorian Winchester. His younger friend, Tom Stopher, also a Liberal, was his successor in terms of local patriotism. His interest in, and concern for, Winchester's past was only matched by that of Alderman Jacob and a future mayor, Alfred Bowker, whose work in organising the millenary celebrations of his namesake, Alfred the Great, produced the famous statue in the Broadway by Hamo Thornycroft.[11]

Chapter Fourteen

Winchester in the 20th Century

By the beginning of the 20th century the condition of the cathedral was proving a major cause for concern, not only in the city but throughout the world; cracks and other signs of movement were discovered in some of the walls and in parts of the vaulting, particularly at the east end. A major scheme of repair had to be embarked upon, and Dean Furneaux made several national appeals for the money needed, first asking for £20,000, then £30,000, then £87,000 – the final bill amounted to nearly £120,000. At first it was thought that the foundations of

81.   From left: William Walker (diver), Francis Fox (engineer), J.B. Colson (cathedral architect) and an unknown worker.

82.   One of the divers who laid concrete bags under the cathedral during repairs to the foundations.

the cathedral were drying out, though this interpretation was challenged by experts at the time. Whatever the cause, the timber baulks on which the eastern end rested had to be replaced with masonry, new foundations being carried down to the firm gravel below. Much of this work had to be done in extremely difficult conditions under water, for the structure had to be supported on bags of concrete laid by divers. The cathedral's architect, the younger Colson, died whilst the work was in progress, and Thomas Jackson, the eminent architectural surveyor to the Diocese of Winchester who had first been called in to advise merely about the foundation problems, was eventually made responsible for the preservation work on the rest of the fabric. During an operation lasting six years subsidence was stopped, walls were bonded and tied, much of the foundation was underpinned, and parts of the vaulting were reconstructed. A great pageant was held in 1908 to help raise funds.

In 1908, too, the 'Winchester Gun Riots' took place. The crisis achieved national notoriety when a mob assembled in the Broadway in order to prevent the removal of Winchester's souvenir of the Crimean War.[1] Order and good humour prevailed only after three days of rioting and window-breaking. Ironically, the gun, which had served as a sort of Speaker's Corner, eventually disappeared unnoticed in 1939 as scrap metal. In 1912 Winchester had a royal year: in May, Alfred Gilbert's Jubilee statue of Victoria, which had been moved to the Great Hall from its first position in Abbey Gardens, was unveiled for the second time, by Princess Henry of Battenberg; two months later, on St Swithun's Day, a thanksgiving service attended by King George V and Queen Mary marked the completion of the work on the cathedral, and in the afternoon the new king was received *ad portas* at Winchester College. It was the last royal day of Winchester's peaceful years before the Great War.

The city had always been a garrison town, but the wars of the 19th century, fought by professional soldiers, had affected comparatively few Winchester families. The garrison was no longer housed in the shell of Charles II's palace, as a major fire had gutted the building in 1894. Although the site was re-used and the barracks rebuilt with stylistic features inherited from the earlier building, nothing remains of Wren's work on the western hill except for two drawings, some fragments of the stone capitals, and a piece of the staircase, all in the city museum's collections. The purpose-built museum was constructed in the Square in 1902. A plan has been submitted for the redevelopment of the barracks site: Italian in style, it suggests a series of residential squares.

It is not difficult to distinguish the major factors which changed Winchester in the 20th century. In the first place, the cumulative effects of the two World Wars were fundamental. Those who returned to Winchester had seen the world, and in the Second World War, though there was some damage and, sadly, a small number of casualties when the only bombs to be dropped on Winchester exploded on the corner of Hyde Street and North Walls, a vast influx of evacuees and troops from almost every allied nation had a great effect on the life and thinking of the citizens. Service establishments in the neighbourhood (at Flowerdown and Worthy Down) remained, though at Worthy Down the Fleet Air Arm was replaced by a substantial development of the Royal Army Pay Corps. In the centre of Winchester, on the old Peninsula barracks site, the army groups particularly associated with Winchester's county regiment and riflemen were amalgamated with other units, and only token forces now remain. In 1989 the queen opened the Royal Greenjackets' new museum there, alongside the Light Infantry museum; nearby are the new regimental museums of the Gurkhas and the Royal Hussars.

Secondly, population movement to and from the city was encouraged by the Second World War; after 1951 the number of citizens steadily grew, and improved means of transport brought about an increase in the number of people able to work outside Winchester. Fewer and fewer people, however, were living in the centre of the city. The drift to the outskirts continued throughout the first 60 years of the present century, and in the late 1920s was accompanied by a slight decline in the population. Before the outbreak of war in 1939 empty houses were a frequent feature of the town, both on council estates and in the privately-owned sector.[2] Houses in Christchurch Road were changing hands for about £400 each, while large houses in the centre of the city stood empty or were sold very cheaply indeed. The total number of inhabitants increased steadily and significantly at each census, but since the war only a small proportion continues to live within the old city walls.

There were other kinds of change too. Problems of increasing traffic before the Second World War had resulted in the construction in the mid-1930s of a by-pass on the eastern side of Winchester. This was a highly controversial decision, opposed by a number of people including the Bishop of Winchester, Cyril Garbett. Not only did the new road separate the city centre from St Catherine's Hill, a favourite local beauty-spot, it was also considered to be on the wrong side of the city, which still suffers from the lack of a western by-pass. The controversy was renewed in the 1970s when it was proposed to enlarge the by-pass to form a section of the M3 motorway: a powerful local action group was formed and after nearly 15 years of bitter wrangling it was agreed that the motorway should be re-routed over Twyford Down, further to the east. This decision proved no less controversial, and at the time of writing the argument continues.

Other substantial changes took place within the city, where many familiar landmarks disappeared. *The Black Swan* was demolished in 1935, in an effort to improve the High Street/Jewry Street bottle-neck, and *The George Hotel* was taken down after the war. Chesil railway station was closed, the Didcot and Newbury line was taken up and the area redeveloped, with the recent construction of a car-park in 'supermarket vernacular' style, complete with turrets and fake corn-hoists. In 1959 the Westgate was closed to traffic so that the Romsey Road

83 & 84. *The Plume of Feathers* (*above*) and *The Black Swan*, two inns which have been demolished in the 20th century.

passed alongside the old city gate rather than through it, and at the same time, on the site of the old *Plume of Feathers* public house (which had been taken down in 1940) the new County Offices, Queen Elizabeth Court, were constructed. They had been designed 23 years previously by C. Cowles Voysey – a formidable brick-built neo-Georgian construction balancing the 19th-century Castle Hill offices by Blomfield on the other side of the road. The law courts were rebuilt by the Louis de Soissons partnership and were opened by the High Chancellor, Lord Hailsham, in 1974. There have been changes in other parts of Winchester too. Most of Tower Street has been demolished and replaced by the new offices of Hampshire County Council and a gigantic multi-storey car-park. At the time of writing, extensive rebuilding is taking place in the High Street opposite the Pentice. An 18th-century independent chapel (later a corn-chandler's, then Woolworth's) used to stand here: only a replica of its façade remains. The old *Carfax Hotel*, which once stood near the city station, has also been demolished recently. In contrast, the vast United Reformed church in Jewry Street has been renovated, marking a welcome change in attitude towards development – careful alteration instead of complete destruction. The changing pattern of religious belief is a factor which has greatly affected other city churches: St Maurice has been pulled down, St Peter Chesil turned into a theatre, and St Michael handed over to Winchester College. Two new Anglican churches, St Luke's at Stanmore and St Mark's at Weeke, have been built in recent years

Although Winchester acquired a reputation between the wars as the home of predominantly retired people, the average age of inhabitants was, and still is, too low. After the war the city's education system was drastically reorganised. With two notable exceptions, St Faith's and All Saints', all the parochial schools were shut, and most of Winchester's children of primary school age now go to a large school at Stanmore or to St Bede's, a new Church of England primary school off North Walls, where there is also a modern Roman Catholic primary school, St Peter's. Older children attend the two comprehensive schools, Henry Beaufort and Kings. Peter Symonds (named after Winchester's 16th-century benefactor and previously a grammar school) has become a sixth-form college, and there is a school of art.

In 1904 local government was reorganised so that the electors were grouped in six wards instead of three. The duties of local government, however, remained vested in the mayor and corporation until the major reform by the Conservative government in 1974. Responsibility for a separate police force and fire service had already been handed over to the county during the Second World War, and the city had ceased to be an educational authority in 1974. Winchester became the centre of a large new 'city' spreading from Denmead in the south to Micheldever in the north.[5] Hyde, Sparkford, Weeke and Winnall were all submerged. The old city council, the effective ruler of Winchester since 1155, gave way to a new District Council with 51 members, of whom only 18 represented the old city area.

85. Proclaiming King Edward VII at the City Cross.

Perhaps it is not surprising that the new council is sometimes regarded by Wintonians as remote. Aldermen were abolished, the city ceased to be a highway authority, and the public library was removed to the care of Hampshire County Council. Despite all these changes the corporation's work increased in depth, detail and complexity; the mass of statutory requirements and regulations which are issued by central government do not make the art of local government any simpler, especially when there are increasing numbers of people to govern and more local services required. Perhaps the most striking innovation in the corporation after 1918 was the election of the first three woman councillors, followed inevitably in 1946 by the election of the first woman mayor in Winchester. She was Mrs. Crompton, who remained in office for 18 months, rather than the usual 12, as the beginning of the municipal year was changed at this time from November to May. Since that date Winchester has had 16 woman mayors.

The technical advances, new architectural skills and engineering processes which had been used to rescue the cathedral were characteristic of the years of change which followed. It became increasingly possible to build cheaply and repetitively in the centre of Winchester and on the outskirts of the city. One of the most striking developments in the years after the Great War was the provision of council housing on the fringes of the city, chiefly on land which had belonged to the ecclesiastical commissioners. A start was made in 1920 in the area historically known as Stanmer.[3] By 1936, 736 houses had been erected there to a plan by William Dunn, the individual house types being designed by the architect William Curtis Green. The area, soon known as Stanmore, was considerable, and it was thought that any further council building should take place in other parts of Winchester. In 1926-7, 300 houses of different types were added to Highcliffe, on the slopes of the eastern hill, and 42 were built on the hill itself in a group called Fairdown. In 1929 another small group was built further north at Winnall, near St Martin's church, called St Martin's Close. By this time over 1,000 houses had been built, and to a large extent the initial demand for council housing had been satisfied. This meant that people moving to Winchester had a choice of home as, overall, the population was declining.

The Second World War permanently increased the demand for houses, and considerable developments were built in the post-war years. Work began on 'new' Stanmore in 1946 (624 houses), additions to Highcliffe were started in 1948, and large new estates were built at Weeke and Winnall.[4] Weeke, in particular, was heavily developed with private buildings in the Teg Down area, and the old village centre, consisting of St Matthew's church, the pond and a few old houses, was virtually submerged, although it still survives today. At Winnall the situation was different: St Martin's church was pulled down and a large industrial estate was built; between 1948 and 1960 this became the home of more than a dozen local industries, including builders' merchants, makers of agricultural machinery, a greenhouse manufacturer, various engineering works and the depot of the Hampshire Fire Service. More recently there has been a further extension in the Winnall Valley Road area. During the last 15 years a large estate of private houses, the Badger Farm estate, has been built in the area near Oliver's Battery.

Post-war developments in Winchester included important changes in the centre of the city. Redevelopment on a massive scale began in the Brooks area after 1953 because it was felt that areas of slum property should be cleared, and a private Act of Parliament was obtained by the corporation. The first plan for the area was prepared by Sir Patrick Abercrombie, who died before he was able to submit detailed designs for the flats and houses that he envisaged. This was undertaken by his successor as architect consultant, Peter Shepeard, F.R.I.B.A. Brooks streets were probably the most densely populated area of Winchester, and it was deemed necessary to pull down many houses, provide a large central car-park, and encourage the movement of industry to land outside the centre of the city. Together with poor-quality tenements mainly of 19th-century date, a number of fine medieval buildings, admittedly in poor repair, were cleared on one side to form a riverside walk, continuing a similar path further down the river. In this kind of redevelopment the density of population tends to be lower than it was previously.

The development of central Winchester has provided many opportunities for archaeological excavation. During the 1960s large areas of central Winchester were excavated under the direction of Martin Biddle by the newly-formed Winchester Excavations Committee, starting with the investigation of the former cathedral car-park, on which *The Wessex Hotel* was constructed in 1961-3. The site of Old Minster was discovered under Cathedral Green, the Brookes street area was excavated, as were the castle precincts, the Iron Age enclosure at Oram's Arbour and the late Roman cemetery at Lankhills School. The results are currently being published in the prestigious

86.   The Brooks development.

'Winchester Studies' series. One result of the excavations of the 1960s was the creation in 1972 of the post of city archaeologist, whose offices are now situated in the Historic Resources Centre in Hyde Street, headquarters of the Winchester Museums Service.

More recently the appearance of the Brooks streets area has been further altered by the construction of a large shopping centre, complete with underground car-park. Before any building work took place the area was excavated by the city archaeologist's team, and remains of several medieval houses were discovered, notably the substantial property of a Tudor merchant, John de Titing. Several of the streets in the vicinity of the Brooks development have been pedestrianised, including an area used for the thriving local market. This work continued the city council's policy of removing vehicular traffic from central Winchester: a large section of the High Street was closed to traffic and repaved in the 1980s, and more recently the closure of the Kingsgate Arch and the erection of a barrier outside Wolvesey Palace have further reduced the flow of traffic through the city's streets. Some may miss the former bustle of the High Street,

87. The interior of Hunt's chemist's shop, which has been re-erected in the City Museum.

but pedestrianisation has created an area where street entertainers give great joy (or annoyance, depending on one's point of view) to the passer-by. The annual Folk Festival attracts a predominantly youthful audience, and Winchester can now boast the country's longest-running yearly Hat Fair.

The development of central Winchester has, unfortunately, been accompanied by the closure of many long-established businesses. The construction of a huge supermarket on the Badger Farm estate may have contributed to the demise of the traditional small food shops, though one traditional butcher's shop and two greengrocers' stores survive in the High Street. Increasingly, the shops of Winchester High Street tend to display the familiar fascia boards of national retail firms and building societies, and only a handful of older businesses remain, notably the offices of the *Hampshire Chronicle* and Whitwam's music shop. Two of Winchester's more interesting small shops have been re-erected in the city museum in the square: Hunt's the chemists and Foster's the tobacconists.

As a result of an appeal in the later 1970s the Theatre Royal in Jewry Street was refurbished, but Winchester's only cinema, in neighbouring North Walls, closed in 1989. Other facilities to have made their appearance in the past decade include the new Recreation Centre at North Walls, which replaced an earlier swimming pool destroyed by fire in 1988, and the new golf course at Pitt on the Romsey Road.

Despite all these changes to the physical appearance of Winchester much of its essential character survives. To the south of the city the broad corridor of water-meadow and downland remains undeveloped – a priceless amenity – and a more enlightened attitude towards the conservation of Winchester's architectural heritage, backed up by a thriving civic society, the Winchester Preservation Trust, ensures that the city's finer buildings will remain for posterity. Increasing numbers of visitors are attracted to Winchester, and an expanding team of city guides conducts groups around its wealth of historic buildings.

Abbreviations

H.C.R.O.	Hampshire County Record Office.
W.C.R.O.	Winchester City Record Office.
D. and C.	Dean and Chapter Library.
D.R.O.	(Winchester) Diocesan Record Office.
P.R.O.	Public Record Office.
H.R.S.	Hampshire Record Society.
Milner	Milner, Rev. J., *The History, Civil and Ecclesiastical, and Survey of the Antiquities of Winchester* (James Robbins, Winchester, 1798), in 2 vols.
V.C.H.	*Victoria County History of Hampshire* (Constable, Westminster, 1900-12), in 5 vols.
C.C.W.	Herbert, J. A., *Calendar of Charters* (Jacob and Johnson, 1915).
D.N.B.	*Dictionary of National Biography.*
Anon his	The History and Antiquities of Winchester (J. Wilkes, Winton, 1773), in 2 vols.
Bailey	Bailey, Charles, *Archives of Winchester* (Hugh Barclay, 1856).
B.B.	Bird, W. H. B. (ed.), *Black Book of Winchester* (Warren & Son, 1925).
Usages	Furley, J. S. (ed.), *The Ancient Usages of Winchester* (Clarendon Press, 1927).
City Government	Furley, J. S., *City Government of Winchester from the records of the 14th and 15th Centuries* (Clarendon Press, 1923).
Locke	Locke, A. A., *In Praise of Winchester* (Constable, 1912).
C.R.	*Cathedral Records* (Friends of Winchester Cathedral).
Proceedings	*Proceedings of the Hampshire Field Club and Archaeological Society.*
H.N.Q.	*Hampshire Notes and Queries.*
Hogs	Carpenter Turner, B., *Hampshire Hogs* (Cave, 1977, 1978), Vols. 1 and 2.
H.H.	Carpenter Turner, B., *History of Hampshire* 2nd edn. (Phillimore, 1978).
C.M.W.	Carpenter Turner, B., *Churches of Medieval Winchester* (Warren and Son, 1957).
Portal	Portal, Melville, *The Great Hall of Winchester Castle* (1899).

A Note on Sources.

Most of the primary material used in this book is to be found in the City
Archives, and the writer would like to acknowledge the kind help always given
by the City Record Office. Grateful thanks are also due to the Winchester
College Fellows' Librarians. The chief sources are as follows:

1. Charters, with J. C. Furley's transcripts and the present writer's introduction, compiled in 1954.
2. Books of Ordinances, 1552-1835.
3. Tarrages, 1417-1726.
4. Proceedings of Paving Commissioners, 1771-1886.
5. Rents from dissolved monasteries.
6. Proposal books.
7. Peter Symonds' documents.
8. Account Rolls, 1352-1881.
9. Court Rolls, 1269-1841.
10. St John's Rolls, 1294-1701.
11. Somers' rentals.

Other material is to be found in the leases and minute books of the Dean and
Chapter, the Archives of Winchester College, and of the Duke of Norfolk. Permission to use these sources is most gratefully acknowledged.

Appendix A: The Soke

Temp. Bishop Henry Woodlock[1]

Street and other place-names indicating the widespread extent of the Bishop of Winchester's property interests in the city, and from which rents were collected by the bailiff of the soke:

a) 'Outside Eastgate', 'outside Kingsgate', 'outside Northgate', 'outside South-gate', 'outside Westgate', 'before the gate of the Castle'.

b) Buck Street, Wongar Street, Tanner Street, Mullane, 'Senctwythene', 'Paillirdestwychene', Parchment Street, Colbrook Street, High Street, Gar Street.

c) Le Est-Barr, Forge at the Bar, Forge set up in the way to St Giles' Hill, House of Newbrigge, Land 'next la Broketychene', Land on the ditch of the city, Spark-ford, La Floudstock, Mill outside Durngate, Mill of Abbess of Winchester, Mill of William le Wayte, Mill of Thomas de Thornecombe.

Appendix B: Population

Figures for the population of the city before the first census of 1801 need to be approached with the greatest caution. They rely on incomplete material and differing assessments of the number of people per household. The following suggestions have been made at various times by different writers:

1086	more than 5,000[1]
Early 12th century	c.8,000[2]
1148	7,200[3]
1348	8,000[4]
After c.1353	c.5,000[5]
1377	2,700[6]
1416	c.3,431[7]
1604	c.3,120[8]

Census figures are accurate, but need to be used in relation to the physical expansion of the city boundary:

Year	Source of figure	Population (civilian)	Population (civil and army)
1801	Registrar-General's census	6,194	8,171
1811	Census	6,705	
1821	Census	17,739	
1831	Census	9,212	
1841	Census	10,733	11,083
1852	Census	12,079	13,704
1861	Census	14,776	
1871	Census	17,003	
1881	Census	17,690	
1891	Census	19,073	21,346
1901	Census	20,919	21,635
1911	Census	20,128	24,144
1921	Census	23,791	24,123

1931	Census	23,523	23,523
1938	Registrar-General's estimate	24,460	
1941	Source unknown – not census	25,550	
1948	Registrar-General's estimate	26,790	
1949	Electoral Roll estimate	26,950	
1949	Registrar-General's estimate	26,990	28,140
1951	Registrar-General's estimate	25,280	26,400
1952	Registrar-General's estimate	25,032	25,790
1953	Registrar-General's estimate	25,083	26,300
1956	Registrar-General's estimate	26,269	27,580
1957	Registrar-General's estimate	26,253	
196	Census	28,770	
1961	Registrar-General's estimate	28,477	28,920
1962	Registrar-General's estimate	28,621	28,650
1971	Census	31,107	
1979	County Council estimate	33,221	
1982	County Council forecast	33,650	
1985	County Council forecast	33,150	

It is permissible to ask if the expectation of life fell in the late 14th and 15th centuries. In 1373 an inquiry into St Cross Hospital produced 28 witnesses including men of 60, 65, 70, and two of 80 years of age.[9] In 1551, at another local inquiry, there were six witnesses all between the ages of 44 and thirty-six. In both cases, the object was to produce witnesses of as great an age as possible.[10]

Appendix C: Reprisals, 1660

Jacob's Scraps No. 5 and P.R.O. E/178.

A commission of inquiry sitting at *The White Hart* on 1 August 1662 turned out parliamentarians from civic office, and restored royalists.

Royalists

1. John Colson — 'ejected for loyalty', to be restored, with precedence over Benjamin Clarke, as alderman

2. Peter Symonds) for constant loyalty
3. William Cradock) forthwith to be chosen freeman
4. John Fletcher)
5. Godson Penton) for like loyalty, 'forthwith
6. John Warner) of one and twenty one'
7. Thomas Cropp)
8. John Tipper)
9. Thomas Grantham)
10. John Clure)
11. Phillip Ruddesbye) to be freemen
12. Thomas South)
13. William Horwood — to be and remain 7th Alderman

Parliamentarians

'To be expelled and removed out of the said Corporations ... for being disloyal and non-conformist to the Church Government.'

1. Cornelius Hooker, Esq., Pretended Recorder
2. Robert Wallop, Esq.
3. Sir William Walker
4. Sir Henry Mildmay
5. Nicolas Love
6. John Lisle
7. John Hidesley
8. Thomas Bettesworth
9. John Woodman
10. Laurence Lampard

11. John Byrch
12. Benjamin Smith
13. Guy Badcock
14. Philip Jones
15. Lancelot Bignell
16. John Boes
17. Philip Stone
18. Thomas Muspratt   )
19. John Champion   ) Not to be Governors
20. Thomas Lambert   ) of the Blew Hospital

There have already been commissions of enquiry into the estates of John Lisle and Nicolas Love, both exempted by parliament from the Act of Indemnity: both had fled the country, all their property was confiscated, and Lisle was murdered by royalists in Switzerland in 1664. The inquiry into Love's estate had also been held at *The White Hart* before a jury headed by Essex Powlett. Lisle's property was assessed by an Isle of Wight commission sitting at Newport; he was particularly hated as Bradshaw's deputy at the trial of Charles I.

Appendix D: 17th-Century Historians

The first local historian, as distinct from the monastic writers of the past, was John Trussell (d. *c.*1648), the son of refugee papists who settled in Winchester in the early years of the 17th century. Trussell was not only a good historian who made use of original documents, but a rough and ready poet. He was a royalist, deeply involved in local politics, a lawyer, and mayor in 1624 and 1633. Not very skilled as a palaeographer, his mistranscription of medieval documents produced a number of mistakes which long remained a feature of Winchester's written history. His most striking creation was Florence de Lunn, an entirely mythical first mayor. Trussell's chief work, the manuscript *Touchstone of Tradition*, has recently been purchased by the corporation; its apparent introduction, 'The Origin of Cities', contains a valuable account of early Winchester, and his so-called 'Book of Benefactors', a miscellaneous volume, much of which must have been written during the Civil War, is particularly interesting for its accounts of contemporary events and its critical verses on Trussell's civic contemporaries. The 'Origin' was bequeathed to the city by the late Miss A. Johnson. 'The Benefactors', in a single volume which includes a long narrative poem 'Caer Gwent', was lent to the city in 1955 for the exhibition of that year by its owner, the American collector, Mr. James Osborne.

It is the cathedral, however, not the city government, which can claim the honour of the first printed history, for one result of Charles II's interest in Winchester was the compilation by a courtier, Henry Hyde, the second Earl of Clarendon, of *Some account of the Tombs and Monuments in the Cathedral Church of Winchester*. Finished in February 1683, it was brought up to date and published in 1715 by Samuel Gale, with a dedication to Jonathon Trelawney, Bishop of Winchester. Its many illustrations, though they need to be interpreted with caution, make this a delightful book, and Gale added a list of cathedral charters, 'from the Tower of London', a catalogue produced by F. Holmes, deputy record keeper there.

Appendix E: Early Dissent in Winchester[1]

Date	Meeting Place	Denominations, and Ministers if known
c.1645-60	Cathedral	Humphrey Ellis[2]
	St Maurice's church	Leonard Cooke[2]
	St Thomas' church	
1652-55	St Peter Chesil church	John Brayne[3] 'Minister'
1657-60	Cathedral	Theopilius Gale[4]
1672	House of Ann Complin 'over Market House'	Samuel Tomlins[5] Presbyterians
1700	'new Chapel then building in Parchment Street'	(Successors to S. Tomlins, including Edward Pain)[6]
1737	Winchester[7]	
1749	Parish of St Peter Chesil	Quakers[7]
1752	Parish of St Maurice	Presbyterian[7]
1752	Parish of St Mary Kalander	'Protestant' Dissenters[7]
1763	Parish of St Peter Chesil[7]	
1768	High Street[7]	

Appendix F: Winchester's Royal Charters

The city's charters fall into several well-defined groups, though some can be placed in more than one section. An asterisk indicates that the original grant is no longer in the city archives.

A: Charters concerned with the ancient privileges of the city and the Merchant Guild, and with the continuance of the privileges.

Grantor	Date
Henry II (to Guild Merchant)	c.1155-61
Henry II (to citizens)	c.1155-61
Richard I	1190
John	1215*
Henry III	1227
Edward I	1290
Edward II	1324
Edward III	1327
Edward III	1336
Richard II	1378
Henry IV	1401
Henry VI	1438-9
Edward IV	1462
Henry VIII	1489
Henry VIII	1514
Edward VI	1549-50*
Philip and Mary	1554*
Elizabeth I	1561

B: Charters giving various forms of economic aid.

Grantor	Date	Subject
Henry VI	1439-40	Licence to hold in mortmain to the value of £40 etc.
Henry VI	1442	Appointment of J.P.s*
Henry VI	1449	Licence to hold fair and market
Edward IV	1462	Appointment of J.P.s (Confirmation of 20 Henry VI) (and *inspeximus*)

Henry VIII   1516   Mayor's oath
Henry VIII   1518   Two fairs
1 & 2 Philip   1554   Monastic rents
and Mary   (17 Sept.)

C: Grants from the Ulnage, in respect of payment of the fee farm.
Henry VI   1451-2   40 marks for 50 years from ulnage
Edward IV   1461-2   Confirmed
Richard III   1484   Confirmed
Henry VII   1486   Confirmed
Henry VII   1504   Renewed for 60 years
Henry VIII   1514   Confirmed
Edward VI   1549-50   Confirmed
Philip & Mary   1554   40 marks for 60 years ulnage*
                  (1 Sept.)
Philip & Mary   1554   Farm of ulnage given to mayor and
                  (5 Sept.)   bailiffs*
Elizabeth I   1561   Confirmed
James I   1604   Farm of ulnage confirmed

D: Grants reducing the fee farm.
Philip & Mary   1554   10 marks from fee farm for 10 years*
                  (8 Sept.)   50 marks from fee farm for 50 years
James I   1604   50 marks from fee farm for 60 years from 1613
Charles II   1673-4   Renewal for 60 years
George II   1734   Renewal for 28 years
George III   1763   Renewal for 31 years

The farm of the city could be used by the king in various ways. It rarely reached the exchequer as a complete sum. Deductions from it were made at the royal command to make local purchases, to give alms, or to pay small pensions and stipends. A hermit was maintained out of the farm in John's time, and from time immemorial the Hospital of St Mary Magdalen received regular royal help, paid before the money left the city. The farm formed part of the jointures of both the queens of Edward I, and of later royal consorts. From the late 14th century the number of people receiving small stipends from this source greatly increased. Thus in September 1448 William Shirley, a king's sergeant, was granted 6d. a day for life from the city fee farm.[1] In 1452 a grant of £10 a year was made to Gilbert Par, 'esquire of the body', and his wife Agnes.[2] Other grants included those to John Parker (12d. a day, 1454),[3] and Henry Crane (6d. a day).[4] The final grant was to the first Marquess of Winchester, who was given a permanent annuity of 50 marks by Edward VI as his creation fee.[5]

It will perhaps be of some use to show here in tabular form the grants obtained by various groups in Winchester before 1290, when Edward I confirmed the city's privileges, as did almost every successive monarch. Reference 'C' numbers relate to Herbert's *Calendar*.

Nature of grant and grantors, form (e.g. charter) and date

	HENRY II	RICHARD I	JOHN	HENRY III
Ancient customs of citizens as in time of Henry I	Confirmed to citizens, 1155 (C.2)	By charter, 1190, confirmed to members of G. Merchant (C.3)	By charter, 1215, confirmed to citizens as in times of my ancestors (P.R.O. C.53/14/m.4)	As John by charter 1227 (C.4)
Power to hold purchases, mortgages & tenements according to custom of city as they were held in the time of Henry I	Confirmed to citizens, 1155 (C.2)	Confirmed to members of G. Merchant 'they shall have their lands, tenures & mortgages of debts whosoever wes them to them' C.3)	As Richard I but confirmed to citizens (P.R.O. C.53/14/m.4)	As John (C.4)
Unjust customs levied in time of war to be quashed	Confirmed to citizens 1155 (C.2)	Confirmed to members of G. Merchant (C.3)	By charter, 1215, confirmed to citizens (P.R.O. C.53/14/m.4)	As John (C.4)
Alien and Denizen Merchants coming to Winchester to trade to have the King's sure peace	Confirmed to citizens 1155 (C.2)	Confirmed to members of G. Merchant (C.3)	By charter, confirmed to citizens (P.R.O. C.53/14/m.4)	As John (C.4)
Members of Merchant Guild to be free of all toll, passage and custom	Charter to G. Merchant (C.1)	Confirmed; quit of toll, lastage pontage in and out of fairs and in sea-ports (C.3)	By charter, and Confirmed to M. Guild only, with freedom from passagium (P.R.O. C.53/14/m.4)	As John (C.4)
Farm by local officials (e.g. sheriff excluded)	1155-7 (*Pipe Rolls* a) Returned by reeve of the city, Stigand	–	City allowed return its own farm for limited periods	As John

	HENRY II	RICHARD I	JOHN	HENRY III
Weavers' Guild had right to elect own aldermen	On payment of one mark of gold to Crown (*Pipe Roll* 1166)	–	–	–
Fullers to have their liberties	–	–	Grant by (lost) charter, 1194 (*Pipe Rolls*, s.a.)	
No member of the Merchant Guild to plead outside (C.3) the walls of the city	–	Grant by Richard I	As Richard I (P.R.O. C.52/14/m.4)	As Richard I (C.4)
No member of the Merchant Guild to fight a duel (i.e., no ordeal by battle) 'and in pleas of the crown they shall deraign themselves according to the ancient custom of the city'	–	Grant by Richard I (C.3)	As Richard I (P.R.O. C.53/14/m.4)	As Richard I (C.4)
No member of the Merchant Guild to be judged of an amercement of money except according to the law of the city	–	Grant by Richard I 'the law of the city which they had in the time of my ancestors' (C.3)	As Richard I (P.R.O. C.53/14/m.4)	As Richard I (C.4)
Preservation of Judicial Customs concerning lands & tenures 'according to custom of the city'	– Richard I (C.3)	Grant by (P.R.O. C.53/14/m.4)	As Richard I (C.4)	As Richard I
Retaliation for toll wrongly taken from members of M. Guild	–	Grant by Richard I (C.3)	As Richard I (P.R.O. C.53/14/m.4)	As Richard I (C.4)
No scotale to be levied by any sheriff or bailiff	–	Grant by Richard I (C.3)	As Richard I (P.R.O. C.53/14/m.4)	As Richard I (C.4)

	HENRY II	RICHARD I	JOHN	HENRY III
Mayor & Commune recognised	–	–	1200, Chancery enrolments (Charter Roll, 5 April, 1 John. Liberal Roll, 4 Oct. 1200)	
Citizens to have site of two mills at Coitebury	–	–	Grant by John, 1215, (P.R.O. C.53/ 14/m.4)	As John (C.5)
Mint and Exchange to be forever in Winchester	–	–	John 1215 (P.R.O. C.53/ 14/m.4)	As John (C.4)
No one to be distrained for any debt outside city unless he is capital debtor or security	–	–	John 1215 (P.R.O. C.53/ 14/m.4)	As John (C.4)

Appendix G: Mayors of Winchester District 1973-90

(*name of ward given at time of mayoralty – in some cases this has subsequently changed.)

Date	Name	Ward*
1973	Alderman Cyril Arthur Taylor O.B.E. (Con.)	Winchester (St Thomas)
1974	Barbara Dorothy Mary Carpenter Turner (Ind.)	Winchester (St Michael)
1975	Alan Cotterill (Con.)	Winchester (St Maurice)
1976	Gwendoline Annie Shave (d.1989) (Con.)	Curdridge
1977	David George Ball (Con.)	Winchester (St Bartholomew)
1978	John Derrick Flook (Ind.)	Upper Meon Valley
1979	John David Green (Ind.)	Swanmore
1980	Melus Pamela Pitt (Con.)	Itchen Valley
1981	Ian Robert Bidgood (Lib.)	Owslebury and Colden Common
1982	Albert Joseph Donald Austen (Con.)	Wonston
1983	Frederick Hinton Peachey B.E.M. (Ind.)	Micheldever
1984	John Frederick Charles Hartgill Broadway (Con.)	The Worthys
1985	Jean Doreen Freeman (Con.)	Winchester (St Barnabas)
1986	Susan Margaret Gentry (Lib.)	Bishops Sutton
1987	Douglas Frederick Covill M.B.E., D.C.M. (Con.)	New Alresford
1988	Brian Hall M.B.E., R.N. (Con.)	Wickham
1989	Frederick George Allgood (Con.)	Denmead
1990	Pamela Grace Peskett (S.D.L.P.)	Winchester (St Bartholomew)

Notes

Introduction

1. Hawkes, C. F. C., Myres, J. N. L., Stevens, C. G., 'St Catherine's Hill', *Proceedings* Vol. 11 (1930).
2. Cunliffe, B., *Winchester Excavations, 1949-60* (City of Winchester Museum and Libraries Committee, 1964), Vol. 1, pp. 1-17. *Prospect*, pp. 3-12.

Chapter One: Roman Winchester

1. *H.H.*, pp. 17-21. *Prospect*, pp. 13-19.
2. Cunliffe, B., 'The Winchester City Wall', *Proceedings*, Pt. 2, Vol. 22 (1962).
3. The Southgate reconstructed after its excavation by B. Middle in 1971. *Prospect*, p. 16.
4. Johnson, David E., *Sparsholt Roman Villa*, 2nd edn. (1972).
5. *V.C.H.* Vol. 1, p. 292.
6. Collis, John (ed.), *Winchester Excavations* Vol. 3 (forthcoming).
7. *V.C.H.* Vol. 1, p. 291.
8. *Winchester Excavations* Vol. 3 (forthcoming).
9. *See* the notes by Frank Cottrill in *Sixty Generations* (Winchester City Council, 1955), pp. 5-67, a catalogue compiled for the visit of H. M. The Queen in 1955.
10. *Roman Burials in Winchester* (Guildhall Exhibition, Pamphlet, n.d.).
11. *Milner*, p. 73.
12. *Locke*, p. 14.

Chapter Two: Wintanceaster

1. The earliest reference to Winchester appears in the *Chronicle* under the year A.D. 642. Whitelock, Dorothy (ed.), Douglas, David C., Tucker, Susie, *The Anglo-Saxon Chronicle* (Eyre & Spottiswoode, 1963).
2. Meaney, A. L., and Chadwick Hawkes, Sonia, 'Two Anglo-Saxon cemeteries at Winnall', *Society for Medieval Archaeology*, Monograph Series No. 4 (1970).
3. *A.S.C. s.a..*
4. Biddle, Martin, *The Oldminster; Excavations near Winchester Cathedral, 1961-69* (Warren & Son, 1970). Biddle, M., *Winchester: the development of an early capital* (Vanden Noech & Ruprecat in Gottingen, 1972).
5. de G. Birch, W. (ed.), *An ancient manuscript* (H.R.S., 1889).
6. de G. Birch, W. (ed.), *Liber Vitae: Register and Martyrology of New Minster and Hyde Abbey* (H.R.S., 1892), p. 157.
7. The stone was first seen by John Carter, Milner's architect, in a garden in St Peter Street.
8. Quirk, R. N., 'Winchester Cathedral in the Tenth Century', *Archaeological Journal* Vol. 114 (1959).
9. Oakeshott, W. F., *The Sequence of English Medieval Art* (Faber, 1950), pp. 14-16.
10. Hunter Blair, Peter, *Anglo-Saxon England*, 2nd edn. (C.U.P., 1960), pp. 292-4.
11. Mack, R. P., 'The Winchester Mint', *Proceedings* Vol. 20.
12. Wilde, Edith E., 'Weights and measures of the city of Winchester, *Proceedings* Vol. 10 (1931).
13. *Prospect*, pp. 22-8. *V.C.H.* Vol. 1, pp. 527-37. Round, J. H., 'Winchester Survey' texts in *Domesday Addidamenta* (Record Commission, 1816), pp. 531-62. Biddle, M. (ed.), *Winchester Studies* (Clarendon Press, 1976), Vol. 1.

Chapter Three: The Struggle for Freedom, 1066-1215

1. John, Eric, 'The church of Winchester and the tenth-century reformation', *Bulletin of the John Rylands Library* Vol. 47, No. 2 (March 1965).
2. The archives of the Soke, to be found, *inter alia*, in the Pipe Rolls of the Bishopric of Winchester. Proceedings in Cheyney Court, in Soke Books, and Cheyney Court Proceedings, all in H.C.R.O. on deposit from Ecclesiastical Commissioners. *See* Appendix A. The divisions of east and west soke appear clearly in the 17th-century Hearth Tax Assessments.
3. Winchester is not surveyed in Domesday Book, which has only incidental references to the city under its descriptions of property owners. The so-called *Winchester Domesday* contains two surveys of the city, made in 1110 and 1148.
4. de G. Birch, W. (ed.), *Liber Vitae of Newminster and Hyde Abbey* (Hyde Register), (H.R.S., 1892), pp. 1-2.
5. *V.C.H.* Vol. 5, p. 530. B.C.T., *H.H.*, p. 36.
6. *Book of Fees* (H.M.S.O., 1920-1), Vol. 1, p. 77.
7. Chrimes, S. B., *Introduction to the Administrative History of Medieval England* (Blackwell, 1952), p. 23. Joliffe, J. E. A., *Angevin Kingship* (Adam & Charles Black, 1955), p. 229.
8. Lech, A. F., *A History of Winchester College* (Duckworth & Co., 1899), pp. 36-7.
9. *A History of Recent Events in England* (Cressent Press, 1964), translated by G. Bosanquet, p. 19.
10. Knowles, David, *The Episcopal Colleagues of Thomas Becket* (C.U.P., 1951), pp. 34-7. B.C.T., 'Henry de Blois and his Cathedral Church and city', *C.R.* (1961), pp. 13-20. Round, J. H., 'The Citizens, headed by their Bishop', *Geoffrey De Mandeville* (London, 1892), pp. 56-7.
11. Hunter, J. (ed.), *Pipe Roll, 31 Henry I* (Record Commission, 1833).
12. B.L. Add MS. 153114, f. 124. (Cartulary of St Denys) Southampton.
13. *C.C.W.*, No. 1.
14. *C.C.W.*, No. 2.
15. *C.C.W.*, No. 3.
16. *C.C.W.*, No. 7.
17. P.R.O. C.66/86/m.17.
18. Harvey, John H., 'Hyde Abbey and Winchester College', *Essays in Honour of Frank Warren*, pp. 51 & 22. Chitty, Herbert, *Mayors and Bailiffs of Winchester* (Jacob & Johnson, 1930): in *The Wykehamist*, No. 26, 24 July 1923, Mr. Chitty disposed of Florence de Lunn, the mythical first mayor.
19. Dunn Macray, W. (ed.), *Selbourne Charters* (H.R.S., 1894), Vol. 2, p. 74, *et seq.*
20. Not preserved in city archives, but on Charter Roll. P.R.O. C.53/14/m.4.
21. Restated in Henry III's grant, *W.C.C.*, No. 4.
22. Brown, R. A., Colvin, H. M., Taylor, A. J., *The King's Works Vol. II, The Middle Ages* (H.M.S.O., 1963). Some Saxon buildings were destroyed in this area by the Normans who built a massive earthwork there. *Prospect*, p. 23, and *see* J. Harvey's discussion of 14th-century 'view', *C.R.* (1958), p. 9.
23. Pugh, Ralph B., *Imprisonment in Medieval England* (C.U.P., 1968), numerous references to the Winchester Gaol.
24. Adler, Michael, 'Inventory of Property of Condemned Jews (1285)', *Miscellanies of the Jewish Historical Society of England*, Pt. 2 (1935). Adler, Michael, 'Benedict the Gildsman', ibid. Pt. 4 (1942). Richardson, H. G., *The English Jewry under Angevin Kings* (Methuen, 1960).

Chapter Four: Church and Society

1. For the whole subject *see* B.C.T., *Churches of Medieval Winchester* (Warren & Son, 1957).
2. It also had a connection with the Abbey of Tiron; Round, J. H. (ed.), *Cal. Docs. preserved in France*, pp. 358 & 527.
3. Wavell, Vol. 1, p. 180.
4. Sites of the Friaries in *C.M.W.*
5. B.C.T., 'The Historians of Winchester Cathedral', *C.R.* (1979).
6. Atkinson, T. D., 'Winchester Cathedral Close', *Proceedings* Vol. 15, Pt. 1 (1941), is the standard account.

7. W.J.C.T. and B.C.T., *Pilgrims' Hall.*

8. Goodman, A. W. (ed.), *Register of Bishop Henry Woodlock* (Canterbury and York Society, 1940), p. 568.

9. Harvey, John H., 'Essays in Honour of Frank Warren', *Proceedings* Vol. 20 (1956), p. 51.

10. Edwards, E. (ed.), *Liber Monasterii de Hyda* (Rolls Series, 186), p. lxxvi *et seq.*

11. *V.C.H.* Vol. 2, p. 193 *et seq.*

12. *V.C.H.* Vol. 2, p. 197 *et seq.* Wavell, Vol. 2, pp. 155-211.

13. B.C.T., 'St John's House and the Commonalty of Winchester in the Middle Ages', *Proceedings* Vol. 19, Pt. 1 (1955).

14. cf. *also* Paid 12s. to widows of St John's 'For dressing the founder – usual custom'. 12 Sept. 1783. Jacob Scraps. No. 6, W.C.R.O.

15. W.C.R.O. St John's Rental, 1294.

16. *See* Frontispiece in Cook, A. K., *About Winchester College* (Macmillan & Co., 1917).

Chapter Five: Aspects of the Medieval Economy

1 Leases of this mill from Wherwell Abbey in B.L. Egerton 2104, f. 180, f. 183 (v).

2. Deposition of the Prioress of Wintney, P.R.O. E.178/2018.

3. Willis, A. J., *Catalogue of Deeds before 1850* (1958), No. 62 (Diocesan Archives).

4. W.C.R.O. C. Rolls, pp. 37-8 HVIII.

5. *V.C.H.* Vol. 5, p. 36 *et seq.*

6. cf. Payments by fullers of Winchester for their charter, p. 104. *P. Roll 3 John, 1201* (P.R.S., 1936) and earlier examples in *V.C.H.* Vol. 5, p. 41. The craft guild records have gone.

7. Furley, J. S., *The Usages of Winchester* (Clarendon Press, 1927).

8. *I.P.M. Vol. V. Edward II 1-9 No. 338*, pp. 189-90. His heir was his niece Alice la White of Buckingham, from whose family the Clothselde eventually passed to the Priory of St Swithun.

9. B.C.T., *Hogs* Vol. 1.

10. B.L. Add 15314 (St Denys' Cartulary), p. 490.

11. This brief summary is derived chiefly from the many private charters in B.L. Stowe 846.

Chapter Six: A City of Alliances

1. Pelham, R. A., 'Medieval Southampton', *A Survey of Southampton and its region* (British Association, 1964), p. 212.

2. Adler, op. cit. (*Benedict*).

3. *C.C.W.*, No. 6.

4. *C.P.R. (1338-40)*, pp. 180, 212 & 281.

5. *C.P.R. (1340-3)*, p. 580.

6. *See* J. S. Furley's classic *City Government.*

7. The fundamental right was 'No Citizen ought to Plead or to be Impleaded outside its Walls', *C.P.R. (1281-90)* (Case of July, 129a).

8. The old method continued: cf. Court Roll of 1412-13 (M. 28), which contains important decisions about the walls and the M.P.s.

9. Goodman, A. W. (ed.), *Cartulary of Winchester Cathedral* (Warren & Son, 1927), No. 149.

10. Goodman, A. W., *Manor of God-Begot* (Warren & Son, 1928).

11. Holt, N. R. (ed.), *Pipe Roll of the Bishopric 1210-11* (Manchester University Press, 1964), p. 42, xxii.

12. Beresford, M., *The Six New Towns of the Bishop of Winchester, 1200-55*, pp. 187-215. Titow, J. Z., *Mediaeval Archaeology* (1959), Vol. 3, *English Rural Society* (Allen & Unwin, 1969), p. 33 *et seq.* Drew, J. S., *Compton* (Warren, 1939), p. 22 *et seq.*

Chapter Seven: The Years of Decline and Revival

1. D.R.O. Edington's Register.

2. *C.M.W.*

3. Wykeham's *Register* (H.R.S., 1899), Vol. 2, pp. 121, 125 & 495.

4. *City Government*, p. 99. The city's decline was accompanied by disasters in the countryside; at Silkstead, Compton and Morstead there were vacant holdings, the plough acreage went down

and the Prior's model farm had to be let. Goodman, F. R., *Winchester, Valley and Downland* (Warren, 1934), pp. 27-9.

5. P.R.O. E101/344/12.

6. P.R.O. E101/344/10.

7. W.C.R.O. Tarrage of 1417.

8. *C.P.R. (1377-81)*, p. 221.

9. P.R.O./K.B.9/107 f.8(d).

10. Reville, Andre, *Le Soulvement des Travailleurs D'Angleterre en 1381* (Paris, 1898), pp. 278-9.

11. *W.C.C.*, No. 37.

12. D. May, 'The Somers Rentals', *Proceedings* Vol. 18 (1954), Pt. 3.

13. *C.C.W.*, No. 29.

14. *C.C.W.*, No. 20.

15. *C.C.W.*, No. 21 (Appendix IV).

16. *C.C.W.*, No. 38 (Edward IV, confirmed by Richard III, 16 Feb. 1484).

17. *C.P.R. (1476-85)*, p. 381, No. 15.

18. *Rot. Parl* Vol. 3, p. 640 (6): 641/a/(Petition of 1410).

19. B.L. Royal MSS. 18(6) Vol. 22 (c.1475).

20. Carr, A., *John de Campeden and St Cross Hospital* (University of York, unpublished thesis).

21. *Catalogue 1951 Exhibition* Vol. 4, St Mary's College, p. 10.

Chapter Eight: The Reformation

1. 'Arthur, Prince of Wales', *H.H.* Vol. 2, p. 24 *et seq.* Portal, Great Hall, p. 25 *et seq.*; pp. 135-6.

2. Bird, W. H. B. (ed.), *The Black Book of Winchester* (Wykeham Press, 1925), from a transcript by F. J. Baigent.

3. *C.M.W.*, p. 21.

4. *Black Book*, p. 132.

5. *C.C.W.*, No. 35.

6. *C.C.W.*, No. 36.

7. H.C.R.O. Inventories of intestates found since 1955.

8. H.C.R.O. Inventory, 1575.

9. 'Dame Elizabeth Shelley, last abbess of St Mary's': John Paul, 60, H.F.C. *Proceedings* Vol. 23, Pt. 2 (1965).

10. P.R.O. E/315/400: and for Hyde, Pennell, R. F., *The Parish of Hyde* (Gilbert & Son, Winchester, 1909).

11. B.C.T., 'Changes in the Cathedral Fabric, 1538-71', *C.R.* (1957), and B.C.T., *C.R.* (1974 & 1975).

12. Watson, A. G., 'A Sixteenth-Century Collector: Thomas Dackomb 1496-*c*.1572', *The Library* (Sept. 1963), pp. 204-17.

13. Hurd, D. G. E., *Sir John Mason* (printed, Parchment (Oxford) Ltd., 1975).

14. P.R.O. E/315/400.

15. 'William Pescod', *H.H.* Vol. 11 (H.C.R.O., Mildmay Papers).

16. (anon.) 'An Alderman's Household Stuff in 1545', *H.N.Q.* Vol. 8 (1896).

17. Pennell, op. cit.

18. P.R.O. E/315/?

19. Susterne chapel. Appendix: *Wykehamica*: H. C. Adams (J. Wells, 1878).

20. Frere, W. H. (ed.), *Register of John Whyte* (Canterbury and York Society, 1930: Registers of Gardiner and Poynet in same volume), and Chapter 19, Leach, A. F., 'Winchester and the Dissolution', *A History of Winchester College* (Duckworth, 1899).

21. P.R.O. E.321/24/75, and E.321/39/25 St John's and St Mary's Charnel.

22. E.321/24/No. 79 and E.321/37/23 St Mary Magdalene: E.321/30/77 (Chantries).

23. P.R.O. Church Goods inventories: E.117/2/69/St Mary Kalendar: E.117/2/70 and 70. (St Laurence, St Thomas, All Hallows): E.117/2/72 – 73 – 74 (St Peter, St Clement, St George): E.117/2/76 (St Peter Colebrook): E.117/2/78 (St Maurice).

24. B.C.T., 'The City's preparations', *Hampshire Review* (July 1954): Spanish accounts, Himsworth,

Sheila, 'The Marriage of Philip of Spain with Mary Tudor', H.F.C. *Proceedings* Vol. 22 (1962), Pt. 2.

25. P.R.O. E.321/39/25.
26. *C.C.W.*, No. 39.
27. W.C.R.O. Rents from dissolved monasteries, 1555-6, 1556-7.
28. St John's Hospital: 9. J. Deverell (London, 1879).
29. *C.C.W.*, No. 40.
30. *C.C.W.*, No. 41.
31. *D.N.B.* Flemyng had the house (in the soke) now called The Soke.
32. Atkinson, T., *Elizabethan Winchester* (Faber & Faber, 1963), p. 136 *et seq.* Winchester Scraps, Vol. 2, p. 46.
33. *H.H.* Vol. 1.
34. *V.C.H.* Vol. 5.
35. 'Sessions arrangements for setting rogues to work', *S.P.D. 1581-90*, pp. 51-2 and p. 205 (Abuses in House of Correction, 1584).
36. Paul, John, 'Hampshire Recusants' (unpublished Ph.D. thesis, Southampton University) and King, Archbishop John, *The Martyrs of Hampshire* (n.d.).

Chapter Nine: Winchester under the Stuarts
 1. W.C.R.O. Chamberlain's Roll.
 2. *H.N.Q.* Vol. 8, pp. 52-3: 95 *Sir Henry Withed's Letter Book* Vol. 1, p. 84 (H.C.C., 1976), cf. Mrs. Clarke's many Jewels. (Will, 1618, H.C.R.O.).
 3. *W.C.C.*, 42(a): 42.
 4. Sason's Charges, W.C.R.O. *C.R.* The river between the city and Woodmill was surveyed by John More of Farnham in 1618: his map, 102 M71/P1 (H.C.R.O.). In September 1681, the city lottery under 'Mr. Barber, master of the Lottery, produced £20, towards making the river navigable'. Scraps, No. 5, p. 83: W.C.R.O.
 5. Chamberlain's Rolls suggest 1620, as in Young's *Diary*, p. 68. Perhaps followed by making of Market Street. 'Origin of Cities', *Trussell.*
 6. The palace was otherwise empty of bishops and their furniture. *Relation of a short survey of the Western Counties*, pp. 1-128, Camden, *Miscellany*, 3rd Series, Vol. 16. Hall, Great Chamber, Galleries, Lodging Chamber, Chapel, 'all as void of furniture as entertainment'.
 7. Goodman, F. R. (ed.), *Dean Young's Diary* (S.P.C.K., 1928): passim.
 8. *Young's Diary, passim*: Stephens, W. R. W. (ed.), & Madge, F. T., *Cathedral Documents*, Vol. 2, 1636-83 (H.R.S., 1897), pp. ix-xiii.
 9. Commons' *Journal.* B.C.T., 'Unhappy differences of the city', *Hants. Observer* (26 March, 1952). W.C.R.O. Book of Ordinance, Vol. 5, 17(a) – 'Edmund Riggs Mayor ... Appointed, by Act of Parliament'.
10. Leach, op. cit. p. 326 *et seq.*
11. W.C.R.O. Ordinances, Vol. 6, 140(a).
12. *Cathedral Documents* Vol. 2, p. 75.
13. Bailey, *Archives*, pp. 60-6.
14. Commons' *Journal.*
15. Wavell, Vol. 2, p. 202.
16. 'Unhappy Differences'. H.M.C. Appendix to 7th Report. Lords' *Journal* Vol. 11, p. 60.
17. *Calendar of Compounders.*
18. MSS. John Woodman's Accounts (Dean and Chapter Library).
19. B.C.T., 'The Return of the Church', *Record* (1960).
20. Bailey, *Archives.*
21. Williams, J. F. (ed.), 'Plague Accounts', *Early Church Wardens Accounts of Hampshire* (Warren & Son, 1913), pp. 229-36.
22. *W.C.C.*, p. 43.
23. B.C.T., 'A Royalist Chapter Clerk', *Record*, p. 19.
24. Scrap Book, No. 5, p. 95.

25. Arundel Castle Archives: MD 786, p. 359. M24.
26. *W.C.C.* Nos. 44 & 45.
27. The ceremony cost the Corporation £5 2s. 8d. C.A., 1683 Emes' Diary. W.C.M. The 2,000,000 bricks required were burnt from earth from Painters' Field, and the ashlar from the castle was to be reused with some Isle of Wight or Portland stone. *King's Works* Vol. 5, pp. 304-16.
28. W.C. Muniments NR14 (Buckingham): B.C.T., *Wessex Life* (October 1970, Clobery).
29. He himself lived in the house now called Moberley's. (W.C.M. NR14).
30. B.C.T., 'Return of the Church', *Record* (1960).
31. B.C.T., 'A Winchester Scandal', *Wessex Life* (December 1969).
32. Wolvesey can hardly have become completely uninhabitable. It was taxed for 23 hearths in 1664 (P.R.O. E.179/176/524).
33. Smallpox 'Hott', and 1,000 inhabitants said to have it in 1694. Emes' Diary. W.C.M.
34. Scrap Book (5).
35. P.R.O. E.179/247/30.
36. The elder Sir Robert was a Winchester M.P. in 1627-8. *D.N.B.*; for Pawlett, Pennell, R. F., *The Parish of Hyde* (Gilbert 1909), p. 46.

Chapter Ten: From Queen Anne to Queen Victoria

1. W.C.R.O. MSS. Godson's Maps: D. & C. Archives.
2. W.C.R.O. Proceedings of Paving Commissioners: 10 Vols. 1771-1866.
3. Jacob, W. H., *The Westgate, Winchester* (Warren & Son, 1899). Bailey, *Archives*, pp. 9-10.
4. *Great Hall*, p. 68.
5. Leroy, A. C., & Bramston, A. R., *Story of Wolvesey* (Jacob & Johnson, 1895), p. 35.
6. Edwards, E. (ed.), *Liber Monasterii De Hyde*, Rolls Series (1866), p. ixxv *et seq.*
7. Milner, *Survey*, p. 184, *Q.R.* (May 1863).
8. B.C.T., 'A notable family of artists', *Proceedings* Vol. 21 (1961), Pt. 1.
9. Bailey op. cit., pp. 162-5.
10. Detailed Building Accounts. Jacob's Scrap Book, No. 5.
11. W.C.R.O. Rate Books.
12. H.C.R.O. Mildmay Papers, 1260: Mr. Shenton's objects. He supplied the East India Company.
13. D. & C. Minutes.
14. D. & C. Minutes.
15. Locke, pp. 113-14 and Mr. Twynham's letter in *H.C.*
16. Blore, G. H., *Thomas Cheyney, Dean of Winchester.*
17. Holt-White, R. (ed.), *Letters of Gilbert White ... to the Rev. John Mulso* (R. H. Porter, 1906).
18. D. & C. Minutes.
19. A collection of papers relating to the County Hospital for the sick and lame, etc., at Winchester (London, 1737).
20. Ranger, P., 'Lost theatres of Winchester', *Proceedings* Vol. 31 (1976). B.C.T., 'A notable family of artists', *Proceedings* Vol. 22 (1961), Pt. 1.
21. *V.C.H.* Vol. 5 (Sports).
22. W.C.R.O. Whist Club Minutes.
23. Hatchard, J., *Report of the Committee (on) ... The state of Hampshire County Gaol and Bridewells* (1817).
24. William Pescod, *Hogs* Vol. 2. B.C.T., '29 Jewry Street', *H.C.* (15 Nov. 1969).
25. Information from the late Sir Lewis Namier.
26. Namier, Sir Lewis, & Brooke, John, 'Members', *The Commons, 1754-90* Vol. 3 (History of Parliament Trust. H.M.S.O., 1964).
27. *H.C.* (September), *s.a.*
28. B.C.T., 'A notable family of artists', *Proceedings* Vol. 22 (1961), Pt. 1. W.C.R.O. Ordinances, *s.a.*
29. Ordinances: Vol. 11, p. 164(6); Vol. 12, p. 140 (96); Vol. 13, p. 52(6). Payment to Robert Clarke's widow for 'his' papers, 1792, Vol. 13, p. 77(a).
30. Clark, K., *The Gothic Revival* (Penguin Books, 1964), pp. 87- 90.
31. 'S.M.F.', *Hidden Wheat: The Story of an enclosed Franciscan Community* (Franciscan Monastery, Woodlands St Mary's, Newbury, 1971).

32. *D.N.B.* John Milner. *Hampshire Registers* Vol. 1. *Winchester* Vol. 42 (Catholic Record Society, 1948), pp. 12-14.

33. *Dissenters' Meeting House Certificates, 1702-1844*, Hants. Miscellany, Vol. 3 (compiled and published by A. J. Willis, 1965).

Chapter Eleven: Reformers

1. Deverell, John, *History of St John's Hospital* (Davis, 1879), pp. 49-57.
2. Ordinances Vol. 13 (19 April 1833 – to Reform).
3. *See* Appendix B (Population). Holladay Philbin, J., *Parliamentary Representation in England and Wales, 1832* (Newhaven, Connecticut, 1965), p. 7.
4. *Return of Members of Parliament, Pt. II* (Printed by Order of House of Commons, 1878). V. Bonham-Carter, *In a Liberal Tradition* Vol. 10 (Constable, 1960), pp. 87-9.
5. W.C.R.O. Treasurer's Accounts, 1838-9. Watch Committee Minute Book, No. 1.
6. 'Union' Archives in H.C.R.O.
7. W.C.R.O. Proposal Books, Vols. 1-9 (160-1855).
8. Deeds of (Former) Westminster and National Provincial Banks, owned by the banks.

Chapter Twelve: Progress and Change

1. *Dulce Domum*, pp. 75-6, 140-1, & 149. C. A. E. Moberly (John Murray).
2. W.C.R.O. Minutes of Water Works Company.
3. Furley, J. S., *Winchester in 1867* (Warren, n.d.), pp. 41-2.
4. W.C.R.O. Minutes of Museum Committee.
5. B.C.T., 'Henry Moody', *H.C.* (1971).
6. B.C.T., *Winchester 100 Years Ago, 1879-80* (Cave, 1979).
7. D. & C. Minutes.
8. Garnier, A. E., *The Garniers of Hampshire* (Jarrold & Son, 1900), pp. 38-43.
9. Rannie, Alan, 'St Thomas' Church', *H.C.* (2 August 1969).
10. B.C.T., 'Christchurch, a New Parish', *Christ Church Parish Magazine* (1961).
11. *Winchester Quarterly Records* (1850-64) have much information about all these kinds of activities: edited and printed by William Tanner, followed by his widow.
12. B.C.T., 'William Budden', *H.C.* (12 Sept. 1959).
13. Carpenter, F., *Winchester Congregational Church Centenary* (published W.C.C., 1962).
14. 'C.J.B.', 'A House in Winchester', *The War Cry* (22 Aug. 1964).

Chapter Thirteen: The Expansion of Winchester

1. W.C.R.O. Paving Commission.
2. Walker, Charles, *Thomas Brassey, Railway Builder* (Frederick Muller, 1969).
3. *Transport in Hampshire ... A guide to the Records* (Hampshire Archivists' Group, 1973), pp. 45-6.
4. *Hogs* Vol. 2.
5. W.C.R.O. Water Works Company Minutes.
6. Minutes, Building Committee, Royal Hampshire County Hospital.
7. D. & C. George Forder's 'Long Book': Forder drew up the specification for the sale particulars.
8. *Q.R.*, p. 6 (13 May 1857).
9. B.C.T., *Winchester 100 Years Ago* (Cave, 1979).
10. *Great Hall*, Portal.
11. Bowker, Alfred, *The Alfred Millenary* (Macmillan, 1902).

Chapter Fourteen: Postscript: Some Aspects of Recent Development

1. Watt, A., *History of the Hampshire Constabulary* (Hants. and I.O.W. Constabulary, 1967), p. 1.
2. Winchester College demolished houses on the north side of College Street and replaced them with gardens. *H.O.* (26 Oct. 1935).
3. The Prince of Wales 'opened' the estate and was given the freedom of the city. *H.C.* (10 Nov. 1923). *Country Life* (3 Nov. 1923). H.R.H. planted the beech trees at Airlie Road corner (Airlie Road is named after the Countess of Airlie).

4. Details kindly supplied by Mr. L. M. Perkis, formerly Winchester's chief engineer and planning officer.

5. Its status as a city, and the continuation of the mayoralty, confirmed by the last royal charter.

Appendix A: The Soke
1. Based on Pipe Rolls.

Appendix B: Population
1. Brooke, C., *Alfred to Henry III*, p. 127.
2. *Prospect*, p. 27.
3. Russell, J. C., *British Medieval Population* (Albuquerque, 1948), p. 285.
4. Russell, op. cit., p. 285.
5. Furley, *City Government*, p. 101.
6. Russell, op. cit., p. 285.
7. Atkinson, *Elizabethan Winchester*, p. 30.
8. Atkinson, op. cit., p. 33.
9. *Winchester College*, pp. 32-3.
10. P.R.O. E.321/39/25.

Appendix E: Early Dissent in Winchester
1. For whole subject, excellent summary in Carpenter, F., *Winchester Congregational Church Tercentenary*, 1662-1962 (published by the Congregational Church in Winchester, 1962): and D.R.O. Applications for meeting house licence, 1702-61: E/GA/i(a): ibid B.K.2.
2. B.C.T., 'Return of the Church', *C.R.* (1960).
3. Book of Institutions, D. & C. His widow, Dorcas, given pension 7 July 1655 (P.R.O. Warrants).
4. *D.N.B.*
5. *V.C.H.* Vol. 2, p. 95.
6. Carpenter, op. cit. This chapel, on site of later primitive Methodist chapel, was rebuilt in 1807, and the congregation moved to Jewry Street in 1853. In Pain's time (1715-47) the congregation was perhaps 330 persons.
7. Applications.

Appendix F: Winchester's Royal Charters
1. *C.P.R. (1446-51)* (5 Sept. 1448); 2. *C.P.R. (1452-61)* (20 Sept. 1452); 3. Ibid (p. 162); 4. Ibid (p. 644); 5. P.R.O. EM8/2461.

Index